Commerce and the World Outside

Commerce and the World Outside

L. C. BOND, A.C.I.S.

Senior Lecturer in Business Studies,
The Harrogate College of
Further Education

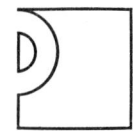

Pitman Publishing

Second Edition 1971

SIR ISAAC PITMAN AND SONS LTD
Pitman House, Parker Street, Kingsway, London, WC2B 5PB
P.O. Box 6038, Portal Street, Nairobi, Kenya

SIR ISAAC PITMAN (AUST.) PTY. LTD
Pitman House, Bouverie Street, Carlton, Victoria 3053, Australia

PITMAN PUBLISHING COMPANY S.A. LTD
P.O. Box 11231, Johannesburg, S. Africa

PITMAN PUBLISHING CORPORATION
6 East 43rd Street, New York, 10017, U.S.A.

SIR ISAAC PITMAN (CANADA) LTD
Pitman House, 381–383 Church Street, Toronto, 3, Canada

THE COPP CLARK PUBLISHING COMPANY
517 Wellington Street, Toronto, 2B, Canada

ISBN: 0 273 40812 7

Printed in Great Britain
at the Pitman Press, Bath
G1—(B.860)

Preface

This book has been written in an attempt to broaden the study of *commerce*. Few young people realize how important a knowledge of this subject is to them in their future lives.

The book sets down in a logical sequence the many and diverse activities which play an important part in our working and personal lives. Although the importance of commerce as a vocational subject has been fully borne in mind, an attempt has been made to give a much wider view than hitherto thought necessary. Certain additional topics have been included in the book so that it may help students, as part of their general education, to span the gulf between life at school or college and life in the world outside.

The facts have been set down so that young persons studying the subject for the first time will not find it too difficult to understand the business and industrial world and, indeed, their own place in society. Although the non-vocational aspects of commerce are extremely important, it must not be forgotten that many young persons will be required to take an examination at the end of their course of studies, and that success in their examination is a prime object. With this in mind, the author has included a wide range of examination-type questions and practical work at the end of each chapter. This book, therefore, will be useful for pupils in secondary schools, including those taking the Certificate of Secondary Education examination, and first-year students in colleges of further education, many of whom will be taking an examination in commerce at the end of their year, including R.S.A. (Stage I) examinations. It will also be found useful for students preparing for G.C.E. "O" level examinations, and O.N.C., O.N.D. and C.O.S. students, as a primary book in commerce. In addition students taking a course in social studies will find that the book has been designed to help them in their understanding of society and their place in it.

There is a great deal of correlation between commerce and other subjects, such as arithmetic, geography and social studies, and it is hoped that the topics have been dealt with in a manner that makes possible co-operation between subject teachers.

Preface

The author wishes to thank all those individuals and organizations who have helped in any way to make this book possible; in particular Mr. C. J. Booth, F.C.B.I., F.S.C.T., of the Stockton/Billingham Technical College, Mr. G. Badderley, B.A., of the Clarendon College of Further Education, Nottingham, and members of H.M. Inspectorate for their valued help and encouragement.

The author's thanks are also due to the Metropolitan Regional Examinations Board and the Middlesex Regional Examining Board for permission to reproduce specimen examination questions; also to all those organizations which have given permission for the reproduction of illustrations, and which have provided information on their work.

The second edition of this book attempts to ensure that material is kept up-to-date, and decimal currency is used throughout. An additional workbook section has been included at the end of the book, and it is hoped that teachers and students will find the questions of value to them.

With the raising of the school leaving age, schools will, perhaps, have more time for including in the curriculum, studies which provide pupils with an insight into the world outside. Indeed the Newsom Report emphasizes this important aspect of our work, and it is hoped that the matter contained in this book goes some way towards helping pupils in gaining a knowledge of the vital work of commerce and industry in Great Britain.

Contents

Contents

LIST OF PLATES

1 The World Outside

How many of us ever sit down and think of all the things that we need in life, or what makes it possible for all these many things to be brought to us so that we may enjoy them?

If we were to spend only a few minutes of our time in bringing to mind all those many and varied requirements, we should be able to appreciate better just how dependent we are on others. If we consider the needs of the average family, we should think not only in terms of foodstuffs and a house, complete with all its necessary furnishings, but also of the ownership of a motor-car, a tape recorder, or a record player. These, although at one time regarded as luxuries, are now thought of as necessities.

Apart from all those needs which we now regard as essential if we are to live comfortably, there are other things provided for us, such as entertainment in the form of "pop" records, bowling-alleys and the like. They are all available to us because people, not only in this country but in many different parts of the world, have helped in some way to make them possible.

Progress in the World: How Our Needs are Satisfied

There is a tendency for us to take for granted all the luxuries we need in order that we may enjoy life to the full. Perhaps we all tend to live in our own little world, forgetful of the contribution that many other people, not only in this country but in others too, make towards our personal comfort and well-being.

If we could turn the clock back, even only fifty years, we should realize just how much progress has been made in the world during this time. Factories have been built in many different parts of the country. Plant and machinery have been installed in the factories to help make our jobs easier. Today the working day is much shorter and many people now enjoy the benefits of the five-day week. A direct result of this is that we have far more leisure time.

More families today can enjoy the benefits of an annual summer holiday, or a week-end by the sea. There are fast express trains and coaches to take us to our destinations, should we not own a car of our own. More people are going abroad for their holidays than ever before.

Shopping for our family and for our own personal needs has been made much easier for us today. Most towns now have department stores, where a large selection of goods of all types is on view in the various departments. Shopping at Christmas, for instance, is made much easier because of the wide choice offered to us. Even if we prefer to do our shopping in a smaller shop there is a good choice, and the little local shop is very handy if on returning home we find we have forgotten that packet of sugar or that loaf of bread.

Many services are now provided which are beneficial to us throughout our lives. In our towns and villages we have attractive parks and facilities for playing our favourite sports. Youth clubs are often available for us to enjoy table-tennis, drama, woodwork, and a host of other activities. Public libraries now contain a wide selection of books, including those of general educational and instructional, as well as fictional, interest. All are provided for our use.

Colleges of further education and colleges of art are situated within easy reach of us all. No matter what our hobbies or interests, or what qualifications we seek to attain to help us in our future work, help is provided for us. In this country health and welfare services are available to those needing them. Should we be unemployed or off work through sickness, help is given until we can begin work again.

One word sums up all these changes that have taken place during the past fifty years—that word is *progress*. It is this progress, and how it has come about, that we shall be reading about in this book.

It is no longer possible for a person in this modern world to say that he is not dependent to some extent on other people, doing a variety of jobs in many different occupations. Taking a look at the world outside may help us to appreciate, perhaps, just how much we rely on help from others, and how each person in his own particular way is of benefit to many other people. Even primitive peoples learn that it is usually more efficient for the various jobs that have to be carried out to be shared amongst the different members of the community, and there is this same sense of dependence on one another in more progressive communities.

In order that we can live, much produce has to be grown on the land, and minerals have to be extracted from the ground. Factories are needed to help to produce all those things which are so necessary to us in life.

2

Coal and oil are but two commodities needed to provide us not only with fuel, but with help in the manufacture of many of our wants.

TRADE

Very few countries can be said to be self-supporting, and because of this it becomes very necessary for all nations to exchange many of the things that they produce in return for the products of other nations. This exchange, not only of goods but of services also, between the countries of the world, is called *trade*. Great Britain has to buy many of its foodstuffs from other countries. In return we supply other nations with manufactured goods, such as motor-cars, television sets and record players. We build some of the finest ships and the greatest bridges in the world. Our steel-works sell steel to many nations, who use it to produce a vast range of goods.

We can now appreciate that without this exchange of goods and services between people and between nations life would hold few joys for us. We should exist rather than live. Without trade we should not have a market for our products and the wheels of industry would grind to a halt. A direct result of this would be high unemployment amongst all types of workers, no matter what their jobs. Goods would be dear, and it would not be possible to obtain the luxuries of life because we should not be able to afford them. Trade has made possible, then, to a very large extent, the progress that has been made generally in the world today.

THE AIDS TO TRADE

Because of the increasing trade between the peoples of the earth, many different activities have become necessary to maintain and improve our relationships with one another. Today we live in a world of "big business," and time is important. Modern techniques have to be used extensively if progress is to be maintained. During the years many *aids to trade* have come into being, aids that are necessary to the business world and to ourselves as individuals so that our lives may be made more comfortable and secure.

For instance, when starting work you may find that you wish to deposit part of your wages with a bank, partly because you know that your money will be safe but also because you know that your money can earn interest as long as it is kept in the bank. Eventually you may decide that you can afford a motor-cycle or a motor-scooter, but unless you take out a policy with an insurance company, you will not be able to

3

use your vehicle. This is because our laws state that a driver must compensate any person or persons who suffer in any way as a result of his negligent driving.

Do you ever consider what events have made it possible for us to go into a shop and purchase an article such as a box of chocolates? Before the chocolate factory has been able to manufacture the chocolates, raw materials have been transported from other countries. The bank will have helped, perhaps, in making payment for the raw materials. If after manufacture the chocolates were not required immediately, they would have to be stored until they could be sold. At this stage the help of the wholesaler may be required. He is the person who buys the chocolates in bulk from the manufacturer, and then supplies them to the shopkeepers on demand. And it is the shopkeeper who, having made sure that he has a good stock of chocolates, will sell them to us.

No matter what articles we purchase, it is quite probable that all these activities have played some part in ensuring that we receive them, when required, and in good condition.

We must also remember that it is quite possible that we may purchase particular products simply because we have seen them advertised on the television or in the newspapers.

The Meaning of Commerce

The *aids to trade* have a very important part to play in helping to make *trade* possible. In our study of the world outside we deal to a very large extent with these activities, and we have a name which we use in describing them. This name is *commerce*.

Commerce is a term which describes the world of business, and it is necessary for all persons, no matter what their job, to understand its importance. This is necessary because so many people work in occupations which form a part of commerce, and because of its very beneficial effects on the whole of our lives.

Before we can understand fully all the different aspects of commerce, we must know the relationship which exists between them and industry, and a study of Figure 1 will help our understanding.

The Divisions of Commerce

Trade is a term which is used to describe the exchange of goods and services, not only between people, but also between the nations of the world. Trade can be divided into two separate sections:

4

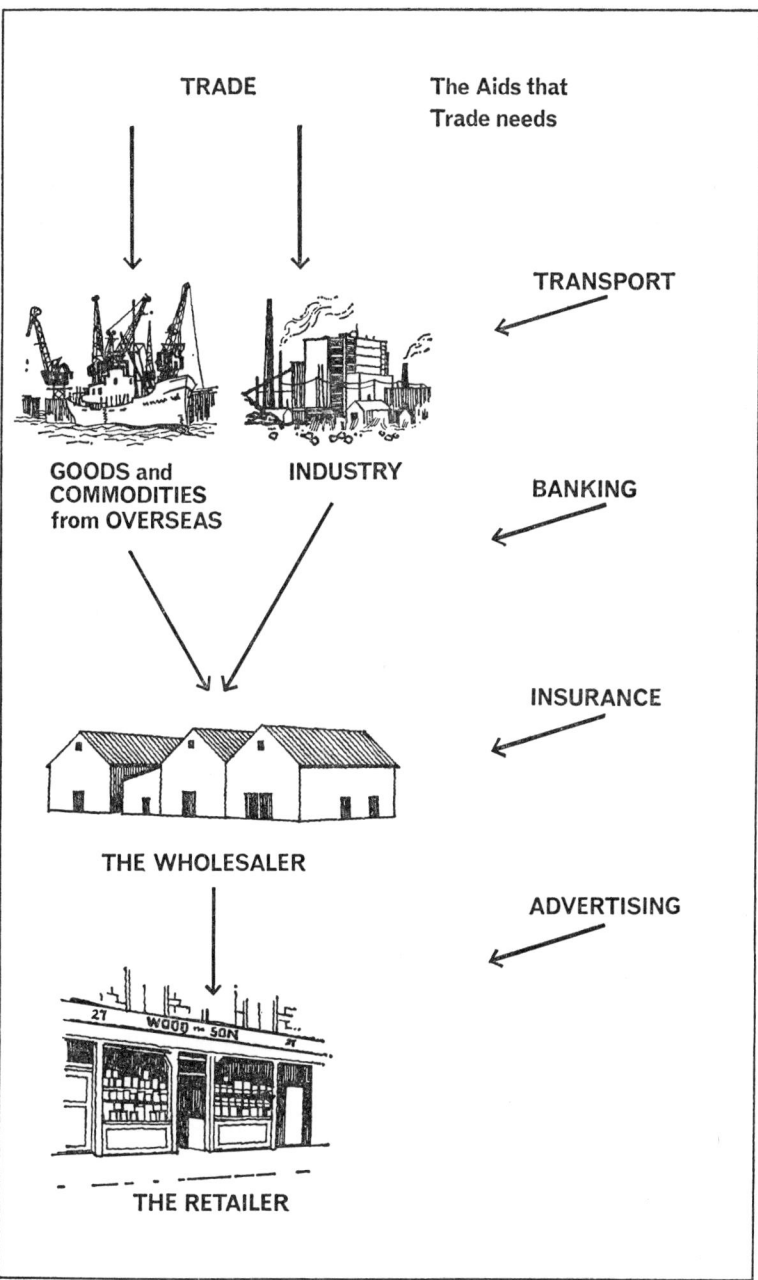

TRADE   The Aids that
               Trade needs

TRANSPORT

GOODS and   INDUSTRY
COMMODITIES   BANKING
from OVERSEAS

INSURANCE

THE WHOLESALER

ADVERTISING

THE RETAILER

Fig. 1. How Commerce Helps in the Supply of Goods and Services

Commerce and the World Outside

1. *Overseas Trade*—which is the buying and selling of many different commodities and services by persons living in different countries, as, for instance, France and Great Britain.

2. *Home Trade*—which is the buying and selling of goods and services by persons living in the same country.

Home trade is a very important function of the business world in this country, and after goods have been produced by the firms of manufacturers, wholesalers purchase the goods in large quantities and then sell them in smaller quantities to shopkeepers (the retailers), who in turn sell them to ourselves (the consumers).

Wholesalers and retailers, then, are *traders*, through whose activities we, the consumers, receive many of our daily wants. Not only do they help to ensure that goods made in the factories in this country are made available to the consumers, but they also supply us with commodities purchased from countries overseas.

It should be borne in mind that the manufacturers (who form a very large part of industry) are also traders, in that they obtain many different raw materials and convert them into products. Eventually, as the goods reach the shelves of the shopkeeper, we, the consumers, exchange (trade) our money in return for the items we require.

We have already read of the activities necessary if our personal wants are to be satisfied, and it is the function of *banks, insurance companies* and *transport concerns*, together with the help of *advertising*, to enable the traders of the world to carry out their work efficiently.

Questions

1. List the family's needs in life. Describe the part commerce plays in helping to satisfy these needs.

2. Distinguish between commerce and trade. Into what main branches may trade be divided? Write a short note on each one.

3. Discuss the progress that has been made in the world during this century, mentioning the part industry and commerce have played.

4. What is commerce? Discuss its purpose.

5. What are the aids to trade?

Practical work

1. Draw a diagram which will show the links between the different functions of commerce.

2. Select a country with which Great Britain trades. Prepare a statement listing some of the goods and services we receive from that country. Show also the goods and services with which Great Britain provides that country.

2 Going to Work

From a very early age we talk about the kind of job that we should like on leaving school. Very often, of course, we take up work in an occupation vastly different from our first choice. Often there are arguments expressed both for and against different kinds of jobs. Certain people may suggest obtaining a job in which you will learn a trade and become skilled in a particular craft, such as engineering, electrical work, shipbuilding or joinery. To do this you will perhaps be apprenticed to a local firm until the age of twenty-one, to learn the skills of the trade you have chosen. Other advisers will suggest that you should try to obtain a "clean" job, in an office perhaps. We often call office workers "white-collar workers."

The Importance of all Occupations

If we were to sit down and compile a list of all the occupations that we could think of, it is probable that the final result would be very lengthy. There are hundreds of different occupations. How useful are all these occupations? Is there any one job which could be regarded as being far more important than another?

Possibly the best way of trying to find the answer to this problem is to consider the people employed in a firm in your own area. What different kinds of occupations do they follow?

A typical firm engaged in the engineering industry will need many workers, skilled in their own particular crafts, a number of examples being—

Fitters	Turners	Boilermakers
Welders	Electricians	Blacksmiths
Pattern-makers	Joiners	Bricklayers

In the factory itself there will also be a necessity for labourers, drivers, store-keepers, and packers.

From the above list of occupations, we can see just how many different types of workers are needed for the efficient organization of a factory. There are, however, a number of other people who will be necessary if the business is to run smoothly.

The Works Manager—to co-ordinate all the activities needed in producing the goods. He will require a great deal of help from production engineers, progress clerks, and general works clerks.

The Works Engineer—who, along with his team of assistants, is responsible for the maintenance of the factory buildings, in which the plant and machinery are housed.

The Company Secretary—may be responsible for organizing many of the commercial activities of the firm. His department may include accountants, shorthand-typists, order clerks, costing clerks, wages clerks, sales clerks, and other general clerical workers.

The Sales Manager—who, with his team of sales representatives, will find customers for the firm's products.

The progress that a firm makes, in manufacturing and selling its products, will not depend on any one man or woman. The general prosperity of the firm will depend upon a number of factors. Perhaps the most important factor is how well all the employees of the business work together. Each one, in his or her own way, is doing an important job of work, and making some contribution towards the firm's success.

Even in these days of increasing mechanization in industry, all jobs are important. No person can claim that *his* job is more important than that of another person. No matter what our work, whether we are accountants or fitters, clerks or shorthand-typists, each one of us has a contribution to make towards the well-being of the rest of the community. Every job is constructive in that it has a useful purpose, no matter how menial it may appear to be.

Many people have jobs which cannot directly be related to industry, and we say that these persons provide us with *services*. Doctors and nurses, although not concerned in the manufacturing of products, are providing services which are vital to the rest of the community. When buying a home, we may need the assistance of a solicitor and an architect. The services of teachers, policemen, bus drivers, hairdressers, and a host of others are essential to the community in that they have arisen from the public's demand for them.

Today we have a reasonable amount of leisure time, and many people, in a variety of occupations, help us to enjoy it. The "pop" stars of stage and television, the producers, and the stage hands, all play their part.

Classes of Occupations

Life today offers an enormous variety of occupations, and we choose the one for which we think we are best suited. All occupations can be classified into four main groups, of equal importance—

1. Persons who work on the land, whether they are farming, or engaged in forestry work, or extracting minerals such as coal from the earth, are engaged in *extractive occupations*. This class of occupation also includes fishermen.

2. Persons employed in extractive occupations provide the raw materials for another group of workers, who in their work convert these raw materials into a huge variety of products, ranging from ships to television sets. This group of workers are employed in what are termed *manufacturing* and *constructive occupations*.

Although persons employed in manufacturing and constructive occupations have been grouped together, there is a difference between them. Whereas workers in the manufacturing side of industry convert the raw materials into finished goods, such as motor-cars, television sets, etc., people employed in the constructional trades are concerned with the construction or building of such things as houses, shops, factories, bridges, and roads. Both types of workers, together with the extractive workers, form that large group who work in *industry*.

CLASSIFICATION OF OCCUPATIONS

1. *Extractive*	2. *Manufacturing*
Miner	Weaver
Farmer	Tool-maker
Fisherman	Electrician
Quarryman	Joiner
Forestry worker	Fitter
3. *Commercial*	4. *Direct Services*
Bank clerk	Dentist
Shop assistant	Solicitor
Van driver	Recording star
Insurance agent	Teacher
Warehouseman	Nurse

3. We must now consider the third group of occupations, which consists of persons engaged in *commerce*. If the raw materials that are required by industry have to be transported from overseas, help will be required from people in the world of shipping. Banks will assist in making the necessary payment for the materials, and insurance companies will provide cover, in the event of any damage or loss to the materials. After the products have been manufactured, the services of those people employed in the wholesale and retail trades may be required if the goods are eventually to be sold to the consumer.

4. Our fourth group of workers are employed in occupations which provide *direct services* of one kind or another.

Those engaged in *commercial occupations* play just as important a part in helping to provide us with the necessary things in life as persons employed in the other occupations. In our study of the "world outside" we shall examine their many and varied activities.

Production

The term *production* is used to describe all those processes which take place, and which ensure that the community has its needs satisfied. As we have read earlier in this chapter, all jobs are productive, or constructive. All those persons working in industry, commerce, and those providing direct services form part of the production process, and as such come under the heading of production. It is quite wrong to think that only those following extractive, and manufacturing occupations are involved in production. All those persons providing the many vital services, are of equal importance to the industrial workers. It is the joint effort on the part of all of these people which ensures that our needs are satisfied.

Questions

1. List the different classes of occupations. Give two examples of each class of occupation, mentioning why such a job comes under the heading chosen.

2. Discuss the reasons why all jobs are equally important.

3. Why are persons engaged in commerce performing a job just as important as those in industrial occupations?

4. Using an actual product as an example, write briefly on the links between the different occupations, and how all the persons in the

11

occupations mentioned contribute towards the consumers' eventually receiving the product.

5. Which of the following is engaged in an "extractive occupation"?

(i) A miner,

(ii) A doctor,

(iii) A lathe operator in a manufacturing firm.

Practical work

1. Make a list of thirty different occupations, and then arrange them into their correct groups, according to the class of occupation to which they belong.

2. Draw a diagram or chart showing how all the different classes of occupations are linked together.

3. Draw a map of your own local area, marking the sites of —

(i) extractive industries,

(ii) manufacturing industries,

(iii) constructive industries.

3 The Help Industry Needs

The Interdependence of all Persons

If we bear in mind that all occupations are important, and that everyone throughout his life needs a great deal of help from others, we shall realize that there is a necessity for all persons, no matter what their job, to work together in a spirit of co-operation and joint effort. The reason so much progress is being made in the world today is that the peoples of the earth are coming to appreciate that, by working together in a co-operative effort, each one of us ultimately benefits in his personal life.

The Help that Industry Needs and Receives from Commerce

It will help us to keep this fact in our minds if we recall the kind of things that the average family needs. Quite apart from our normal priorities, such as a well-furnished home, our requirements embrace a whole range of different goods and services. All the items that we use, both in our homes and outside, we not only expect, but tend to take for granted. We do not always think about all the processes that have taken place so that we can obtain them. Products such as record players, tape recorders, motor-cars, washing machines and records all have to be produced by factories employing many people. We often assume that the factory has merely to obtain a supply of raw materials, convert them into the finished product, and then sell them to the consumers. If we study the following example, we may appreciate that there is far more entailed in helping to satisfy our wants than perhaps we thought.

Let us assume, in our example, that we are studying the needs of a factory producing record players, which not only has to manufacture them, but also has to ensure that the consumer is able to make a purchase easily, by simply going into a shop. Before any factory can commence production, plentiful supplies of raw materials will be necessary, and although certain of them can be obtained from sources in this country, it is quite possible that other materials may have to be shipped from overseas.

13

TRANSPORT

The transporting of these supplies represents a problem which today is overcome quite easily. If the raw materials are being obtained from overseas, arrangements will have to be made with a shipping company for the services of a cargo vessel, in which the consignment will be carried. On arrival at a port in this country the cargo of raw materials will be transferred to waiting rail wagons, and thence transported to the factory. Even in the event of the materials' being obtained from sources in this country, the help of the railways may still be required, as will possibly the services of road haulage concerns also. On paper this may appear to be quite a simple procedure, but a great deal of work and a considerable amount of thought are essential if the goods needed for the manufacture of the products are to arrive safely, and in good time, at the factory.

FINANCE

Assuming that the raw materials have now arrived at the factory, we must consider the question of making payment for them. Many people now make use of the extensive services offered by the commercial banks, which have branches in most of our towns and cities. The manufacturer of the record players will need to use the services of the banks, not only in paying for the materials that have been supplied to him, but also in ensuring that he can pay the weekly wages of employees working in his factory.

ADVERTISING

During the manufacture of the record players, the factory will be seeking ways in which to sell its product. It is probable, therefore, that it will need to advertise in newspapers, periodicals, and on television, so that we, the consumers, will know that such a record player is available for us to purchase.

INSURANCE

The services of an insurance company will be needed by the manufacturer, for eventualities such as damage being caused to goods and materials through fire, or the payment of compensation to employees in the event of their having an accident whilst at work.

MARKETING—INCLUDING DISTRIBUTION

The problem of ensuring that the consumer receives an adequate supply of many different kinds of goods is an extremely complex one.

14

Although there are some instances today of manufacturers selling their products direct to the consumer, these transactions still form a very small proportion of total sales and most manufacturers of *consumer goods* will need assistance in ensuring that their products reach the consumer. It is the function of wholesalers situated in different parts of the country, to provide goods such as our record players when required by the retailers.

The *marketing* of products today is a vast operation. Most firms do a lot of research in trying to ascertain just what the consumer really wants, and then attempt to provide the consumer with the type of product he wants. A lot of money is spent on *market research* today by firms of manufacturers who need to find out consumer preferences. There is, for instance, no point in a manufacturer producing vast quantities of ginger flavoured chocolate, unless he is certain that there is a substantial demand for this type of product.

A good deal of thought goes into other aspects of the product, including packaging, and product design. Often, a product which is attractively packaged, and well designed, will sell far better than another brand where no apparent thought has gone into its design and packaging. Price too, is extremely important, as the public will not usually buy one particular product if another brand will do the job just as well, and is sold at a lower price. Marketing of products, which includes the distributive process, is an involved operation and persons employed in this field carry out a very important function.

COMMERCE AND INDUSTRY

If we think carefully about all that has gone into providing us with our record players, bearing in mind that the same procedure applies to the manufacture and distribution of hundreds of products of all types, we can perhaps appreciate the part played by a great many people, in all walks of life, who are working together in a joint effort to provide us with many of our needs. All this activity on the part of industry and the business world ensures that all of us are helped in our daily lives. They provide us with the necessities of life, and also with goods and services which help us to enjoy our leisure hours.

Commerce is the world of business, and it is through the joint efforts of industry and commerce that life as we know it exists. Commerce is not merely a term which we use in describing the world of business; it has a far more special significance for us. It is that very large part of the community which devotes a great deal of time to ensuring that we have our wants satisfied, and that industry is given all the aid possible in producing and supplying the goods.

The world of commerce also does a great deal in helping to stimulate demand by the consumer for many products. Industry is helped by the banking houses in the form of financial aid so that it is able to equip itself with modern machinery which can produce goods quickly and cheaply, to be sold with the assistance of large-scale national advertising through the medium of television and the newspapers. Goods will be manufactured in large quantities as a result of the use of modern equipment and the increase in consumer demand owing to advertising. Because of these factors, costs of producing many products are reduced, and this will lead to lower prices being charged to the consumer. Everyone benefits because of this. Factories can use their facilities to the full, and we in turn are provided with many of our wants at a fair price.

Great Britain is not only a great industrial nation, but a commercial one too. One has only been able to progress because of the aid of the other. Through the years, our standard of living has increased and the luxuries of yesterday are regarded as being essential today. This has come about as a result, not of any one factor, but of a number of factors. Mechanization and the use of new techniques in industry have made possible its development and growth. Only if industry can be assured of a great deal of help from the commercial world can progress be maintained and our own personal wants in life be satisfied.

The Distinction Between Producer and Consumer Goods

We are all consumers in one way or another, but it is important that we should appreciate the difference between products which are manufactured for consumers (shoppers) and those which are not intended for our own personal use but are to be used by factories to aid them in the production of other articles.

Consumer goods are items which are consumed (or used) by the general public. Producer goods are really technical products such as tools and machinery which are used in the manufacture of other products.

Producer goods

Machinery, such as lathes, drilling machines, etc.	Textile machinery
	Ships
Boilers for power stations	

Consumer goods

Motor-cars	Clothing—
Television sets	suits, skirts, coats, stockings,
Sweets	etc.

Questions

1. Describe the commercial activities necessary to get a can of soup from the manufacturer to the consumer.

2. Explain the differences between industry and commerce, mentioning the work that each does.

3. Describe briefly the relationship between industry and commerce.

4. What is the difference between producer and consumer goods? Use examples to illustrate your answer.

5. What part do manufacturers of producer goods sometimes play in ensuring that the consumer receives many important consumer products?

6. Describe how the various commercial activities help in the different stages through which the raw material passes until it finishes as a garment in the shop.

Practical work

1. Prepare a chart or diagram which illustrates the links between industry and commerce.

2. Using as an example a factory in your own area, draw a diagram which illustrates all the commercial activities necessary if the final product is to be manufactured and then made available to the consumer.

3. Make a list of the different factories in your own district, and then prepare for each factory a list of products manufactured.

4 Trade

How many families take the time to sit down and list all the items of expenditure on which they spend their income each week? Many families will, in fact, do this, and we term it *budgeting*, which really means the planning of how they will spend their money. All expenditure is analysed, and an estimate is made of how much will probably be spent on their various requirements. This is a form of good housekeeping, and we shall be discussing budgeting, and the necessity for it, in a later chapter.

Wages and Prices

The following examples of a family budget will help us to understand how our needs have altered over the years (and how prices have risen).

FAMILY BUDGET FOR ONE WEEK—TWO ADULTS AND TWO CHILDREN

	£	£
Weekly wage, and family allowance		25·00
Expenditure		
Housekeeping allowance for food, etc.	9·00	
Rent or mortgage, rates	4·00	
Electricity, gas, fuel	1·75	
Clothing	1·75	
Tobacco, etc.	2·50	
Hire purchase or credit payments	1·25	
Fares	1·50	
Insurance	0·50	
Entertainment, including cosmetics, etc.	1·00	
Sundries	0·75	
Savings (holidays, etc.)	1·00	
		25·00

If we analyse this expenditure, it will be apparent that we spend a high proportion of our wages on food and other essentials. We still have

18

sufficient left over, however, for items such as entertainment, tobacco, and the buying, on credit perhaps, of a television set or a washing machine. A small amount each week may be saved for any future contingencies, or for a particular object such as a holiday or a new car.

It is interesting to compare our present day expenditure with a typical family expenditure budget of fifty years ago.

BUDGET FOR THE SAME FAMILY—FIFTY YEARS AGO

	s.	d.	£	s.	d.
Weekly wage			1	15	0
Expenditure					
Housekeeping allowance for food, etc.	13	6			
Rent	4	0			
Clothing	4	0			
Gas and fuel	4	6			
Tobacco, etc.	1	0			
Doctor's panel	1	3			
Entertainment	2	3			
Sundries	3	0			
Savings	1	6			
			1	15	0
(Equivalent to £1·75 in decimal currency)					

It is noticeable that wages were far smaller fifty years ago, but our different items of expenditure were smaller too. It is not our intention to look too deeply into the reasons for these changes in value, but from these figures we can conclude that, as wages increase, so do our expenses. It does not follow that increased wages will ensure that we are better off financially.

We hear and read a great deal about wage earners wanting rises and this poses many problems for the Government who watch the national situation very closely and try to ensure that wages do not rise too steeply, with a consequent increase in the prices of the many commodities we need. For example, if we know that, today, £1 will buy a joint of meat sufficient for a family of four, an increase in wages will only be of *real value* if it is not swallowed up by increases in the price of meat. An increase in wages will improve our own standard of living only if this increase is not spent in paying higher prices for our wants.

An examination of our respective budgets will reveal that today we spend proportionately more of our wages on items which, many years ago, would have been either unobtainable, or classed as luxuries which we would have found difficult to afford.

The Development of Trade

Today, we have come to accept the many things in life which are available to us—the latest films, perhaps, from the United States of America, holidays abroad, or the latest in "pop" records—a whole range of products, produced not only in this country but in many overseas countries. One of the reasons for our having available such a wide variety of products today is that, through the years, the countries of the world have exchanged many goods and services. Goods which are not obtainable in this country may be provided for us by other countries, and in return we supply these nations with our products. This is a process known as *exchange* or *trade*.

BARTER

Many centuries ago man was said to be self-supporting. A family may have had a small piece of land on which they farmed. The wife would perhaps make the family's clothing, by weaving cloth in the cottage. Life in those days was generally very simple and primitive by our standards. Eventually, people living in the same village commenced exchanging different articles and commodities with one another. If one family was short of food, clothing would be exchanged with another family in return for supplies of foodstuffs. This exchange was called *barter*, and it is from this bartering that families conducted, one with another, that the whole process of trade had its beginnings.

THE INDUSTRIAL REVOLUTION

In this country, during the eighteenth century, we had the beginnings of what is called the "Industrial Revolution." Workshops or factories were built, which were, of course, very small compared to our industrial giants of today. New machines were invented, to help in the manufacture of different products, and workpeople were engaged and trained to operate the machinery. Life for the people of this country was changing. Towns were springing up near to the factories, and exchange between people was increasing.

INTERNATIONAL TRADE

Trade between people in this country grew very quickly as new techniques were introduced into the factories to help speed up production,

20

and to produce in larger quantities. Although for many years this country had been recognized as a trading nation (our mariners sailing to foreign lands, and exchanging various goods for spices and silks), with the increasing growth of industry it was found that we could manufacture more than we needed for our own requirements. It was quite logical, therefore, that we should trade our excess products in exchange for the goods of other nations that were needed by us.

Great Britain is a small country, with a large population for its size, and it has never been able to grow foodstuffs in quantities sufficient to feed all its population. Trade has always, therefore, been necessary. Through the years we have received not only supplies of necessary foodstuffs from other nations, but also many raw materials, such as wool, cotton, and oil.

All the peoples of the world are *traders*, in that they exchange what they have to offer, in return for something they need. No matter what our occupation in life, we exchange our labour for a reward known as wages or profits. A great deal of the progress that has been made in the world is due to trade, and it has been realized that it is impossible to live in isolation from one another. The nations of the world have traded with one another to some extent because they wanted to, but mainly because it was, and still is, absolutely vital to their well-being.

Because all the natural resources of the world are limited, countries tend to exchange with one another the goods and services which they are best suited to produce. Great Britain, a powerful industrial nation, supplies other countries with products such as ships, motor-cars, and engineering goods of all descriptions. We are also an important commercial nation, and our banks and insurance companies provide many people in all parts of the world with these important services. In return, we in this country receive supplies of wool from Australia and elsewhere, cotton from the United States of America and dairy produce from Denmark.

Imports and Exports

When we send our products to other countries of the world, we say that we are *exporting*. Goods we receive from other countries are called our *imports*. The ideal situation is to try to ensure that over a period of time the total value of goods imported into this country is equalled by the total value of the products we in Great Britain export or sell to other nations. It is only if we can achieve this state of affairs that it can be said that, as a nation, we are paying our way or, to put it another way, to say that we are balancing our trade.

Balance of Trade and Payments

Each month, the Department of Trade and Industry, which is responsible for looking after the affairs of commerce in this country, publishes a statement setting out the total values of goods exported and imported during that period, which informs us of our *balance of trade*. It tells us whether we have balanced our exports of goods against our imports, or whether there is a difference, and one has exceeded the other.

Because Great Britain needs to import an enormous quantity of goods and foodstuffs, it is usual to find that we in this country never achieve a perfect balance between, on the one hand, the goods we receive from other countries, and on the other hand, the goods we sell to them. The balance is thus often an adverse one, our imports exceeding our exports. This, however, is not the only consideration, because we should also take into account the many *services* that countries provide for one another, such as transport, insurance, and banking facilities. It is necessary therefore, that we think not only in terms of goods, but also in terms of the provision of services. Great Britain provides many nations with a great variety of services.

The overall trade position must recognize, then, the exchange of goods and services, and any difference between our total imports and exports is known as the *balance of payments*. Because Great Britain usually provides other nations with more services than it receives from them, this helps considerably in ensuring that the two sides of the scales balance.

VISIBLE AND INVISIBLE IMPORTS AND EXPORTS
Goods and commodities that are imported and exported are known as *visible* imports and exports. Services are called *invisible* imports and exports. Consider the following example—

Margaret Jones sold Carol Watson a brooch which she no longer required. An actual article was thus exchanged between the two girls. Should, however, Margaret have offered to deliver Carol's suitcase to the railway station, a service would have been performed.

How The Balance of Trade and The Balance of Payments are Calculated

Month of............. 19.	
	£
Total goods exported by Great Britain	250,000,000
Total goods imported from other countries	270,000,000
Balance of Trade (adverse)	20,000,000
We must now take into account the many services exchanged between countries:	
Total services exported by Great Britain	25,000,000
Total services imported from other countries	10,000,000
Balance (favourable)	15,000,000
Adverse balance of trade	20,000,000
Reduced by a favourable balance in considering exchange of services	15,000,000
BALANCE OF PAYMENTS (the overall balance, taking into account both goods and services) is adverse	5,000,000

A country's imports and exports are separated in exactly the same way. An exchange of actual goods is classed as visible, whereas the exchange of services is regarded as invisible.

It is always the concern of the Government of this country to try to ensure that we can pay our way as a trading nation and so provide the community with all its wants.

So that you can better understand the importance of the trade position between Great Britain and other countries, it is informative to collect each month the appropriate cuttings from the national newspapers in which our trade figures are given, so that a constant record is kept of the situation.

THE STRENGTHENING OF TIES

Because of the increase in trade, the bonds of friendship between countries have strengthened, and because of this friendship and reliance upon one another, the threat of war diminishes to some extent, and cultural exchanges are arranged. Each nation develops an increasing

23

appreciation of the way of life of other nations. The worlds of industry and business have a common *aim*, which is to ensure that there is work available for all, with consequent trade amongst all peoples, and a share in the general prosperity.

Customs Duty

Many goods that are imported into this country from abroad are subject to a form of taxation known as *customs duty*. Those of you who have returned from a holiday abroad, having brought with you articles such as perfume, cameras, and watches know that the customs officer will charge duty on each of these articles (if in excess of the allowance).

Customs duty may be levied on certain goods, such as tobacco and spirits, for the purpose of raising revenue. Certain imported goods are subject to duty because the Government wishes to reduce the quantities being brought into the country.

BONDED WAREHOUSES

Bonded warehouses are used as places for storing goods on which duty must be paid. As the goods are taken out of the warehouse, the amount of duty which the goods have to bear is paid by the person desiring their release. The warehouses are supervised by customs officers, and a careful check is made of all goods entering and leaving the warehouse so that payment of duty cannot be avoided.

Questions

1. Describe the changes that have taken place in this country during the last century.

2. Why are increases in wages only useful provided that prices of the goods we purchase do not rise correspondingly?

3. Explain the importance of trade to this country.

4. Explain why increased trade helps us all in our own lives.

5. What is meant by imports and exports? Why is it important that this country should continue to increase its total exports each year?

6. Explain the difference between the balance of trade and the balance of payments. Explain how each is calculated, using examples to illustrate.

7. (i) What is customs duty?
   (ii) What are bonded warehouses?

8. What are the reasons for charging customs duty?

9. (i) What is another word for exchange?
   (ii) Give one example of a raw material imported into this country.
   (iii) Name an important British export.

Practical Work

1. Compile a budget for the average family today, and one for the average family of fifty years ago. Write briefly on the differences.

2. Draw a chart (e.g. a bar chart) which will illustrate why increases in wages do not necessarily mean that a person is better off.

3. Make a list of any articles used personally by you that come from overseas countries. Write briefly on their importance to you.

4. Collect newspaper cuttings of last month's balance of trade and balance of payments figures. Show these figures in the form of a diagram (e.g. a bar chart or graph) and then collect each month's figures for the rest of the term and show them on your diagram.

5 Money

Have you ever considered just how you spend your pocket money? Although we all have different preferences, the following example is typical of our monthly expenditure—

SCHOOLGIRL—15–16 YEARS OF AGE

	£	£
Pocket money for one month		3·00
Spent as follows—		
Sweets	0·50	
Nylons	0·45	
Cosmetics	0·45	
Dancing or records	0·90	
Fares	0·15	
Sundries	0·15	
Savings	0·40	
	——	3·00

SCHOOLBOY—15–16 YEARS OF AGE

	£	£
Pocket money for one month		3·00
Spent as follows—		
Sweets	0·50	
Records	0·45	
Fares	0·25	
Cinema	0·60	
Refreshments (youth club)	0·30	
Sundries	0·30	
Savings	0·60	
	——	3·00

The Necessity for Money

How you spend your own pocket money will depend to a large extent on what your personal priorities are. Some girls may prefer to spend a great deal each month on dancing, or listening to their favourite "pop" group. Others may spend a large proportion of their pocket money on records by their favourite artists. Whereas one boy may spend a large amount each month on periodicals, another may have a hobby on which he spends his pocket money. It does not really matter how our pocket money is spent. What does matter to us is that we do have a regular supply of money, in order that we may buy all those things that we need.

It is difficult to imagine life with no money, and without the means to enjoy life in the way that we wish. We do, of course, often hear people say that money is not everything, and this is quite true. Nevertheless, it is equally true that there is a necessity for us to have sufficient money to pay for the things we need in life. From the previous chapter you will recall that trade really commenced with people bartering goods with one another. One person had something that somebody else needed, and consequently people made exchanges. In this way everybody benefited.

Development from the Days of Barter

Eventually, it was realized that this particular system of exchange was not always practicable, and a measure of value for this exchange of goods and services had to be devised, such as a token, which was valuable in itself and which could be used to measure the individual values of the goods and services that were being exchanged. With the discovery of valuable metals such as gold and silver, it became possible for people to sell what they had in return for this token, which we today call money, and use the token to buy the things they needed. Through the centuries, as exchange grew, not only between people living in the same village or town, but also between people living in different countries, money was the measure of the value of all the goods and services that people had to offer. It was the only fair method of ensuring that individuals received good value in their exchanges with one another.

Although at one time, when gold and silver were used extensively, money was regarded as valuable in itself, the need for more money led to the introduction of bank-notes, based, of course, upon paper, which is of little value in itself. Yet the bank-note is a far more convenient form

27

Fig. 2. The Goods and Services Money Buys for Us

of money, in that it can be carried more easily, and is less bulky. It is hardly possible even to imagine the situation of having plenty of money, but nothing to spend it on. Nor can we imagine the effect on our personal lives if this situation were to arise, and our money were to become valueless because the goods and services we needed were not obtainable. It is no longer the money itself which is important, but the things we can buy with it.

How Money is Used

When you leave school or college you will need to go out to work in order to earn money, so that you will be able to afford all those things that are so necessary. You will exchange your own personal skills in return for wages so that you can support yourself, and perhaps your family when you marry. It is exactly the same with the countries of the world. Goods and services will be exchanged between nations, one with another, money being the measure of their value; but it is only if we can exchange the money we have received for goods we have provided, in return for commodities from other countries, that it will have any value for us. Because there is in existence a "measure of value," exchange between people has been made possible.

Questions

1. Describe the uses of money, explaining the development of the use of money from the days of barter.
2. Why is money acceptable to people, when in itself it is practically valueless?
3. Why is money in itself valueless as a means of exchange between countries trading with each other?

Practical Work

1. Prepare a statement showing how you spend your pocket money. List the materials used in the manufacture of the goods you purchase out of your pocket money. In another column on your list show the origin of these materials.
2. Draw a diagram which illustrates the necessity for money in the exchange of goods and services between people.

6 The Nation

We are now living in a changing world, and as science makes important new discoveries, and researchers discover new methods and techniques, our way of life is changing. Many of our factories are installing machinery and employing new methods which are bound to affect many people in their working lives. Whilst some people may argue that increasing mechanization in industry, and in other spheres too, will create greater unemployment, this is not necessarily so, and the reasons why will be explained later in this chapter. Apart from the changing industrial world, there have been other developments. In this country we now have many different kinds of shops, all with one purpose in view—to provide the consumer with the best possible service. New developments such as the growth of self-service shops, supermarkets, and the increasing use of automatic-machine vending, have given the retail trade a new look. A whole range of services (which are regarded as so essential to us in our everyday lives) are now provided for us by our local town councils and the Government.

The Development of Industry, Commerce and Social Services— The Industrial Revolution

To discover the reasons behind this story of development through the years, we must go back to the eighteenth century. At that time there was a bloodless revolution in this country. Prior to this most families lived a very simple life, farming their own plots of land, and weaving the cloth for their clothes in the cottages where they lived.

Our story really commences at this point, because, with the discovery of the coalfields and the invention of the power-driven loom and other machinery, came the beginnings of industry as we know it. Workshops and factories were built near the coalfields, because coal was (and still is) a very important commodity for the producing of power, and is a necessary aid in the manufacture of iron and steel. The people of this country started to leave the rural areas in order to obtain jobs in the factories, and we had the beginnings of towns.

The factory age, or the "Industrial Revolution," had commenced, and for a long time conditions in industry were very bad. Young children were sent out to work in the factories and the coal mines. The working hours were long, and conditions poor; wages were low, and the general picture was one of distress and almost unbelievable suffering. Eventually, people began to rebel against the terrible conditions, and as a result of the courageous action of a number of citizens, Parliament passed various laws, all designed to improve the working lives of the people. Employment exchanges were set up. Help was given to those out of work, or unemployed because of sickness. A great deal of progress was made in improving working conditions for people, and in the provision of many State services.

In the early stages, industry tended to be concentrated in particular areas of the country, because factories at that time had to be situated as near as possible to the source of the raw materials used in the manufacture of their products. Many of our major steel-works are still sited near the coalfields; this helps to keep the cost of transporting coal, a bulky material, as low as possible. Climatic conditions and the proximity of the coalfields led also to the development of our great textile industries in Lancashire and the West Riding of Yorkshire.

Specialization of Industry and Manpower

With the introduction of electricity into factories and homes, and the improvement in transport facilities, industry generally began to spread to other areas. This led to the growth of industry in other regions, such as the London area. There has, however, always been a tendency to concentrate particular types of industry in the same area, for example the north-east, which is famous for its steel plants and shipyards, or the Midlands, renowned for the manufacture of motor vehicles. This concentration of particular types of industries in the same areas is called *specialization*, because these particular districts are said to specialize in the making of certain products. This has been advanced as a possible reason for the pockets of unemployment that occur, from time to time, in certain parts of the country. A lack of demand for the products produced in areas where manufacture is restricted to certain types of goods will in turn affect other industries which are supplying the raw materials for these products. An instance of this kind occurs when a decline in the shipbuilding industry leads to a decline in the steel-producing industry also.

31

Today, however, efforts are made to situate in the same area factories producing a large variety of different products. This often ensures that, should there be a lack of demand for a particular product, not all the factories in a particular area will be affected.

Since the days of the "Industrial Revolution" a great deal of mechanization has taken place in our factories. Machines which work at high speed and with great accuracy have been invented, and installed in many factories. The articles produced in factories which are equipped with this type of modern machinery are not only made in less time, but are manufactured in much larger quantities.

The days have gone when one man did a variety of entirely different operations in his work. It has been realized that, if a person can concentrate in his work on performing one operation only, personal skills will develop, and the speed at which the work is carried out will improve also. Because of this improvement in skill and the increased speed at which an employee can work, higher wages can be paid, and there are also greater economies for the factory owners. We have, therefore, not only specialization in the sense that industries of one type tend to be found in the same areas of the country, but we also have workpeople who specialize in their own particular jobs, as in the instance of an employee in a factory producing motor-cars, whose sole job it might be to fit the tyres on to the wheels.

Mass Production and its Benefits

In this country, certain industries have developed extensively techniques for the *mass production* of goods. In other words, the manufacture of motor-cars, television sets, telephones, shoes, and a whole range of other goods, is carried out in very large quantities. Mass production has developed very largely because specialization, the principle of one man doing one job, has helped to make it possible. Another important factor has been the use made of modern machinery in speeding up production.

Henry Ford, of the United States of America, originated the manufacture of motor-cars by these methods, and today Ford's of Dagenham are a very good example of a firm using these same methods in this country. The various components necessary in the building of a motor-car are either manufactured in one of the many departments at Ford's, or are brought in from outside sources. All these components are eventually brought to one of the assembly lines, and in a series of operations the car is built. Some indication of the speed at which a motor-car is built can be gathered from the fact that, on some assembly lines, one complete unit is finished every few minutes.

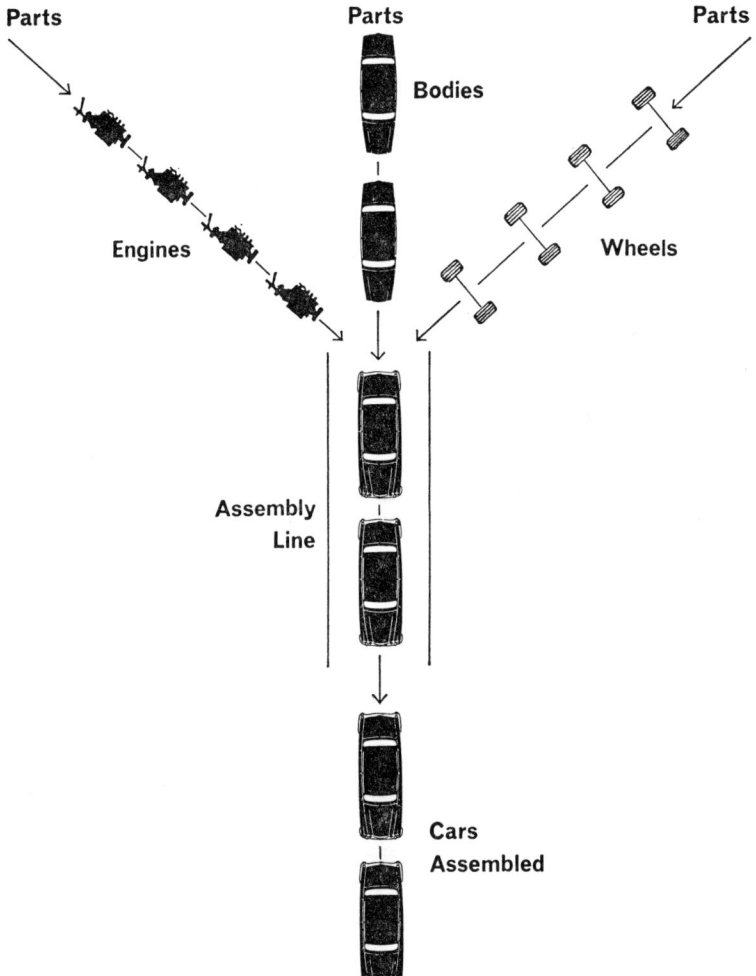

Fig. 3. How Motor-cars are Mass Produced

As we have seen in earlier chapters, we need to produce goods sufficient not only for our own needs in this country but in quantities large enough to enable us to exchange any surplus that we have for the products of other countries. The use of mass production methods of

33

manufacture helps to make this possible. Also, costs of producing goods are kept to a minimum, and ultimately, we, the consumers, benefit from this.

All factories incur certain expenses, which have to be paid whether many articles are produced or only a few. Therefore, the proportion of these costs which each individual product manufactured must bear will vary according to how many are produced. Let us examine the following example.

FACTORY PRODUCING TAPE-RECORDERS

Details of expenses which are incurred by factory in one year.

	£
Rent or mortgage of factory and offices	5,000
Rates	2,500
Salaries for supervisors and office staff	8,000
Wear and tear of machinery	3,000
Stationery, postage, telephones, etc.	1,000
Insurance	500
	20,000

If, in one year, 5,000 tape-recorders are produced, the proportion of the costs that each unit must bear would amount to £20,000 *divided by* 5,000, *equals £4 for each tape-recorder*. If only 4,000 tape-recorders were to be produced, the proportion of the above costs that each unit must bear would be £20,000 *divided by* 4,000 *equals £5 for each tape-recorder*.

In these days of big business and large factories the whole object is, therefore, to try to keep at a fixed level certain expenses that have to be incurred however many units are produced, whilst at the same time endeavouring to increase the number of units produced. In this way prices may be kept as low as possible. Thus, not only do we as the consumers benefit, but the manufacturers sell more of their products to overseas countries because their prices are far more competitive.

Although many people fear that too much mechanization in industry will mean that machines will replace men by doing much of the work previously done by them, this is not necessarily so. The changing pattern of industry as a result of automation may result in fewer employees being required on the work-benches, but there will be an increasing need for people in other occupations, such as administrative work, transport, warehousing, research and maintenance. We must remember that as industry has developed so also has commerce, and an increasing number of jobs are becoming available both in the commercial occupations and in the occupations engaged in the provision of direct services for all sections of the community.

Questions

1. What is meant by specialization?

2. In what ways has the introduction of mass-production methods of manufacture helped us all as individuals?

3. Write briefly on automation in this country. Does increased mechanization in the factory mean that more people will be out of work?

4. Discuss the benefits of the four-day-week. What kind of problems will it pose for the individual?

5. Why do so many small firms continue to exist in these days of large firms and large-scale production?

6. Describe the work of industry in this country. Why have certain industries tended to be concentrated in certain areas of the country? Has this proved to their disadvantage in the past?

7. Write briefly on any manufacturing industry in your area, describing all the processes involved in producing the goods.

8.   (i) Name one industry in which mass production methods of manufacture are used.

   (ii) Mass production means . . .

  (iii) What is meant by mechanization in industry?

  (iv) Name three products which are mass produced.

Practical Work

1. Draw a map of your own local area. Indicate the sites of local industries.

2. From the industries marked on your map, make a list of basic materials used in manufacturing the products made, stating the country of origin.

3. Draw a diagram which will illustrate the features of mass-production methods of manufacture.

4. Find out what type of farming you have in your area. Make a list of the produce sold.

7 Services

It has been stressed in earlier chapters that, throughout our lives, we are dependent on many other persons to help in providing our many and varied wants. Firms of manufacturers also need help in exactly the same way. Whether it be the services of the banking world, the insurance companies, the wholesalers, or the retailers, they are important to both firms and individuals alike.

Local and National Services

At a later stage mention will be made of the very important services provided for us by the business world, but in this chapter we shall deal in detail with those provided for us by the local councils and by the national Government of the country.

If we take a look at a typical day in the life of the average person, it will be apparent that very many services are required by each one of us. An instance of this is the housewife who, after seeing the children safely off to school, sets off to town with her baby, with the intention of visiting the welfare clinic. After alighting from the bus she visits the clinic and then calls at the public library in order to exchange her books. She may then do her shopping and walk home, or perhaps visit the local park.

If we were to list the services benefiting the housewife on this particular day, they would number at least five, all of them being provided by the local council—

1. Maintenance of pavements and roads.
2. Municipal bus services.
3. Welfare clinics.
4. Public libraries.
5. Parks.

In addition to the services mentioned, there are many others which are just as essential, including—

1. Sewage disposal—very necessary for the prevention of disease.
2. Collection of house refuse.

3. Schools and colleges.
4. Museums, swimming baths, sports fields.
5. Police—fire brigade.
6. Houses built by the local authority.

Not only are we being helped by the provision of services which are very necessary for our health and general well-being, but services are also provided which help us in our leisure hours.

In addition to the various services mentioned above there are others provided for us by the central government. These national services are also very essential and include—

(*a*) aid in establishing educational institutions, such as schools, colleges of further education and universities;

(*b*) family allowances, retirement pensions, widows' pensions, and many other benefits to assist families who need them;

(*c*) maintenance of the armed forces.

It has been the concern of successive governments, in this country and in others throughout the world, to ensure that citizens are provided with the help they need if they are to enjoy a comfortable life. Provision for old age, help when illness strikes the family, and the defence of the nation form only a small part of the services provided for all.

People have come to expect a great many services in their daily life, but we should bear in mind that these services have not sprung up overnight; it has taken many years for them to come about. Progress in industry and commerce is not sufficient in itself. Many local and national services are also very necessary.

It must not be forgotten that, although certain countries such as Great Britain have achieved considerable success in ensuring that their peoples have a standard of living which helps them to enjoy life, there are still other countries whose populations, judged by our standards, lead a very primitive life, and it is the long-term object of civilization as we know it to enable such progress to be made in all the countries of the world.

The provision of all these services both by the local authority and by the Government costs a great deal of money and must be paid for by the people of the country. The revenue required is collected in the form of *taxes*, two different methods of tax collection being used.

Revenue required by the local authority in its provision of local services is collected in the form of *rates*. The Government finances national services by the collection of *income tax* and other taxes from individuals and public and private bodies.

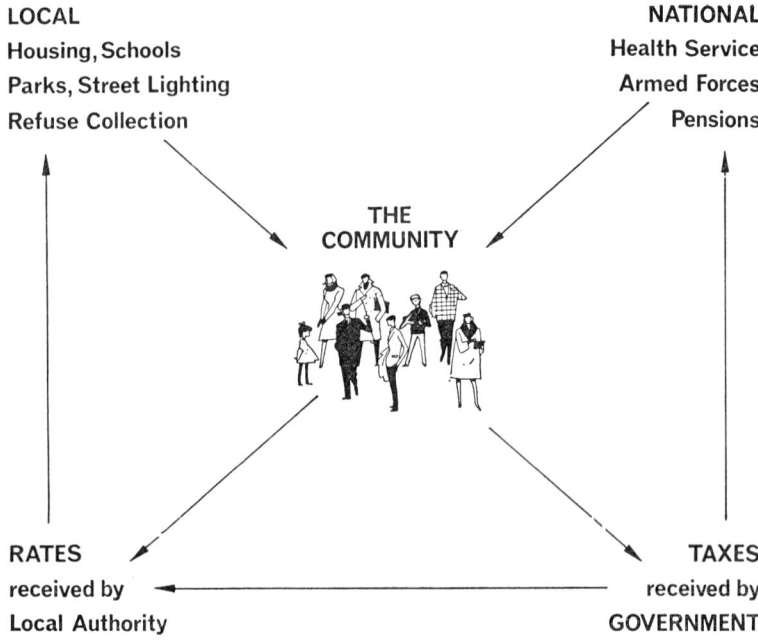

LOCAL
Housing, Schools
Parks, Street Lighting
Refuse Collection

NATIONAL
Health Service
Armed Forces
Pensions

THE
COMMUNITY

RATES
received by
Local Authority

TAXES
received by
GOVERNMENT

Fig. 4. Local and National Services Provided for the Community

The Rates System

It is the responsibility of the local authority to collect rates from owners of all types of businesses, including factories and shops, as well as from private householders. To ensure that the local authority always has adequate supplies of money in order that we may be provided with the many different services necessary, rates are sometimes collected by two equal instalments each year, at six-monthly intervals. Property owners receive a rates demand from the county or borough treasurer showing how much is payable by them.

In order that the treasurer should be able to calculate just how much each property owner must pay each year as his contribution towards the total revenue needed, each building situated within the boundaries of the borough or county, whether it be a private household or a place of business, is given a rateable value. The calculation of this figure is rather complicated; it is sufficient for you to know that the rateable value is based on the value of the property to the owner should it be rented to another person.

At the present time, this system of rates collection and their assessment is considered the only fair means whereby a local authority can obtain sufficient money to meet all the expenses involved in the provision of its public services. The basis of collection of revenue in this way is the valuation placed upon the property owned. The greater the value of the property the higher the rates payable. Persons residing in houses owned by the local council, paying rent each week for the use of the property, also pay rates indirectly, since a certain proportion of the amount charged as rent is in respect of rates.

For a long time it has been thought, however, that the system of collecting revenue in the form of rates is often unfair, since a person such as a widow with only a small income may contribute exactly the same sum as a householder with a much higher income. A great deal of thought as to an alternative system will be necessary before any real changes can be made. In 1966, however, the Government introduced a scheme whereby persons such as pensioners can obtain financial relief in the form of a rebate in respect of rates paid.

Each year the local council meets to consider how much revenue will be required from the ratepayers in order that all the many services may be paid for. In order for it to be able to do this, the council will need to refer to lists provided by the treasurer, which show the rateable value in total of all properties situated within the jurisdiction of the council.

TOTAL RATEABLE VALUES

	£
Industrial premises	500,000
Other places of business including offices, warehouses, and shops	250,000
Private households	250,000
	1,000,000
Estimated amount required to pay for all services for the year being—	1,500,000

Note: *The Government each year provides a local authority with sums of money, termed* **grants,** *towards the cost of providing services such as education, police force, etc.*

39

In the above example we will assume that the Government grant receivable by the local authority amounts to £1,000,000. The council now has the information it needs to calculate how much will be required from the ratepayers if its budget is to be balanced. In this example, the calculation would be as follows—

	£
Estimated amount required	1,500,000
Less Government grants	1,000,000
Amount to be provided by the ratepayers	500,000

It will be evident that if £500,000 is required for the ensuing year and if all the properties within the council's boundaries have a total rateable value of £1,000,000, then for every pound rateable value 50p will have to be paid by the property owner. A rate of 50p in the pound will then be declared by the council, which will authorize the treasurer to collect it in two equal half-yearly instalments. A person owning a house with a rateable value of £100 will, in this particular year, pay the sum of £50, this amount being divided into two equal payments of £25 each. Some local authorities may allow a ratepayer to pay by monthly instalments.

STATEMENT OF SERVICES PROVIDED AND THE COST

	£
Education	0·40
Welfare services, clinics, etc.	0·08
Housing	0·15
Public libraries, museums, etc.	0·05
Police	0·10
Fire service	0·07
Highways, including cleaning and maintenance of roads and pavements	0·25
Public lighting	0·03
Sewerage	0·08
Parks, sportsfields, etc.	0·04
Other services	0·25
	1·50
Less: grants from the Government	1·00
Rate in the pound	0·50

Many local authorities publish a free booklet each year, which is available to all ratepayers. This booklet, obtainable at the local council offices, shows how the revenue collected in the form of rates is spent.

Income Tax

In addition to the cost of maintaining local services, a great deal of revenue is required by the Government for the provision of national services, and to collect this money it has a special department called the Board of Inland Revenue. This particular department is responsible for the collection of income tax from individuals and many organizations throughout the country. The Board of Inland Revenue is divided into two departments for the purposes of collecting income tax, which are—

(*a*) *The offices of the Inspector of Taxes*, situated in all districts throughout the country. This particular branch of the Inland Revenue decides the exact amount of each taxpayer's liability, and deals with any queries that may arise as a consequence.

(*b*) *The offices of the Collector of Taxes*, which are also situated in all districts. The function of this branch of the Inland Revenue is to ensure that all tax payments are received from the various sources.

In the case of a person owning a business, an assessment is made by the Inland Revenue each year, stating the amount of the income tax liability for the year. The amount of the liability will be dependent on the amount of profit earned by the business in that year. Companies and other corporate bodies, which we shall deal with in Chapter 10, pay a special tax known as *corporation tax*.

PAY AS YOU EARN

The vast majority of taxpayers are wage earners employed by many different firms throughout the country, and a special method of tax collection is used for the income tax payable by them. This is called "pay as you earn" or, in its abbreviated form, P.A.Y.E.

Before 1944, persons liable to pay income tax would receive a letter, each year, from the office of the Inspector of Taxes in their area. This would inform them of the amount payable in respect of income tax and that the necessary payment should be made. This was not a particularly satisfactory method of collecting taxes, because many people did not budget for this tax liability week by week, and often found difficulty in finding the money. During the Second World War the Government had to raise a great deal of revenue in order to finance the war effort, and most wage earners became liable to pay income tax. Not only was more revenue required but it was also necessary to collect it far more frequently. Mr. Paul Chambers, a civil servant of that time who later became a very important industrialist, helped to devise the system of P.A.Y.E. The merits of this method are that income tax is deducted from the wage earner's pay on a weekly basis by the employer, and then remitted by him to the Income Tax Collector in the following month. (Persons receiving wages on a monthly basis pay tax each month.)

This particular method is satisfactory from all points of view. The Government receives its taxes more quickly and the taxpayer does not have to budget for future income tax demands.

INCOME TAX ALLOWANCES

Our method of assessing income tax is a fair method since persons with high incomes pay proportionately more tax than those with smaller incomes. The individual's domestic and personal affairs are taken into account, and allowances given for married persons and their children. Persons with dependants (for example, a man with a widowed mother), or those making payments to a pension scheme or to insurance companies under life assurance policies, are also granted relief.

Each year the taxpayer receives a notice from the offices of the Inspector of Taxes, showing the allowances that have been granted for that particular year, which always commences on 6th April. The individual allowances are shown on this notice and, when totalled, will be worth a certain number of points, by reference to which a *code number* is fixed. The more points allotted to the taxpayer in the way of allowances, the higher will be the code number. This code number, when applied by the employer in deducting the income tax, will indicate, after a process of calculation, the total tax due for the week. Each employer is issued with a special set of tax tables from which it is possible to calculate the tax payable for every employee, irrespective of what he earns and the nature of the allowances granted.

The taxpayer pays a set rate of tax on every pound of taxable income. These rates do vary from time to time according to how much income tax the Government needs to collect in a particular year. An example of the rates in one particular year might be as follows—

All taxable incomes—40p (£0·40) in the pound.

42

It can be seen from the example below that the total allowances granted amount to £987 for the year. If we divide this amount by fifty-two, we can see that the weekly allowance will be just under £19, and that wages earned in excess of this amount each week will be subject to income tax.

INCOME TAX ASSESSMENT FOR
MARRIED MAN WITH TWO CHILDREN OF SCHOOL AGE

	£
Personal allowance for man and his wife	465
Allowance for two children (£115 each)	230
Allowance in respect of mortgage interest payable to building society	70
*Earned income relief	222
	987
Wages earned during the present year	1000

Therefore, amount of taxable income for the
present year will be—

		£
	Wages	1000
Less	Allowances	987
		13

Tax paid will be—
£13 at 40p (£0·40) in the pound = £5·20

Note: Wage earners are given a special earned income relief of two-ninths of the net income earned. This could, of course, be varied by the Board of Inland Revenue if desired.

The calculations involved in assessing an individual's allowances and the amount of tax he should pay are rather involved, but it is possible for taxpayers to calculate their allowances on a weekly basis, provided it is borne in mind that they may not be absolutely accurate. The Inspector of Taxes always calculates allowances on a yearly basis, and the tax tables provided for employers allow for breaking down to a weekly basis. As stated previously, the rates of income tax and the amount of individual allowances may vary from year to year, according to the amount of revenue needed by the Government.

Other Forms of Taxation

The amount of money collected by the Board of Inland Revenue in the form of income tax is not sufficient to pay for all the national services that are provided for us, and so the Government must find some additional ways of obtaining revenue.

PURCHASE TAX

This form of tax is really a *sales tax*, and many of the goods we purchase both for our personal use and for use in the home are increased in price by an amount of purchase tax. Hundreds of products of all descriptions cost us far more than the amounts at which manufacturers price the goods, as, at the instruction of the Government, an additional sum of money is added to the price of the goods. Tax raised in this way is called an indirect tax because the person who bears it is the consumer, although it is paid to the Inland Revenue by the seller.

CUSTOMS AND EXCISE DUTIES

We have already dealt with customs duties in Chapter 4. Excise duties are charged on spirits, beer, etc., produced in this country, and the manufacturers must pay this tax before parting with the goods. Both customs and excise duties are, like purchase tax, called indirect taxes.

SELECTIVE EMPLOYMENT TAX

In 1966 the Government introduced this new form of taxation. It is paid by firms and businesses which are not actually *producing* goods, a sum being paid by the employer in respect of each employee.

Direct and Indirect Taxation

We therefore have two forms of taxation: (*a*) *direct taxes*, such as income tax, corporation tax and local rates and (*b*) *indirect taxes*, which we have just been discussing. There are many arguments expressed both for and against the two methods. Some people argue that it is better to abolish all direct taxation and raise the revenue required by increasing

44

the amount of purchase tax on the various articles we buy in the shops and elsewhere. Others favour the abolition of purchase tax and an increase in the general rate of income tax. The whole question of taxation is a very involved one, and the Government must raise its revenue in the way it thinks best. The most important consideration, however, is that whatever form taxation takes, it must be as fair as possible for everybody.

The Budget

Each year the *Chancellor of the Exchequer*, who is the minister who acts as treasurer for the Government, has to calculate, with the help of his assistants, how much money will be needed by the country if it is to pay for all the necessary services already mentioned. Once he knows how much money will be needed, the Chancellor then has to decide what various ways and means he will use to obtain from the British public the required amount of revenue.

Calculating how much money will be required, and from what sources it will be obtained, is really a form of *budgeting* and the annual statement on this subject in the House of Commons is known as *The Budget*. The Chancellor may decide to increase direct taxation and put up the rate of income tax, or he may decide to find his revenue by increasing indirect taxation, and levy greater amounts of purchase tax on many of the goods we need to purchase. He could decide to increase both forms of taxation, if desired, and increase tax rates generally. Taxes could be reduced, of course, should the Chancellor feel he had a surplus of money in a particular year.

The Budget is the planning of the country's financial affairs for an entire year and we are all usually affected in one way or another by the measures that are taken as a result of The Budget.

Questions

1. Describe briefly—

   (i) services provided by local authorities,
   (ii) services provided by the Government.

2. Explain the methods used by local authorities and the Government to obtain revenue so that the many services we need are provided.

3. A man owns a house which has a rateable value of £100. The local council declares a rate of 50p in the pound. Taking into account that the annual rates are collected in two equal half-yearly instalments, calculate the rates payable for each half-year.

4. Do you consider the present system of rates and income tax a fair one? Briefly give your own views, and describe the system of P.A.Y.E.

5. "In this country," said Bill, who was not married, "income tax is not really a tax on income at all, because the amount you pay depends on your responsibilities." How far do you think this is true? Support your opinion with facts about the subject. (*Metropolitan Reg. Exam. Board.*)

6. At an election, one party said that they would abolish income tax and increase purchase tax, with the slogan "Keep all you earn. Spend it how *you* like." Would you vote for such a party? Give clear reasons for your answer and assume that in most other matters you agreed with their policies. (*Metropolitan Reg. Exam. Board.*)

7. Explain—

(i) direct taxes,
(ii) indirect taxes.

8. Write briefly on purchase tax, and its effect on our own personal lives.

9. Describe the purpose of The Budget.

10. James Bloor received an annual salary of £1,000. In a particular year his total income tax allowances amounted to £850. The current rate of income tax was—

all taxable income at 40p (£0·40) in the pound.

(i) How much tax would James Bloor pay in that year?
(ii) How much tax would he pay in each week of that year?

11. (i) What is rateable value?
(ii) Purchase tax is an . . . tax,
(iii) Income tax is a . . . tax.

Practical Work

1. Find out what your own local authority's rates amount to (from the authority's booklet if available), and prepare a tabulated list of where the money goes.

2. Prepare a bar chart showing the above information.

3. Prepare a speech in which you—as Chancellor of the Exchequer—outline how you hope to obtain the revenue needed by your government.

4. Find out the current rates of income tax, and calculate the various allowances due for your own family.

5. Prepare a diagram illustrating how all local and national services are paid for.

8 The Home

It was stated in the previous chapter that a very important service provided by the local authority was the provision of houses that could be rented by families living within the area. In this chapter we shall consider the help given to persons who eventually wish to own a home of their own.

On getting married, young people have to consider the very important problem of finding suitable accommodation. This often proves difficult since rented flats are not always obtained easily and local councils have long lists of people wishing to rent a house. Quite apart from this, there is a tendency today for more people to consider buying a home for themselves.

We all have our own ideas of the type of house we should like to call our own. It may be a small compact house, or perhaps a modern "semi-detached" with garage and garden. Whatever our own particular likes and dislikes, the problem is one of raising the necessary money.

The Help that Building Societies Offer to Home Buyers

The *building societies* can help young couples to buy a suitable property. Provided the societies have funds available, and are given evidence that prospective home buyers will be able to meet future repayments promptly, they will do their best to be of assistance.

These institutions loan money to home purchasers for a number of years, varying from fifteen years for older properties up to twenty-five or thirty years for new houses. Often the condition of the house to be purchased will determine the amount of the loan that the building society may be prepared to advance to borrowers.

Most building societies have branches in many different parts of the country, and also appoint agents, often firms of estate agents, with whom members of the public can deal. The prospective borrower usually has to furnish details of his or her employment and, in addition, the salary or wage being earned. Societies will not grant a loan sufficient to cover all the cost involved in buying a home. They usually insist that the

48

borrower must himself pay a small proportion of the purchase price of the house. This is called the deposit, and will vary from five to fifteen per cent. The fact that the borrower can provide such a sum is often proof that he has been in the habit of saving a little out of his earnings and is therefore the right kind of person to whom the society can entrust a long-term loan of money.

When we enter into an arrangement with a building society, it is usual to engage a solicitor, who will attend to the legal details and also ensure that the property we are buying is free from any "snags." We must provide the society with adequate security to protect its interest in the event of our defaulting with our repayments. We are said to have *mortgaged* our property, the loan of money received from the society being termed the "mortgage." This mortgaging of the house is set down in legal form by the solicitors acting on behalf of the society and of the borrower.

Most building societies appreciate that there may be occasions in the future when borrowers will have domestic difficulties and will not be able to meet repayments at the times specified. It is usually only as a last resort that a building society will take the necessary legal steps to sell the property mortgaged so that it can raise the money owed by the borrower. Building societies usually require borrowers to repay each month over the loan period fixed instalments, which were calculated when the mortgage was granted.

For an extra charge many building societies can arrange for insurance cover, so that in the event of the borrower's death before repayments of a mortgage are completed, further payments are cancelled.

Investors and Borrowers: Rates of Interest

Before a building society can offer loans of money to prospective home buyers, it must have already obtained the necessary funds to make this possible. It follows, therefore, that before there can be borrowers there must be people who are willing to invest their savings with the building societies. They are the "investors," who, before they are prepared to invest in a building society, must be assured not only that their investments are safe but also that they will be adequately compensated by the society for the use of their money. The investor is therefore paid each year a rate of interest for every pound loaned to the society. This rate of interest will vary from time to time, because there is a great deal of competition between many different organizations for the use of the investor's money and the building societies must be governed by this in deciding how much interest they can afford to pay out. The rate of interest is usually in the region of 4 to $5\frac{1}{2}$ per cent per annum on the sum loaned.

Here is an example of how the interest payable to an investor by a building society is calculated—

> Amount loaned to building society
> by investor for period of one year—£100.
> Current rate of interest is 5 per cent.
> Therefore interest payable =

$$\frac{5}{100} \times \frac{100}{1} = £5$$

The building society, having obtained sufficient funds by attracting enough investors, must now calculate how much should be charged to its borrowers for the money made available to them.

There are branch offices to be maintained and staffed, agents' fees to be paid and many other items of expense, such as printing and telephone bills, rates, etc. It is evident that the rate of interest that will be charged to house purchasers (the borrowers) must be sufficient to cover not only the interest payable to investors, but also the many expenses incurred by the society in providing its service to purchasers.

The rate of interest paid by borrowers will usually be two to three per cent greater than that paid by the society to investors. This is normally sufficient to cover all the expenses incurred. An example of how the interest rates function is as follows—

Rate of interest required by investors—$5\frac{1}{2}$ per cent.
Rate of interest that must be charged to borrowers—$8\frac{1}{2}$ per cent.

It is often much easier for a person to obtain a loan from a building society if he has already given proof of his thrift in the past, and this is a very good reason for young couples who wish to save a little out of their earnings each week towards the deposit required for a home to invest this money in a building society of their choice. When the time comes to make application for a loan, the society will already have had evidence of their ability to *manage money*.

We can best illustrate the workings of the building societies by taking the example of a young married couple wishing to buy a home of their own—

	£
Price of house (modern "semi-detached")	4,500
Amount required as deposit from borrowers	500
Loan granted by building society	4,000

Period of the mortgage—*twenty-five years.*
Current rate of interest charged—$8\frac{1}{2}$ *per cent.*

The monthly repayments over a period of twenty-five years at the above rate of interest would be £8·12$\frac{1}{2}$ for every thousand pounds borrowed.

As the amount of the loan is £4,000, this would amount to a payment of £8·12$\frac{1}{2}$ × 4 every calendar month, which would be £32·50.

All the building societies have booklets and leaflets available which can be obtained by calling at their branch offices, or the offices of estate agents. These publications will inform you of the extent of the services available and will set out, in detail, rates of interest charged to borrowers. Sufficient information is given to enable you to calculate the amount of monthly repayments and the probable deposit required from the borrower. The building societies are always pleased to give prospective borrowers the benefit of their expert advice.

The Help that Insurance Companies Offer to Home Buyers

Certain insurance companies also assist home purchasers in obtaining long-term loans. The loan granted is normally coupled with a form of *life assurance*, so that, in the event of the policy-holder's death prior to repayment of the loan, no further payments by the next-of-kin are necessary. This method of obtaining a loan is rather more complicated than borrowing from a building society, but it does offer a great deal of security to the borrower. Representatives of the insurance companies are always pleased to give their expert advice on this matter, so that a choice can be made as to which is the best method of obtaining a loan.

Buying Your Own Home or Renting It

It is at times rather difficult to find a house to rent, which is perhaps one reason why so many young married couples enter into negotiations for the purchase of a home with the help of a building society. Possibly far more people would consider buying their own house but for the

INVESTORS

Investors lend their savings to the Building Societies in return for interest which their savings earn.

BUILDING SOCIETY

The Building Societies use the investors money to enable them to make loans to persons (borrowers) wishing to buy their own homes. The borrowers pay interest on the loans.

HOUSING

Fig. 5. Building Societies—Borrowers and Investors

fact that all the building societies usually require the buyer of the house to place some of his own savings as a deposit, and the finding of this deposit, which might amount to £400 or more, represents a very practical difficulty.

Quite apart from these practical difficulties, a choice may have to be made between renting and buying a home, and the following list of respective advantages and disadvantages may enable you to make your decision more easily.

Advantages of Buying your own Home

1. Eventually the house will be paid for, for instance after twenty-five years, and no further instalments will be paid.

2. For many years in the past houses have increased in value. For example, a house purchased in 1969 at a cost of £4,000 may be valued at £5,000 in 1971. The owner, therefore, will make a profit should he decide to sell. It should be remembered, however, that even if a profit is made on the sale of a house, a new one will also cost more, so that in the short period he will feel no immediate benefit.

3. The owner has the satisfaction of knowing that it is his *own home*, and that within limits he can please himself how he uses it.

4. Because the house will eventually be paid for, it is his, and possibly in years to come his children will have the benefit of living in it with their families, or, should it be sold, they will receive a substantial amount of money for it.

5. The interest paid to the building society for the use of their money is allowable for income tax relief. Those persons not eligible for tax relief can claim a special rebate on mortgage interest paid.

Disadvantages

1. As houses constantly increase in price, the amount of money necessary for deposits is rising all the time.

2. Solicitor's fees normally have to be paid, both when buying and selling a house.

3. For many persons the worry of meeting mortgage repayments for a long period of years may cause considerable distress.

4. If a house is sold and the services of an estate agent are used, a commission has to be paid to him for his services.

Advantages of Renting your Home

1. Some local authorities build houses and let them to tenants at very reasonable rents.

2. No solicitor's fees or estate agent's commissions have to be paid.

3. For some people there may be far less worry, because they pay their rent on a weekly or monthly basis, and are not committed to an agreement for a long period of time, as in the case of a mortgage.

4. Repairs to the house often have to be carried out by the landlord and are not the responsibility of the tenant (the person renting the house).

Disadvantages

1. The house never becomes the tenant's own property.

2. The amount of rent paid each week or month may be high.

3. The landlord or the local authority may impose certain restrictions—for example, the tenant may not be allowed to keep pets.

4. The rent paid does not rank for income tax allowances.

Each person has his own ideas on whether a home should be rented or bought, and there will be individual advantages and disadvantages for the person concerned. The intention of this discussion is to provide some idea of the considerations to be faced.

Questions

1. A thrifty coal miner in Wales has £2,000 invested with a building society. Explain—

    (i) how this helps an electrician in London to buy his own house, and

    (ii) how the fact that the electrician is buying a house of his own makes the thrifty coal miner's investment worth while.

(Metropolitan Reg. Exam. Board.)

2. Describe the work of building societies, mentioning both the investor and the borrower.

3. Why does the rate of interest charged by building societies to borrowers vary?

4. A building society loaned the sum of £3,000 to a borrower who made repayments of £24 per month for twenty-five years. How much interest in all would be paid by the borrower over the twenty-five years?

5. Compare building society loans and assurance company endowment schemes as methods of purchasing a house.

6. (i) Who usually grants house purchasers loans?

  (ii) What is the *deposit* the home purchaser usually has to find when buying a house through a building society?

  (iii) What security does the house purchaser give a building society, in case he is unable, at some time in the future, to make repayment of the loan?

  (iv) What is an investor paid by a building society for the use of his money?

  (v) What is the difference between renting and buying a house?

Practical work

1. Draw a plan of your own "dream house."

2. Visit shops in your own district and calculate how much it will cost you to furnish your dream house completely.

3. Estimate how much your house, as planned, will cost you. Obtain leaflets from a building society and prepare a statement showing how much your repayments off a mortgage would amount to.

4. Prepare a diagram illustrating the work of building societies.

5. Prepare a speech outlining the advantages and disadvantages of—

  (i) Buying your own home.

  (ii) Renting a house.

5—(B.860)

9 Budgeting

Young people do not always consider it a serious matter if they are unable to make their pocket money last the full week. A simple solution to the problem is to persuade parents to make an advance of money so that the latest record can be purchased, or a visit to the cinema made. It is not so easy for them, however, on leaving school or college and commencing work, to get an advance on wages from their employer.

Living Within Our Income

There is only one good method available to us in trying to ensure that we can always *pay our way* and balance our expenditure with our income—and this is to look ahead and *plan* or *budget* for all those expenses which have to be met, and to keep them within the limits of our income.

If we are to budget successfully for all our different items of expense, we must ensure that we have our *priorities* in the right order. If, for instance, a motor-car is owned, this may mean that other luxuries must be forgone. It is quite natural that different people will have different priorities. For some, the most important consideration may be the ownership of a modern house, complete with comfortable furnishings. For others a holiday abroad may be the priority target. It does not really matter what our priorities are, but what is important is that, having decided what they are to be, future planning of expenditure to be incurred must take these considerations into full account.

Most persons are paid their wages or salaries each week or each month, and it is necessary, therefore, that the balancing of expenditure with income be carried out on a weekly or monthly basis. There are some items of expenditure, of course, which arise only once each year, such as holidays and the purchase of clothes, but they also must be taken into account when preparing our budgets.

On what does the typical family spend its weekly income? In addition, perhaps, to the running and maintaining of a motor-car, there may be the following—

Food
Rent—or Mortgage
Clothing
Fuel—light and heat
Rates (if own home is being purchased)
Hire purchase or credit sale repayments
Fund for future purchasing of household furnishings
Insurance
Pocket money for the family
Sundries such as newspapers, fares, etc.
Savings—including provision for gifts at Christmas and on
    birthdays

There can be no set budget suitable for all persons. Each individual or family will have its own particular preferences, but whatever our likes and dislikes, provision must be made for both necessities and luxuries, and amounts must be put aside each week or month out of wages, so that expenses can be paid, or, if a bank account is opened, sufficient money must be paid in to ensure that future payments can be made.

WEEKLY BUDGET FOR MAN AND WIFE
WITH TWO CHILDREN

	£	£
Wage (*after deduction of income tax and National Insurance contributions, etc.*)		24·00
Weekly Expenditure		
Rent	3·50	
Foodstuffs	8·00	
Clothing	1·75	
Fuel	1·50	
Insurance, including life assurance	0·75	
Hire purchase repayments	1·00	
Fares—for family	0·75	
Newspapers, etc.	0·50	
Household sundries, such as soaps, etc.	0·50	
Pocket money for family	3·65	21·90
Amount of money in hand		2·10
Add family allowance for one child		0·90
Total surplus each week is		3·00

The above example will help us to understand how a weekly budget is made up. We can see that the man's earnings are sufficient to cover regular weekly expenditure and that in addition there is a balance remaining which can be used to provide for holidays and still leave, perhaps, a small amount for long-term savings. Because the expenditure has not been allowed to exceed the income for the week, it is said that the budget has been balanced, but it must be remembered that in practice there are many items of expense, such as an unusually heavy fuel bill, or the need for extra clothes for the children, which often crop up unexpectedly, and which have not been budgeted or allowed for.

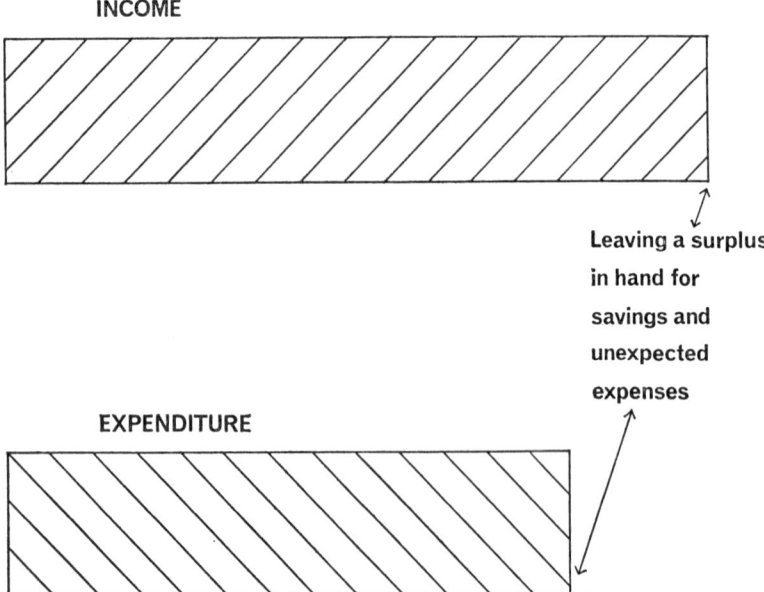

INCOME

Leaving a surplus in hand for savings and unexpected expenses

EXPENDITURE

Fig. 6. We Must Try to Balance our Budgets

Although, as in the illustration, there often seems to be a "margin of safety," and sufficient has been put aside for future commitments, this margin is not always too great and many persons get into serious difficulties because they do not *budget* wisely for future expenditure. For persons who are married, the budgeting for future expenditure is often the joint responsibility of man and wife, and even though the wife may work to provide extra income, there is still a necessity for wise budgeting. Although more money may be coming into the household each week, because she is at work during the day the wife may have to spend more of her housekeeping money on foodstuffs which are pre-prepared and which therefore cost more.

When preparing budgets, we must establish our priorities right from the start. If we own a motor-car we must bear in mind that the cost of maintaining it tends to be high, and accordingly, suitable provision should be made. Once a decision has been made on the family priorities, the income received can then be allocated in a suitable manner. Many people like to set themselves an objective, such as a good holiday. This often helps a great deal, and makes them more determined to save.

Personal Savings

There are always good reasons for being a *saver*, and few people would ever be in a position to make their budgets balance unless they looked well ahead and tried to put to one side a little money each week, or each month, out of their pocket money if still at school or college, or out of earnings if working. There are many organizations today which will welcome your support, no matter how little money you may feel that you can save. Saving—which is really the *investing* of your money, provided it is not kept under the bed in your own home—is one of those practices which once started often become a lifetime habit.

THE NATIONAL SAVINGS MOVEMENT

This is a national organization which enlists the help of many voluntary, and some paid, officials to organize savings groups in schools, colleges, and factories throughout the land. Each group is run by a secretary who sells savings stamps, savings certificates and premium bonds. The National Savings Movement has special booklets available on money management.

SAVE AS YOU EARN (S.A.Y.E.)

In 1969, the National Savings Movement commenced operating a scheme whereby persons agreeing to save a set amount of money each month over a fixed period of years receive interest on their investment, plus a special amount of bonus. This scheme is operated under the Post Office Giro system, Post Offices, and Trustee Savings Banks. Institutions such as building societies also provide similar facilities. You may find it useful to collect leaflets on this scheme from a post office, or a building society. Any person aged 16 years or over may participate in this type of savings scheme.

NATIONAL SAVINGS BANK

A post office can open an account for you with the National Savings Bank. Fixed rates of interest are paid on the money you have invested.

TRUSTEE SAVINGS BANKS

Most cities and towns have Trustee Savings Bank branches, where your money can earn a rate of interest similar to that of the National Savings Bank. Special accounts can be opened if desired, which carry a higher rate of interest; but in this case frequent withdrawals are not encouraged. Many Trustee Savings Banks have special arrangements with employers for the deduction of regular savings from wages. Your affairs are treated quite confidentially and your employer never knows how much money you have in your account. Customers of Trustee Savings Banks can now be provided with cheque books if special arrangements are made.

OTHER ORGANIZATIONS

There are, of course, many other organizations, such as the commercial banks and local authorities, which will pay you interest on your savings. Some persons invest in unit trusts, which purchase shares in many different public limited companies, divide the total investment into small units and sell them to investors.

Of course, an investor can always buy shares or debentures in a particular company.

MAKING THE CHOICE

All these various organizations are available to you for regular savings, and no matter whether you are saving with a special object in view, such as a holiday or a new bicycle, or merely for a future rainy day, your money should be safe. The decision that people sometimes have to make with regard to savings generally is whether it is better to save with safety with bodies such as the National Savings Movement, which give a guaranteed rate of interest, or whether it is preferable to take a risk and invest for a higher rate of interest in other less stable institutions.

Questions

1. What facilities are available for persons wishing to save? What do you consider to be the best methods of saving?

2. Prepare your own *personal* budget on—

   (i) a weekly basis,
   (ii) a monthly basis,
   (iii) a yearly basis.

3. Prepare a budget on a *weekly basis* for your own family.

4. Explain the usefulness of budgeting.

5. What priorities do you think most important when preparing a budget?

6. Describe the activities of the National Savings Movement, and its importance to—

   (i) the individual,
   (ii) the country.

7. Describe the pitfalls ahead for those persons not budgeting for future expenses.

8. (i) What does *balancing the budget* mean?
   (ii) What are priorities?
   (iii) "Paying our way" means ...
   (iv) Name one savings bank.
   (v) For what values can savings stamps be bought?

Practical Work

1. Prepare a personal budget, and from the information obtained draw a diagram showing where the money goes.

2. Plan how you would budget for a holiday from the following information.

You leave school and get a job at the beginning of August. Your wages are £9 a week. You contribute £3 a week to your Mother's housekeeping expenses because you continue to live at home. You have to travel every day by public transport to work. You already have £15 savings.

Write out the budget you would aim at every week on your wages. How much would you save each week for your holiday?

3. Prepare a speech suitable for a debate on the virtues of wise budgeting.

4. Plan a personal budget for yourself. Keep a record of your expenditure in the weeks that follow. Make a list of the amounts of any differences between *actual* and *budgeted* income and expenditure.

5. Obtain a National Savings booklet on "Money Management." After reading it, write briefly about its contents.

10 *The Business*

On leaving school or college we commence our working lives, and look for the job for which we think we are best suited, or for which we may have had special training. It may be in the workshops of a large industrial firm, a warehouse, shop, or perhaps an office. In our working lives we all contribute in some way towards the well-being of our fellow citizens, and it is the owners of the many and varied types of business concerns who help to direct our joint efforts, so that we may all benefit in some way.

It is important that we know something of the structure of the business world today, and in particular of the type of business for which we are going to work, perhaps for the rest of our working lives.

There are *four main types* of business concern, which in commerce are referred to as *business units*; they are—

(*a*) The small one-man business, usually termed the *sole trader*.

(*b*) Small groups of persons in business together called "partners"—the firm being a *partnership*.

(*c*) *Limited liability companies*—both large and small.

(*d*) *State-owned concerns*, which come under Government supervision.

With the possible exception of State-owned concerns, whose prime responsibility is that of providing essential services for the community, all business concerns, whilst ensuring that many sections of the community have a job, have one important object, which is to *make profits*. This is the financial reward that is due to the owners of business concerns as repayment for their efforts in managing and investing their money in the business. It takes a great deal of money and resources successfully to undertake most forms of business enterprise, and unless the owners can make a living themselves and be compensated in the way of profits (financial reward), many jobs that otherwise would be available to us in these firms would be lost. Just as we look for a job that will give us a reasonable return in the form of a regular wage, so too must the owners of businesses seek their reward.

The Sole Trader

This is the type of business operated by one individual, who finances the business himself, perhaps from previous savings or by getting a loan from an institution such as a bank. A typical example of this kind of business concern is the small shop, often to be found at the corner of the street. There are, of course, many other types of one-man business, such as small garages, hairdressing salons, haulage contractors and the like.

It does not always follow that the sole trader's business is a small one, although very many are. But the limiting factor is that the proprietor is not only responsible for providing the necessary finance or capital, but very often for managing the business as well. He may employ the services of assistants to help him with this work, but he is the one who is in full control and has the responsibility of building the business up into a prosperous concern. We can see from this that the size of the business must be restricted if he is successfully to look after all its many aspects. Any profits that are made by the business belong to the owner, but it must also be borne in mind that in any undertaking risks are always present, and that it is the owner who must bear any losses that are incurred.

It is not everybody who has the right qualifications for running his own business, for although the rewards may be high in times of prosperity, so too are the responsibilities and risks. Quite apart from the need to be in possession of adequate supplies of money (called *capital*), the business man must also be gifted with certain very necessary qualities of character.

The Partnership

As already stated, one snag in starting business on your own account is that adequate supplies of capital are necessary, but it is sometimes possible to come to an arrangement with other persons who will each contribute a sum of money towards the establishment of the business. When persons set up business in this way, they are called *partners*. The responsibilities of running the firm, the risks and the rewards, are then being shared jointly.

It is usual, when forming this kind of association, for a firm of solicitors to be engaged to draft out a *partnership agreement*, in which will be stated—

(*a*) The amount of money (capital) contributed by each partner in the business.

(*b*) The proportion in which future profits or losses are to be shared amongst the partners.

An Act of Parliament dated 1890 (the Partnership Act) lays down certain regulations by which partnerships are bound; two important ones (with certain exemptions) are—

(*a*) The number of persons forming such an association must be not less than two and not more than twenty. (Ten in a banking concern.)

Firms of solicitors, accountants and members of the Stock Exchange are not restricted as to maximum numbers.

(*b*) Upon the death of any partner, the partnership will be dissolved. In this event the remaining partners in the business may form a new partnership.

One practical snag with this particular type of concern is that sometimes partners may not always agree with each other on various points that arise in the management of the business, and this could, of course, lead to difficulties. This is one reason why it is now not a particularly popular type of business concern; today, professional people such as doctors, dentists, solicitors, and firms of accountants form a very large proportion of the number of partnerships in existence.

The Difficulties of Running a One-man Business or a Partnership

The chief risk that sole traders and partners take in their form of business enterprise is that of the possibility of running short of money from time to time. Perhaps too much money is being locked up in slow-moving stocks of goods, or personal expenditure has been excessive. This kind of thing could lead to bankruptcy, which is one way of saying that there is nothing in the "kitty" with which to pay the bills that are accumulating. In this event the business may have to be closed down and stocks sold off cheaply so that cash can be obtained quickly. The fixtures and fittings used in the business may also have to be sold, so that the bills can be paid. Should there still not be sufficient funds available for paying the debts of the business, the proprietor or, in the case of a partnership, the partners, would have to sell some, or all, of their own personal possessions to try to meet all the claims that have been made.

We can now appreciate, perhaps, just how serious are the risks when forming a concern of this kind. An alternative is to start a business in association with a number of other people, by forming a limited liability company.

Limited Liability Companies

There are in this country today many business organizations which come under the heading of limited liability companies. Some of them are very large concerns, such as Ford's of Dagenham and Marks and Spencer. Others are quite small in size and may employ only a few people. Limited liability companies include many industrial giants and large retail organizations, and are to be found in all branches of industry and commerce.

It is the practice in this kind of organization for a group of persons each to contribute a sum of money towards the financing of the business venture, and so have a stake in the company's prosperity.

There are two forms of limited liability company—

(*a*) *Public limited companies*

(*b*) *Private limited companies*

The chief difference between them is that whereas in the case of private companies the number of members, excluding past and present employees, must not exceed fifty, there is no such restriction in public companies. Also, whereas members of public companies may freely transfer their financial stake (i.e. their shares) in the company to other persons, this is not so in private companies. It is usual to find, therefore, that many private companies are small family concerns. The giants of business are public companies. An Act of Parliament of 1948, called the Companies Act, later amended by the Companies Act, 1967, ensures that all limited liability companies conform to certain regulations imposed by the State. This is not only in the interest of the companies themselves, but also in the interest of the community as a whole.

A limited liability company has two very important sets of regulations—

The Memorandum of Association, which states:

1. The name of the company.
2. The objects of the company.
3. The country in which the registered office will be situated.
4. The share capital of the company and the number of shares.
5. That the liability of the shareholders is limited.

The Articles of Association, which are the regulations setting out the rules for company meetings and the powers of directors and members of the company, and generally governing the management of the internal affairs of the company.

All limited companies are bound by law to have these regulations.

Persons can invest in limited liability companies by purchasing *shares*. The value of the shares varies, in that if the company prospers and makes good profits and also has the good sense to plough some of its profits back into the business for development purposes, the value of the shares will increase. Should profits decline for any reason, the value of the shares may fall. Persons owning shares in a limited liability company are called *shareholders* and they will naturally expect some recompense for investing their money in the company. Each year, therefore, provided sufficient profits have been made, the company will declare a dividend, based on the amount of profit made in the year.

AN EXAMPLE OF THE AMOUNT DUE TO A SHAREHOLDER

	£
Total number of shares held by shareholders (all valued at £1 each).	1,000
Profit for the year after all expenses of running the business have been met, and which is available for dividend purposes	250
Therefore, shareholders will receive for every £1 share they hold in the company	25p

This is calculated as follows—

$$\frac{\text{Profit}}{\text{Total shares}} \text{ expressed as percentage}$$

$$= \frac{£250}{1,000} \times \frac{100}{1} = 25 \text{ per cent.}$$

Dividend declared is 25 per cent on every £1 share.

Most people today have a stake in the prosperity of the limited liability companies of this country. They may be employed by them, or even if this is not the case, savings they deposit with institutions such as banks and insurance companies may be invested in this form of business enterprise, on their behalf.

Not all companies have limited liability, but *unlimited* companies are rare.

THE MEANING OF THE WORD "LIMITED"

Mention has been made already of the risks that sole traders and partners encounter in running their forms of business enterprise, in particular the risk of having their personal possessions sold in order that debts may be repaid. Shareholders in limited liability companies are also risking their money to some extent because, should the company incur heavy losses and be unable to meet all its liabilities, they may lose a proportion or all of their investment. Yet the risk involved is not quite the same as in the case of sole traders and partnerships, because the shareholders' *liability is limited* to the amount of money they have invested in the business. If the company cannot meet its debts, their personal possessions are quite safe and no further loss is incurred. It is most important that we remember what the term "Limited" (sometimes abbreviated to Ltd.) means.

Shares and Debentures in Limited Companies

ORDINARY SHARES

This type of share is the most common. Usually dividends can be paid on this class of share only after other classes of shareholders have been paid the amounts due to them. When a company has a good year and makes a large profit, the dividend payable to *ordinary shareholders* will often be a good one. Should profits be low, however, a small dividend may be paid or, in some instances, none at all. Ordinary shares, therefore, carry a greater risk than other types of shares.

PREFERENCE SHARES (known as non-cumulative)

As their name implies, these shares have a first claim on the annual profits of a limited company. The shareholders receive a fixed rate of dividend which is usually a low one because of this. This class of share does not carry as great a risk as the ordinary share.

CUMULATIVE PREFERENCE SHARES

This type of share has the same advantage as the preference share since there is a preferential right to a fixed rate of dividend. In addition the shareholder has the right to any arrears of dividend, which may not have been paid out in previous years owing to lack of profits.

PARTICIPATING PREFERENCE SHARES

This class of shareholder receives, in addition to the fixed rate of dividend each year, a share in any profits that are remaining after other shareholders have been paid their dividends.

WHY NOT ONE TYPE OF SHARE?

All the different types of shares, and the above is not the full list by any means, carry their own particular advantages and disadvantages. Some of you may ask, "Why not have *just one type of share*? Surely it would be far better?" The reason for this not being so is that as in all things, and this includes the investing of money, people are different. One person may be inclined to take more of a risk and plump for ordinary shares—sometimes called *equities*—hoping that annual profits will be good and a high rate of dividend declared by the company. Other people tend to be more cautious and buy preference shares, knowing that they will at least receive some form of dividend, even though the rate be lower, provided profits are made by the company.

PRICES PAID FOR SHARES

There are a number of methods of valuing shares but, as a general rule, when times are good for a company and high profits are being made the value of the shares will *increase*. For instance, should George Broom buy, in 1970, 100 ordinary shares in Automation Ltd., manufacturers of electrical machinery, at a price of £1 each, making £100 in all, and decide to sell them in 1972, much will depend on how the company has progressed during these two years in determining the *current market value of the shares* (i.e. at what price they will sell). If the company has made high profits and paid good rates of dividend, 25 per cent for example, yet retained an amount in the business for future "rainy days," the value of the shares will undoubtedly have increased, perhaps to even as much as £1·50 per share. In this event George Broom will make a profit of £50 on the sale of his shares, i.e.—

	£
1970, 100 ordinary shares bought at £1 each	100
1972, the same shares sold at £1·50 each	150
Profit on sale	50

Now work out a problem for yourself—Suppose that in 1972, when George decides to sell his shares, they are worth only 75p each. What will be the loss incurred by him?

Commerce and the World Outside

There are many different factors that can affect the price to be paid for the shares of limited liability companies, and it is always advisable to take the advice of a stockbroker or a bank manager before investing.

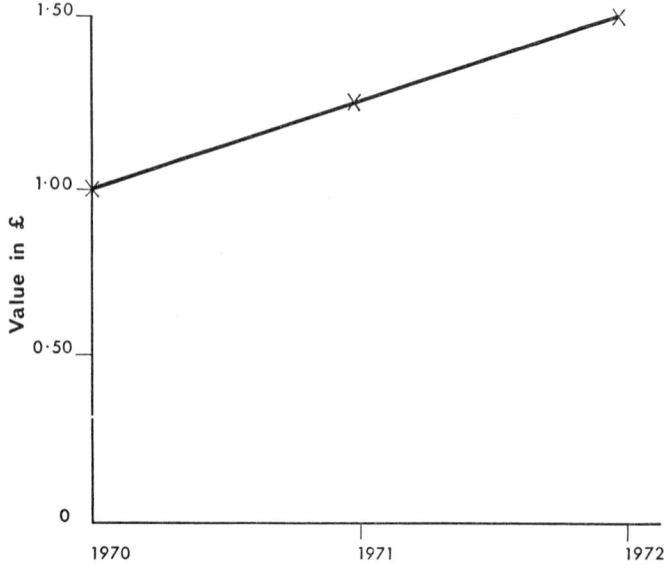

Purchased 1970 at £1 each. Sold 1972 at £1·50 each

Fig. 7. Value of Shares from 1970 to 1972

YIELD (OR RETURN) ON SHARES

The wizards of high finance can calculate just how good or bad an investment are certain types of shares. They do this by taking the price that would be paid for the shares, and working out the amount of dividend receivable as a percentage of the price paid. For example—

1. Share purchased at a price of £1.
   Dividend receivable in any one year is 5p or 5 per cent.
   The yield or return is 5 per cent.

2. £1 share purchased at a price of £2.
   Dividend receivable in any one year is 5p or 5 per cent.
   The yield or return is $2\frac{1}{2}$ per cent, calculated thus—5p divided by £2 times 100 equals $2\frac{1}{2}$ per cent.

70

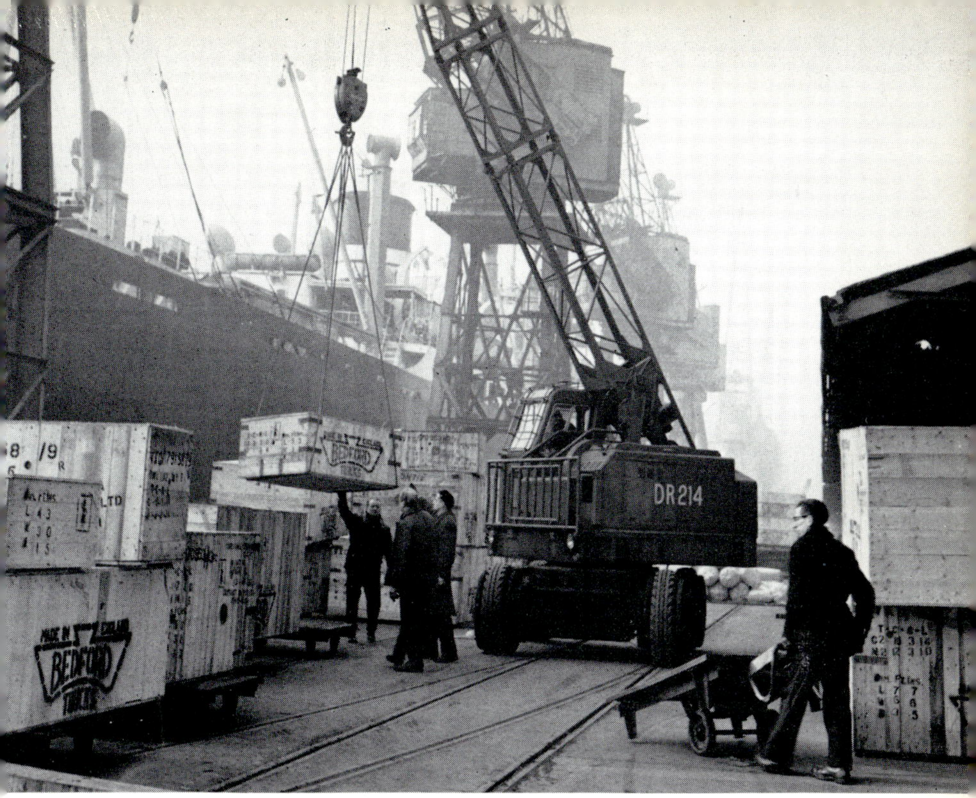

Courtesy of the Port of London Authority

Plate 1. Loading of Goods for Export at the Port of London

Plate 2. Shipbuilding at Sunderland

Courtesy of the Northern Daily Mail

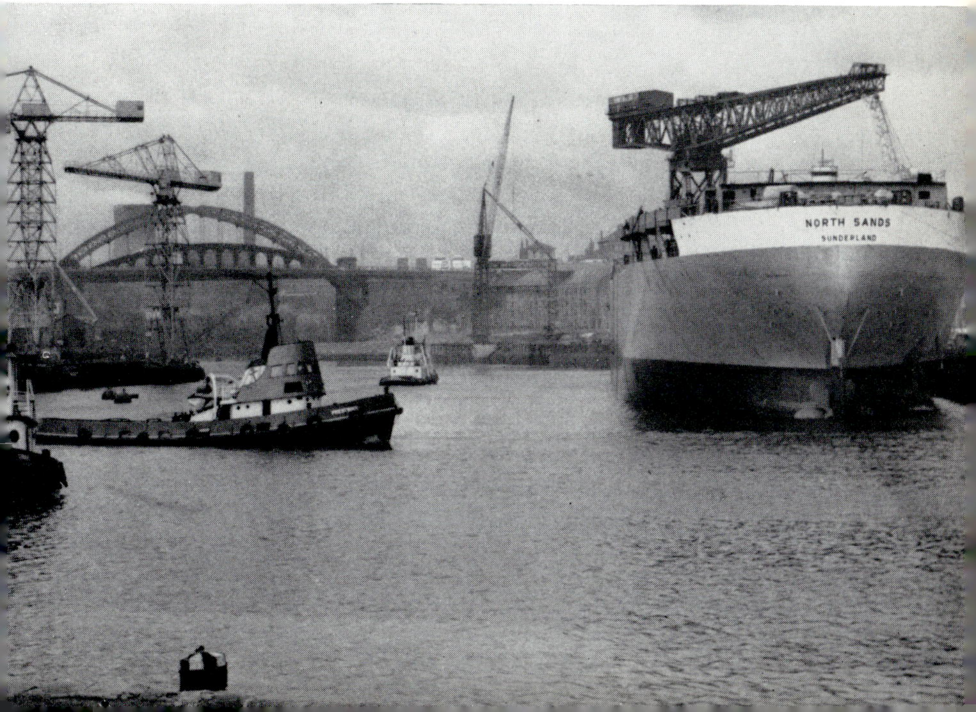

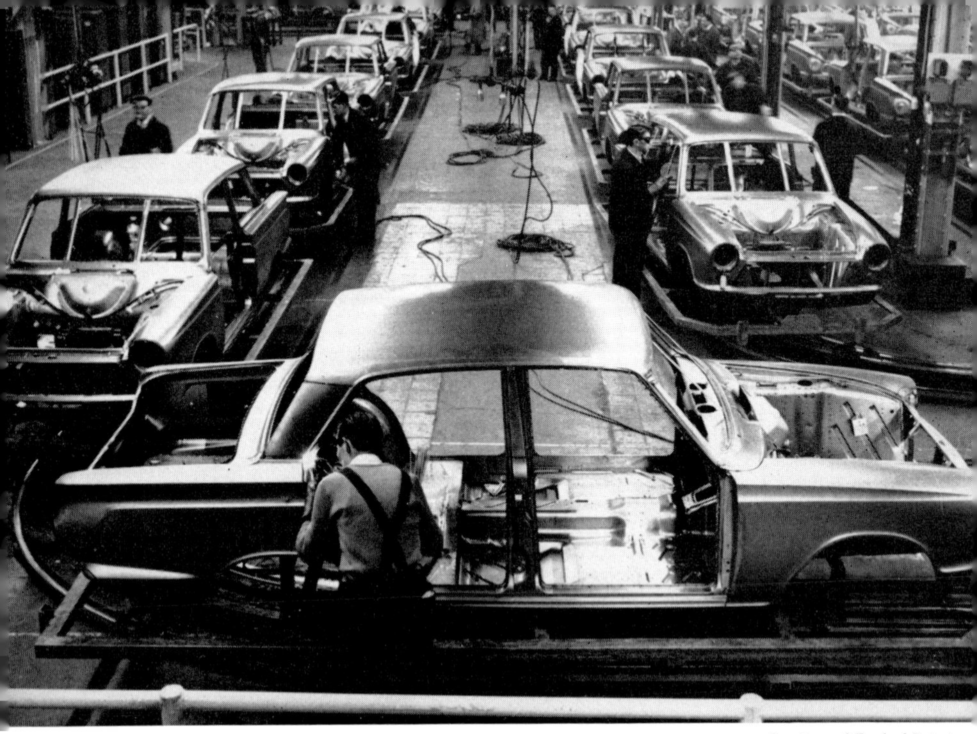

Courtesy of Ford of Britain

Plate 3. Modern Mass Production Methods of Manufacture

Plate 4. A Modern Steelworks in Co. Durham

Courtesy of the Northern Daily Mail

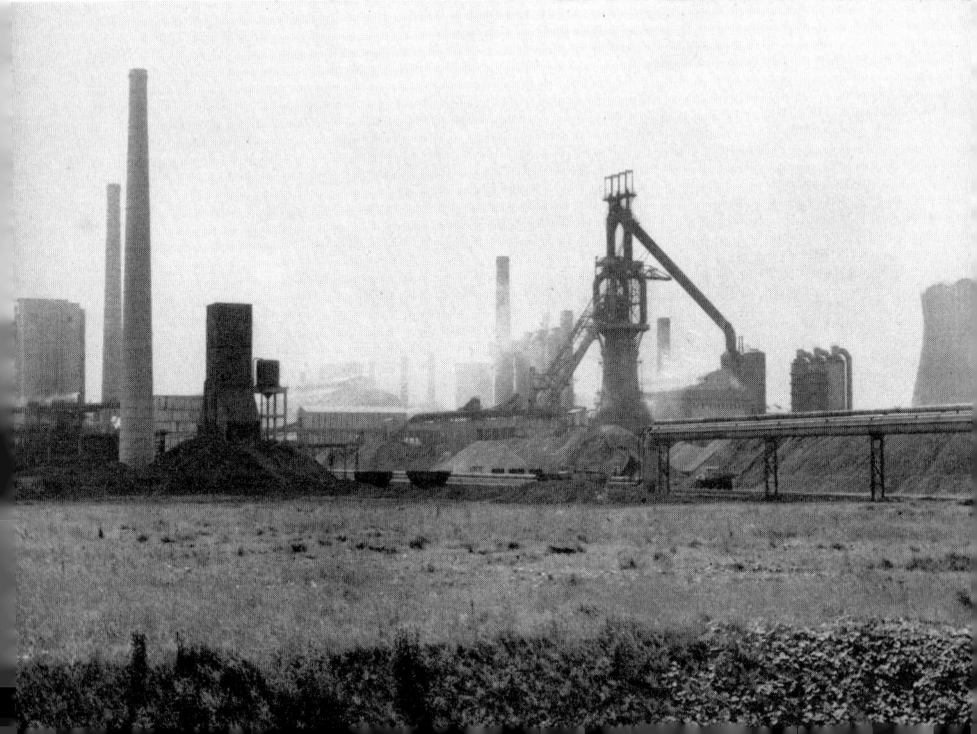

DEBENTURES

Some companies issue *debentures* when requiring fresh supplies of capital. Debentures are *not shares* and carry a fixed rate of interest each year. Persons investing in limited companies by purchasing this form of security do not take the same risk as persons buying shares, as they are classed as *creditors* of the company, and should the company run into financial difficulties, the holders of debentures would be entitled to re-payment of their money before the shareholders receive anything.

The London Stock Exchange

The Stock Exchange is really a market where the shares of many public limited liability companies and government securities are bought and sold. It is not the only market of this type in the country: there are others in many of our provincial cities and towns.

The London Stock Exchange had its beginnings during the seventeenth century when a group of men, whom we now call stockbrokers and stock-jobbers, began to make a living by bringing together buyers and sellers of stocks and shares. For a time they used to carry out their business activities in various coffee-houses situated near Change Alley in London, and in 1773 they took over a building at the corner of Threadneedle Street and Sweeting Alley. Today the London Stock Exchange occupies a large building near the Bank of England and visitors to the Exchange can see for themselves the many transactions taking place, between the representatives of persons wishing to buy and sell stocks and shares.

Members of the Stock Exchange consist of *stockbrokers* and *stock-jobbers*, each performing different functions. It is the stockbroker to whom members of the public go when they wish either to buy or sell shares. The stockbroker then arranges for a member of his firm to go on to the floor of the Stock Exchange and do business with the jobber. The jobber performs an extremely important function because he buys the shares that the stockbroker is offering for sale on behalf of his clients, and then sells to other stockbrokers who desire to purchase shares for their clients. The jobber always gives the stockbroker two prices when asked the price of shares, for example, £1·50 and £1·52. The lower price is the figure at which he is prepared to buy the shares and the higher price is the figure at which he is prepared to sell. He is in fact a dealer in stocks and shares, who buys shares in the hope that he can sell them at a higher price, although he is often forced to sell them at a lower price and so makes a loss; he therefore takes a risk.

71

Jobbers are always very experienced in share-dealing and usually specialize in certain types of stocks and shares. The stockbroker makes his profit by charging his clients, when they wish to buy or sell shares, a commission which is based on the amount of money involved. Members of the public are not allowed to contact jobbers direct, but must always engage a stockbroker to act on their behalf.

In exactly the same way that goods and services of all descriptions are traded between people, so it is with stocks and shares. Many people invest their savings in the stocks, shares or debentures of public companies, and there is always the possibility that at a future time they will wish to sell them. Unless there is a market place where they can be brought into touch with people who wish to buy shares they would have difficulty in disposing of them.

The London Stock Exchange always welcomes the opportunity of showing visitors its activities, and when visiting London it would be well worth your while to go and see for yourself just how this market for stocks and shares works.

State-owned Concerns

There are in existence in this country a number of industries which are absolutely vital, in that they provide services so important that it is considered that they should belong to the nation and not be entrusted to the keeping of companies. Examples of these State-controlled industries are—

British Railways Board
British Road Services
The Electricity Boards
The Gas Boards
The National Coal Board
British Overseas Airways Corporation
British European Airways Corporation
The Post Office (since 1969)

These industries are known as *nationalized* concerns, which means that they belong to the nation, and it was after the end of the Second World War that the Government decided that it would be in the public interest for them to be financed and controlled by the nation. It was felt that all of us might suffer a great deal of hardship should there be any break-down in the services provided by these concerns. This was always

72

regarded as a strong possibility by many people, because it was felt that so much finance would be required in building up their resources after the war that it might prove to be beyond the capabilities of private enterprise firms.

These nationalized concerns are managed by National Boards composed of men and women who are experts in their particular fields and who have a good deal of experience in the work of organizing and operating such concerns.

They differ from other forms of business organizations because the making of profits is not always the prime consideration. It was feared that if they were under the control of private firms and they suffered losses, there would be the possibility of a reduction in the services they offered.

From time to time we read in the newspapers the views of various writers who are often critical of the way in which these State-owned concerns are operated, and who state that it is most unfortunate that the British taxpayer should have to foot the bill for the losses that may have been made. We may even argue amongst ourselves on the merits or otherwise of having to maintain these organizations and whether it would be far better if they were handed over to private enterprise to run. It is rather difficult at times to follow all the arguments expressed on this subject of nationalization, but it must be remembered that, even though as taxpayers we may have to foot the bill, if losses in running these concerns are incurred, it would be far more serious if they ceased to function as efficient public services because of financial difficulties.

It does not always follow that these large nationalized concerns are bound to make losses in helping to provide us with the services we need. Some of them make profits. Then the money comes back to the nation and is used to help the country pay its way, or, perhaps, to assist those national concerns which are losing money.

Questions

1. Explain the meaning of the word "limited."
2. Explain the respective advantages and disadvantages of limited liability companies, as compared with other forms of business organization.
3. Why is there less risk in forming a business as a limited company than a partnership or a "sole trader" concern?

4. What services are made available by the Stock Exchange? What are the functions of—

(i) brokers,
(ii) jobbers?

5. Why has the supply of certain essential services—gas, electricity, rail transport—been undertaken by regional boards or by other organizations set up by the Government? (*Middlesex Reg. Exam. Board.*)

6. We may invest in limited liability companies by buying ordinary or preference shares or by means of debentures.

(i) What is the difference between ordinary and preference shares and how do debentures differ from both of them?

(ii) These three methods of investment are intended to meet the needs of different types of investors. In what circumstances would an investor invest in each of the three types? You should show clearly that you know the advantages and disadvantages of each type of investment. (*Metropolitan Reg. Exam. Board.*)

7. A company has profits of £10,000 available for distribution as dividends. The share capital consists of 40,000 ordinary shares of £1 each. Calculate the percentage dividend that will be paid to the shareholders.

8. Why do shares often rise or fall in value?

9. Miss Caldwell buys 100 ordinary shares in Blackpool Entertainments Ltd., in 1969, at a price of £1·50 each. She sells the shares in 1971 at a price of £1·75 each. How much profit does Miss Caldwell make on the sale of her shares?

10. Spencer Phippin purchases 500 £1 ordinary shares at a price of £3 each. He receives, in the first year, a dividend of 15p, or 15 per cent on every share. What is his yield or return on these shares?

11. (i) Name three types of business unit.
(ii) Whose liability is limited in a limited liability company?
(iii) What are profits?
(iv) What is the name given to an industry which is taken over by, and run on behalf of, the Government of this country?
(v) Name two industries owned by the State.
(vi) Give the name of the type of shares which have a prior claim to the profits of a limited liability company.
(vii) What is the maximum number of partners a normal trading partnership may have?

(viii) Where are stocks and shares dealt in?

(ix) What is a dividend?

Practical Work

1. Prepare a speech *either* supporting *or* criticizing the nationalization of certain industries.

2. You have just been appointed managing director of a limited liability company. Draw up a plan of activities for the coming year.

3. Select the shares of any one company that you would buy, noting the current price. Draw a suitable graph, and keep a note of the fluctuations in value each week, plotting these values on your graph.

4. Obtain information from your public library, or elsewhere, on the numbers of different types of business organizations. Prepare a diagram (e.g. a bar chart) which will illustrate this information.

5. Form a group or syndicate with your friends in class. You have a total of £10,000 to spend on purchasing shares in various companies. Working as a group, keep a record of your fortunes as investors, and show this in chart form also.

11 The Capital of the Business

We have seen in previous chapters how a business raises sufficient money so that trading may commence. This money, or *capital* as it is usually called, is extremely important to a business concern, and in this chapter we shall see how it is used in financing the activities of the business.

Changes In the Form of Capital

When sufficient capital is raised so that the business is able to commence its activities, it will then be necessary to use this initial supply of money in purchasing premises (unless they are to be rented) and all the various kinds of equipment and fittings needed. Stocks of goods or raw materials may also be purchased. Although the original supplies of money have now diminished, the business has equipped itself with its various needs. The business still has the same amount of capital, but its form has changed from being an amount of money only, to include other resources, sufficient cash being retained to cover the day-to-day expenses of running the business.

An example will help us to understand how the original capital of a company or firm may remain the same despite changes in structure—

(a) *Commencement of business—*
Capital (cash)   £5,000

(b) *Position one week later—*
Capital (distributed as follows):

	£
Premises	1,500
Equipment	1,000
Motor vehicle	500
Stocks of goods	1,000
Cash	1,000
	5,000

(c) *Position two weeks later—*

Capital (distributed as follows):

	£
Premises	1,500
Equipment	1,000
Motor vehicle	500
Stocks of goods	1,200
Cash	600
Total	4,800
Add amount owed by customers	800
	5,600
Less amount owed to suppliers	600
	5,000

Note: Although some goods have been sold, additional stocks have been purchased.

On examining the above statements showing the position of the business at different periods of time, we can see that the original capital, although remaining the same in total, is now composed of different items.

The Different Forms Capital Takes

CAPITAL OWNED IN THE BUSINESS AND CAPITAL EMPLOYED

The amount of the original capital, that is £5,000 in this example, is called the capital owned in the business. This is the sum invested in the concern by the owner. Capital employed in the business is the term which describes how much capital is being used or "employed" in the business.

There are different opinions on how the capital employed should be calculated, but one method of calculation can be shown if we examine (c) above. The business now has a number of items which add up to a total of £5,600 (including money owed by customers). These are termed the *assets*. Capital employed is the total assets of the business, £5,600, less the amounts owed by customers, £800, making £4,800. Amounts owed to the business by its customers must always be deducted because these sums are not in the hands of the firm and are therefore not actually being used.

77

If, in addition to the original amount of capital, the business borrows further sums of money, this will have the effect of increasing the capital employed, because whether it adds to the amount of cash held or is used in purchasing other items, it will increase the value of the total assets.

WORKING, FIXED AND CIRCULATING CAPITAL

Working capital is represented by cash plus the value of all those items in a business which can fairly easily be converted into cash, *less* any amounts of money the business owes to others and which will have to be repaid in the near future. It is the amount of liquid funds the business has available to finance its day-to-day trading, and it is extremely important that owners of all business concerns ensure that they have adequate supplies of liquid resources, otherwise there is a danger that they will not be able to meet their commitments.

If we again examine (c) above and divide the assets into separate groups, they may be shown as follows—

	£	
Premises	1,500	
Equipment	1,000	*Fixed Capital*
Motor vehicle	500	
Total	3,000	

	£	
Stocks of goods	1,200	
Cash	600	*Circulating Capital*
Amounts owed by customers	800	
Total	2,600	

You will notice that the various assets of the business have been divided into two sections. One section represents the fixed capital of the business, whilst the other section represents the circulating capital. All those assets that are purchased for use in the business for a *long period of time*, so that the firm is able to carry out its trading activities, as, for example, premises and equipment, represent the fixed capital. Assets such as stocks of goods, cash, and amounts owed to the firm by its customers form the circulating capital of the business. The period of time for which assets are retained in the business will determine to which group they belong. Broadly speaking, assets retained for a long period of time are regarded as fixed, whereas assets which are constantly changing in their value and fluctuate to some extent (circulate) form circulating capital. Items such as stocks of goods or materials and cash never remain in the business for long. On any one day some stocks may be sold or used in manufacture and will be replaced by fresh stocks, and because of this the amount of cash will be fluctuating also. Cash will be paid to persons to whom money is owed, but this will be replaced by cash received from customers owing money to the business. We can now appreciate, perhaps, how apt is the description "circulating capital" for certain of the assets of a business.

Having separated the fixed capital from the circulating capital, we can now calculate the *working capital* of the business. The circulating capital amounts to £2,600, and if we deduct the £600 owed to suppliers we have now calculated the working capital.

A further example of the calculation of working capital is as follows—

	£
Circulating capital amounts to	3,000
Amounts owing by the business include—	
Money owing to suppliers	1,000
Bank overdraft	500
Mortgage on premises	1,500

Because the mortgage on the premises is really a loan of money for a large number of years, and, in determining the working capital, we take into account only those amounts which have to be repaid in the near future, this sum is left out of our calculations. The working capital of the business is therefore—

		£
Circulating capital		3,000
less Money owing to suppliers	1,000	
Bank overdraft	500	
		1,500
Working capital		1,500

Striking the Balance

There is a danger that some business concerns will spend too much money on items which form the fixed capital of the firm, and this will result in a shortage of liquid funds. It should always be the concern of business men to try to strike an even balance between fixed and circulating capital and to spend their money wisely to ensure this. In the past many business concerns have not always achieved this balance between the different forms of expenditure, and, as a consequence, have become bankrupt. Apart from the considerations already mentioned, it may become necessary to try to expand the business in order to meet increased demand from customers, and unless adequate financial resources are available this may not be possible.

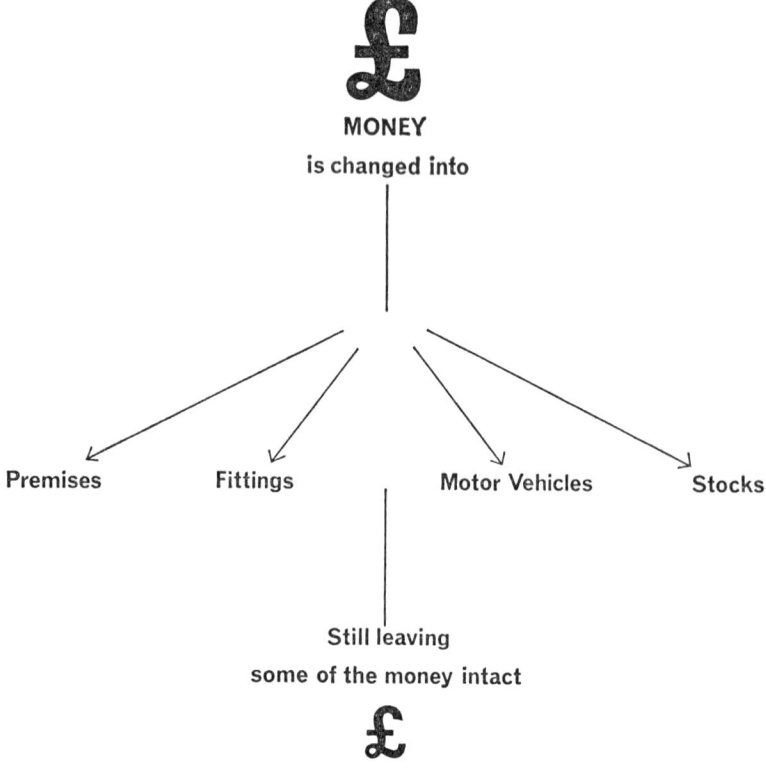

Fig. 8. How the Original Capital of a Business is Used in Purchasing Items for Use in the Firm

Notes For Students of Book-keeping

In book-keeping, circulating capital is referred to as *current assets* and fixed capital as *fixed assets*. In order to calculate working capital, total current liabilities should be deducted from total current assets.

BALANCE SHEET AS AT ...

Liabilities		£	Assets		£
Capital		4,500	*Fixed assets*		
Current liabilities			Premises		2,000
Bank overdraft		500	Equipment		500
Sundry creditors		1,000	Motor vehicle		500
			Current assets		
			Stocks of goods		1,500
			Sundry debtors		1,500
		6,000			6,000

Working Capital is calculated as follows—

	£
Total current assets	3,000
Less total current liabilities	1,500
	1,500

Questions

1. What is the capital of a business?
2. How does capital change its form?
3. Prepare examples which illustrate why the capital of a business changes its form.
4. Explain—
   (i) capital employed in a business,
   (ii) working capital of a business.

5. How is working capital calculated? Illustrate your answer with a practical example.
6. Explain the difference between fixed and circulating capital, using examples.
7. Why are adequate supplies of working capital essential to a business man?
8. A business has the following assets—

	£
Premises	3,000
Stocks	1,500
Cash	500
Fittings	250

The business owes a creditor £50. Calculate—

    (i) fixed capital,

    (ii) circulating capital,

    (iii) working capital.

9. (i) What name is given to capital which is calculated by deducting current liabilities from current assets?

    (ii) Fixtures and fittings, premises, and motor vehicles are examples of what type of capital?

    (iii) Give two examples of items which are part of the circulating capital of a business.

    (iv) Assets retained in the business for a long period of time form part of . . . capital?

    (v) Assets retained in the business for only a short period of time form part of . . . capital?

Practical work

1. You are commencing in business on your own account. Prepare a statement showing how much capital you will need to commence with, and then a second statement showing the position of the business one month later.

2. Prepare a diagram or chart showing the importance of working capital to the business man.

3. Prepare a diagram illustrating fixed and circulating capital.

12 Banks–their Functions and Services

Help for the Private Individual as well as the Business Man

We have already read in a previous chapter that limited liability companies raise much of their capital through their shareholders, who have made a financial investment in the company. Other forms of business organizations, such as the sole trader and the partnership, obtain their capital because the proprietor or the partners have invested their savings in the business. It is often very difficult to obtain adequate amounts of capital for a business, and there are occasions when a visit to a bank is necessary.

The number of people who are using the many and varied services of the banks is growing each year, because it is realized that the banking institutions are able to help both the private individual and the business man with their financial problems. Perhaps a bank loan is required, or there may be doubt as to the best kind of insurance policy to take out, or advice may be needed on how savings should be invested. These are problems which the bank manager can answer for us and so relieve us of a great deal of personal worry. Another factor today is that many people receive their wages in the form of a cheque and this may lead them to open an account at a bank.

We have already learned of the services offered to us by the Trustee Savings and National Savings Banks. These institutions provide very useful services for us, but they are limited in the amount of help they can offer, and it is to the large *commercial banks*, the joint-stock banks, that we turn when a greater variety of services is required.

The commercial or joint-stock banks of Great Britain are very powerful institutions and have branches in most of the towns and cities of this country. They include banks such as—

1. Barclays	3. Midland
2. Lloyds	4. National Westminster

All these banks are limited liability companies and hope to make profits in exactly the same way as other forms of business organizations.

The central bank of this country is the Bank of England, which acts as banker to the Government and with whom all the commercial banks have accounts.

Bank Accounts

Although the services of the commercial banks are of particular importance to persons owning their own business, the general public may also take advantage of the facilities made available by the banks. Having made a decision as to his choice of bank, a person must first consider what kind of account should be opened—a *current account* or a *deposit account.*

THE DEPOSIT ACCOUNT

This type of account is used extensively by people who require their savings to be in a safe place, and at the same time to earn interest. This is credited to their deposit account normally each half-year. The rate of interest paid by the banks to depositors varies from time to time and is at present about $5\frac{1}{2}$ per cent per annum. The interest paid to a depositor is his reward for the use of his money by the bank.

The banks are able to pay interest to depositors who have placed their money in this type of account, since a large proportion of the money is loaned by the banks to other customers who need the use of this money for a time. Amounts deposited are also invested in other ways. A customer who borrows from the bank, in addition to having to repay at a future date the amount of money borrowed, will pay interest on the loan, which is always at a higher rate than that paid by the bank to depositors. The difference between the interest paid by borrowers and that paid to depositors, after taking into account all the expenses paid by the bank in providing services to customers, is the bank's profit.

Depositors are issued with a bank book, which must be taken by them to the bank when they wish to deposit money in their accounts, and when they wish to make withdrawals. Withdrawals of money can normally be made without giving any notice, but for large amounts a period of notice may be required by the bank, although in practice this is usually dispensed with.

THE CURRENT ACCOUNT

It is the current account from which most people (particularly business men) derive the greatest benefit. This type of account is used extensively by people who constantly need to pay money into their bank account at very frequent intervals, and who also need to make constant withdrawals of money. Customers wishing to open a current account with a bank have to provide a reference from somebody known to them, who certifies that they are capable of handling their banking transactions in a proper manner.

Customers using the facilities offered by the current account do not need to give prior notice when wishing to make withdrawals of money and, because they both deposit and withdraw cash very frequently, it is not usual for the banks to pay interest to customers with this type of account. In fact, unless the amount of money in a current account is relatively large, banks charge customers for the use of the facilities provided. For the small depositor these bank charges are not usually very high and are charged by the bank to the customer's account normally twice each year.

Customers opening a current account at a bank are issued with a book of cheques and *when making withdrawals of money for his own use* from this type of account it will be necessary for the customer to complete the details on the cheque, making it payable to himself.

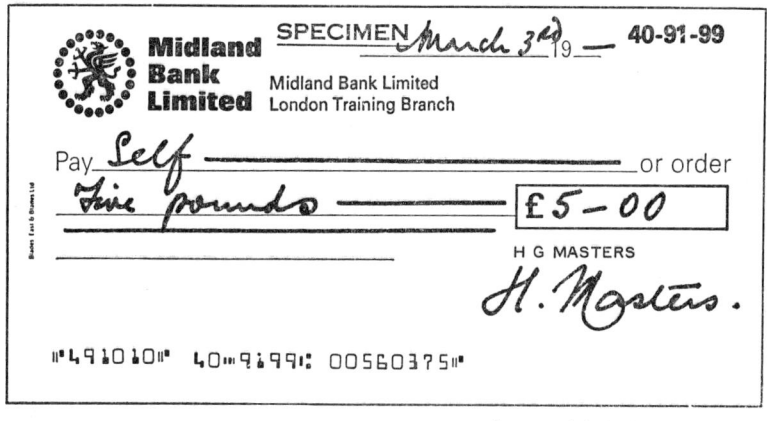

Fig. 9. A Cheque Payable to Self

The virtue of the current account is that the customer, having been issued with a book of cheques, is then able to make payments to his creditors by simply filling in the necessary details on the cheque, including the name of the person to whom it is payable and the amount of money to be paid.

Each cheque has a counterfoil so that the person making out the cheque can make a note of the amount drawn from his account and the name of the person to whom the cheque is payable. It is important when writing a cheque always to make sure that extra figures cannot be inserted on the cheque by someone else. This is the reason for the amount having to be written in words in addition to figures.

All the commercial banks have arrangements with one another so that the person receiving a cheque may pay it into his own bank account. The payer's bank is notified, the cheque is eventually returned to them and they deduct the amount of the cheque from the payer's account. This arrangement between the banks will be referred to in more detail later in this chapter, but it obviously saves customers a great deal of trouble and affords a very quick means of settling debts. This service is, of course, a boon to business men, who have to make frequent payments of money to other firms, often situated in many different parts of the country.

One advantage of the cheque system is that actual cash is not exchanged between people when they are effecting settlement of debts, and as a consequence it is a much safer means of making payment.

There are *three* different parties involved in cheque transactions and it will assist our understanding of the system if we know the terms used—

The drawer is the person who signs the cheque.

The drawee is the bank on whom the cheque is drawn.

The payee is the person to whom the cheque is made payable.

Bank books are not issued to customers with current accounts. The usual practice is to furnish them with *bank statements*, which show details of amounts paid into their accounts, amounts withdrawn, and the balance standing to the customer's credit.

When customers are paying money into their current accounts, they must fill in the details of the cheques, etc., on a *paying-in slip* which is provided by the bank. Provision is made for showing separately cheques, bank-notes, silver, bronze, money orders and postal orders. The paying-in slip is printed in two sections, one part being retained by the bank in order that it may enter the amounts paid by the customer into his account, the other part being kept by the customer for his own record purposes.

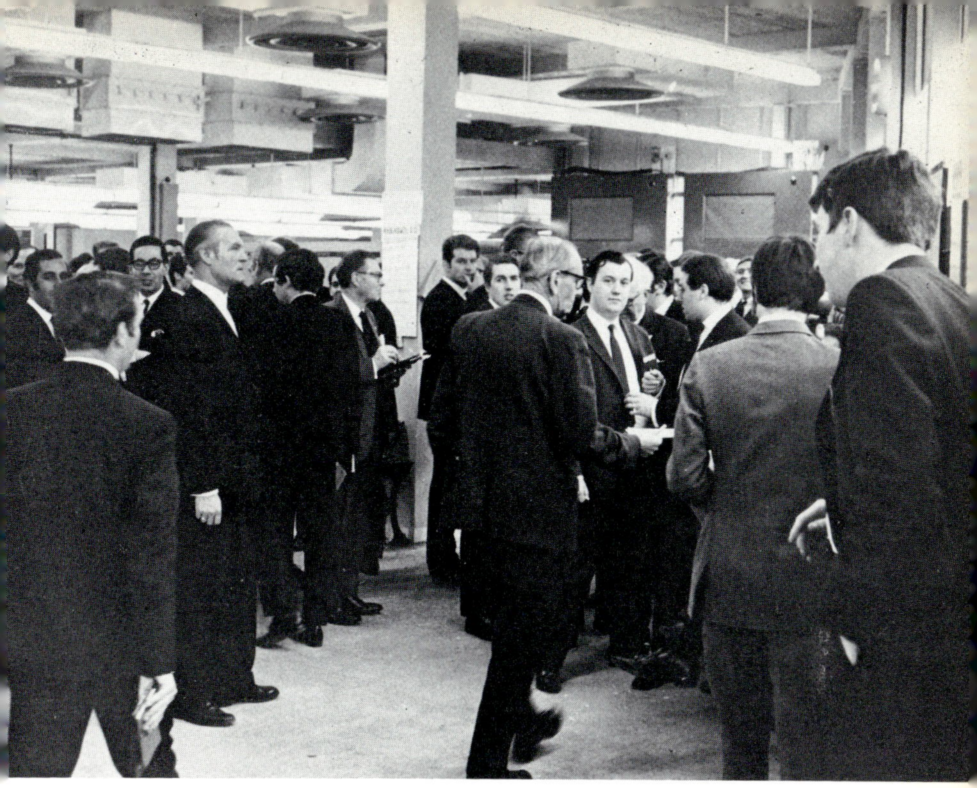

Courtesy of the Stock Exchange, London

Plate 5. The Trading Floor of the London Stock Exchange

Plate 6. The Underwriting Room at Lloyd's

Courtesy of Lloyd's

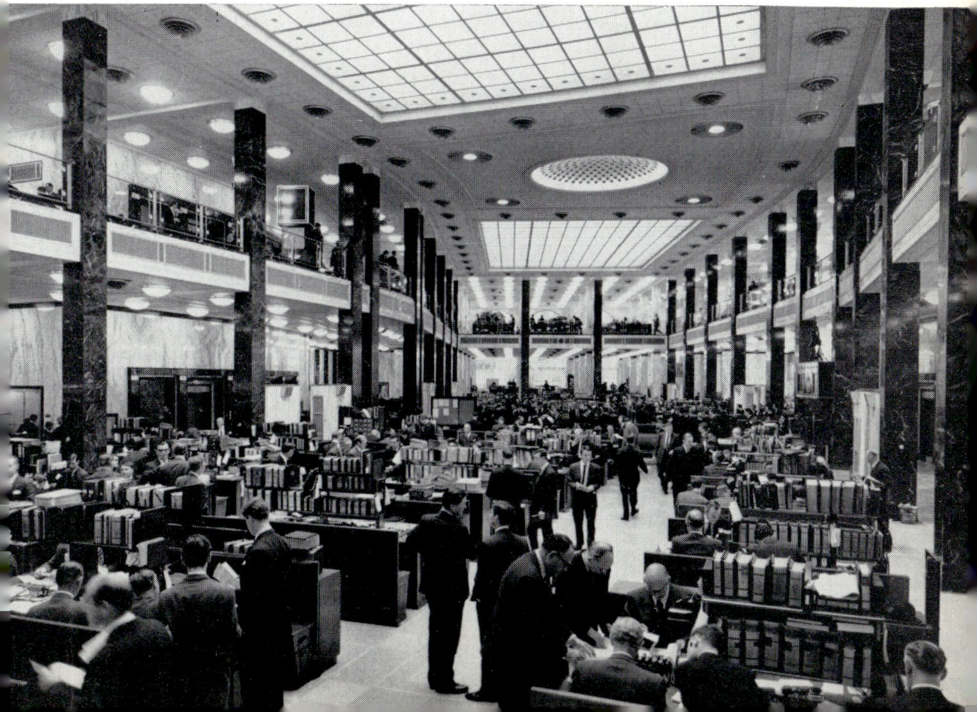

Courtesy of H.M. Postmaster-General

Plate 7. Trafalgar Square Branch Post Office

Plate 8. The Interior of a Modern Bank

Courtesy of the Midland Bank Limited

BANK STATEMENT

Statement of Account Midchester Bank Limited, High Street, Slecombe in account with B. Shaw				

Particulars	Payments	Receipts	Date	Balance (*Dr. in red*)
	£	£	19—	£
			July 1	50·00
212	10·00		3	40·00
213	5·50		5	34·50
		24·50	7	59·00
214	2·10		9	56·90
215	4·15		10	52·75
		3·25	12	56·00
216	5·00		14	51·00

The Clearing House

Each of the commercial banks has an account with the Bank of England, and every day the main banks (the clearing banks) meet at the Clearing House in London, to exchange cheques drawn on one another and to make any necessary settlement of cash.

The Clearing House now consists of seven member banks—

1. Bank of England
2. Barclays
3. Coutts
4. Lloyds
5. Midland
6. National Westminster
7. Williams & Glyn's

The clearing system is very necessary if people in all parts of the country are to be enabled to make payments to one another by the use of cheques. The Clearing House performs an extremely important function in ensuring that the clearing banks can exchange cheques drawn upon one another, and it plays a vital part in helping in the smooth working of the banks' money transfer services. When a person writes a cheque

87

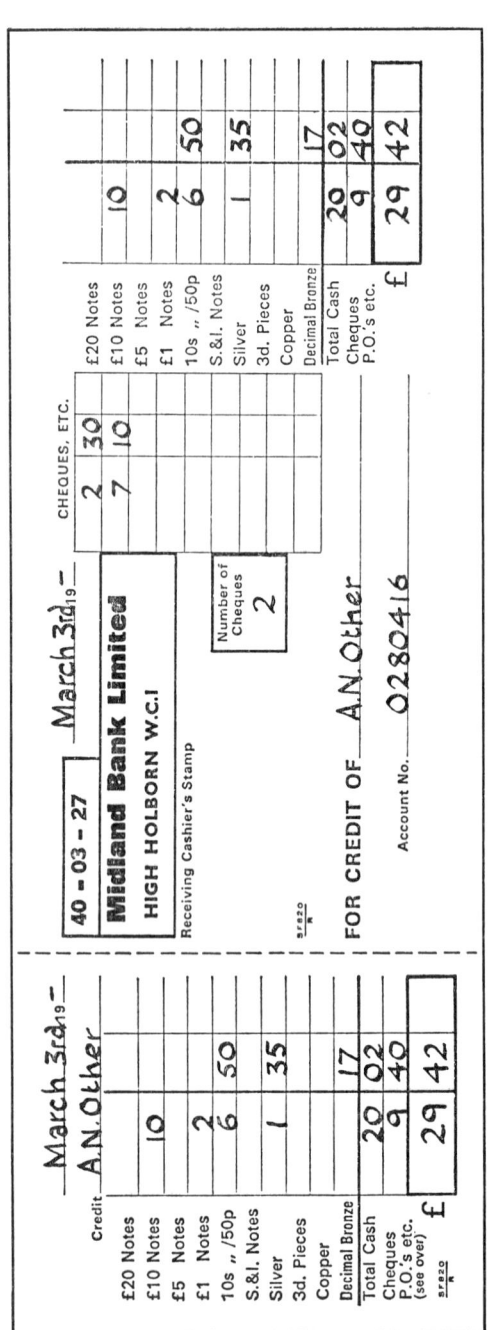

Fig. 10. A Paying-in Slip

payable to somebody with an account at a different bank, the procedure might be as follows—

Mr. Hill with a current account at Barclays Bank, Leeds, sends a cheque for £50 to Direct Supplies Ltd., of Manchester, which banks with the Midland. On receiving the cheque Direct Supplies Ltd. pays it into its current account at Midland Bank, Manchester.

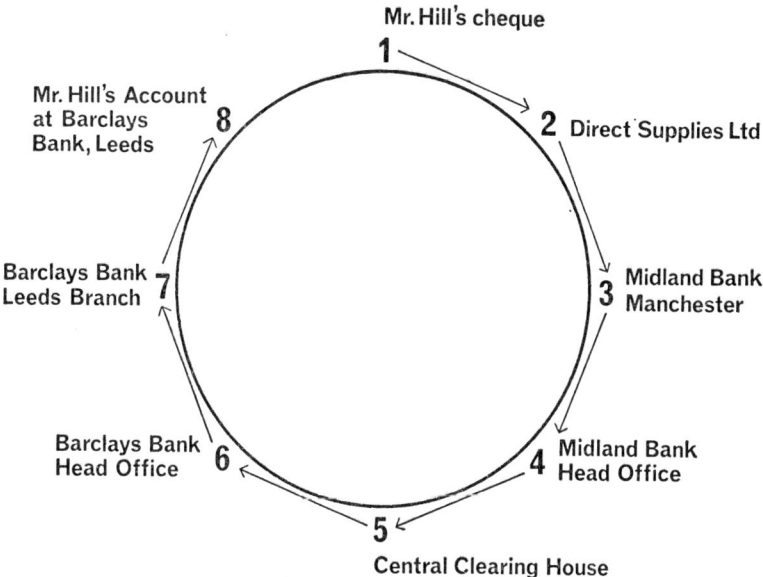

Mr. Hill's cheque

1

8 Mr. Hill's Account at Barclays Bank, Leeds

2 Direct Supplies Ltd

7 Barclays Bank Leeds Branch

3 Midland Bank Manchester

6 Barclays Bank Head Office

4 Midland Bank Head Office

5 Central Clearing House

Fig. 11. The Journey of Mr. Hill's Cheque

The Manchester branch of Midland Bank will then forward Mr. Hill's cheque to its head office in London. The following day, at the Clearing House, the Midland Bank will present the cheque, along with many others, to Barclays Bank's representatives and a settlement will be made in total between the banks. Within the next day or so Mr. Hill's branch of Barclays Bank will receive his cheque back, from its head office, and the £50 will be withdrawn from his current account. The cheque is then stamped, indicating that payment has been made, and Mr. Hill will eventually receive his cancelled cheque when he calls for his bank statement.

Each day the same procedure is carried out by all the commercial, or joint-stock banks, as they are also known, and our one transaction has to be multiplied many thousands of times if we are to obtain some idea of the operation of the bankers' clearing system.

Borrowing from a Bank

The granting of loans by a bank to its customers forms a very important part of its business, and whether it is the business man who wishes to expand his business and needs extra finance, or a private individual who needs a loan for a specific purpose, the bank manager is always available to discuss his customers' problems and to see if he can be of assistance.

THE PERSONAL LOAN

This particular type of bank loan came into being in the 1950's and was first instituted by the Midland Bank, which realized that there were many private citizens who, from time to time, needed a loan to help them provide for such things as furnishings for the home, or who perhaps wanted to exchange their motor-car for a more recent model and were short of the necessary cash. Up to that time there appeared to be no real alternative to hire purchase, which is considered a rather expensive method of buying goods, and for many people the securing of a personal loan from the bank was a very welcome alternative. Certain of the other commercial banks now offer this facility to their customers and will grant a loan of a limited amount of money, normally for a maximum period of two years. The customer makes regular monthly repayments off the loan during this time, the repayments including a certain proportion of interest for the use of the money. This type of loan will, of course, only be given to a customer if the bank is satisfied that he is able to meet future repayments promptly, and that his regular weekly or monthly income is sufficient to warrant it.

We must remember, of course, that the Government sometimes places restrictions on the total amount of money that banks can make available for their customers in the way of loans. If, for instance, the country faces a financial crisis, then private individuals and firms will often have difficulty in obtaining loans of money.

From the customer's point of view, the merit of borrowing money in this way is that, having obtained the loan from the bank, he is then able to purchase the goods he requires from the shop of his choice and may even receive a cash discount from the shopkeeper if it is the custom in the trade.

THE BANK LOAN

A bank loan can be obtained by business men and by private individuals. It is a cheaper means of borrowing money than the personal loan method as the amount of interest repaid to the bank, over the period of the loan, is smaller. Business concerns often make use of this method of borrowing money in order that they may finance the purchase of stocks of goods and other items. Banks will grant loans for varying periods of time, but will not generally make advances of this nature for a long period unless the circumstances are exceptional.

THE BANK OVERDRAFT

This method of borrowing money from a bank is used extensively and is really an arrangement made between the customer and the bank manager, whereby the customer is allowed to draw more money out of his account than he has to his credit. When this happens, we say that the customer's account has been overdrawn, and this excess amount is really in the nature of a loan from the bank. For example, let us suppose that a customer of the bank with £50 to his credit in his current account knows that within the next three months he will need nearly £200 in order to pay some bills. *Provided his bank manager is agreeable*, the customer may be given permission to overdraw his account up to a maximum of £200, within this period of three months.

The bank overdraft is a cheaper method of borrowing money than other methods, as the interest payable by the customer for the use of the money is calculated only on the amount overdrawn from his account. For instance, should the customer overdraw the sum of £100 in the first month and then reduce the amount overdrawn to £50 in the following month, the interest charged to the customer will be reduced accordingly. Interest payable on a bank loan, however, is charged on the full amount of the loan, whether or not some of the money is retained in the customer's account at the bank.

Banks will usually require security from a customer when granting bank loans and overdrafts, such as the title deeds to property or the transfer of interest in life assurance policies. Other types of policies, such as fire and burglary policies, *cannot* be used for this purpose.

Other Services Offered by Banks

There are other services provided for their customers by the banks which are useful for business men and private citizens alike.

HOME SAFES

These can be used to accumulate small savings. They are provided free of charge and are especially suitable for encouraging young persons in the habit of thrift.

SAFE CUSTODY

Customers can deposit with the banks for safe custody items such as documents, jewellery, and other valuables. This is a particularly useful service for customers who wish to keep their important possessions in a safe place.

STANDING ORDERS

People having to make regular periodical payments of fixed amounts such as hire-purchase payments and insurance premiums can have these amounts paid on their behalf by the banks. A small charge is made for this service, but it saves the customer a great deal of time and worry by ensuring that payments are made promptly.

BANK GIRO CREDIT

This system is a means of paying several creditors by making out only one cheque. The bank's customer completes a *bank giro credit slip* for each payment to be made, showing the payee's name, his bank and branch, and the amount to be paid. These bank giro credit slips are then listed on a sheet of paper, and the slips and the list, together with a cheque (payable to the drawer's own bank) for the total sum of all the payments, are sent to the bank. The bank then withdraws this sum from the customer's account and makes, on his behalf, all the payments listed.

This service is an extremely important one for business men as it saves a great deal of time in making out individual cheques, addressing envelopes, and also the expense of postage. It is used by many firms who pay their employees' salaries in this way.

Many private customers of the banks also use this system of making payments. It is convenient for them to pay several bills, e.g. gas, electricity, and rates, simply by writing one cheque, and all the commercial banks now provide this facility. Persons who are not customers of a bank can also use the bank giro credit system, completing the same details that a bank customer does but, in addition, handing to the bank the appropriate amount of cash.

Midland Bank Limited — bank giro credit

Counterfoil (left)

Midland Bank Limited

Date June 12th, 19—

Credit James Bennett

	£	
£20 Notes		
£10 Notes		
£5 Notes	5	
£1 Notes	8	
10s. „ /50p	4	50
S.&1.Notes		
Silver	1	75
3d. Pieces		
Copper		
Decimal Bronze		04
Total Cash	19	29
Cheques, P.O.'s etc.	6	80
see over £	26	09

675   Counterfoil

bank giro credit (right)

Date June 12th, 19—

Code No. 40 – 23 – 12

Bank Midland Bank

Branch Harrogate

Cashiers' stamp & Initials

Credit James Bennett

Account No. 3682411

Paid in by S.K.Johnson

Address 14 London Road, Crewe.   Ref. No.

Fee

Number of cheques 2

675

	£	
£20 Notes		
£10 Notes		
£5 Notes	5	
£1 Notes	8	
10s. „ /50p	4	50
S.&1.Notes		
Silver	1	75
3d. Pieces		
Copper		
Decimal Bronze		04
Total Cash	19	29
Cheques, P.O.'s etc.	6	80
£	26	09

Fig. 12. Bank Giro Credit

Courtesy of the Midland Bank Limited

NIGHT BANKING

Most banks have installed night safes at their branches which enable customers to deposit money at the bank outside normal banking hours. A wallet is supplied in which bank-notes and cheques to be paid into a customer's account may be placed. A key is also provided which gives access to a small door in the outside wall of the bank. The wallet, containing the cheques and money, slides down a chute to a place of safety inside the bank. This service is very useful for shopkeepers, who, after counting their daily takings, wish to deposit their money in a safe place.

Fig. 13. A Cash Dispensing Machine

CASH DISPENSING MACHINES

A number of banks are now providing a relatively new service for customers requiring cash at any time, day or night. The cash dispenser is built into the wall of the bank, and the customer by feeding into the machine a special cashcard or voucher and tapping out his code number on a small keyboard can obtain £10 in cash. Since 1970 an increasing number of banks have been providing this service.

THE MOBILE BANK

Many banks are now represented at most of the large trade exhibitions and shows which take place in different parts of the country and these mobile branches afford a very convenient means of settling debts between persons attending these events.

BANKERS' REFERENCES

A person making purchases of goods and not wishing to make an immediate cash settlement can give his banker's name as a reference. The trader, on taking up this reference, will be given information as to the customer's ability to pay for the goods purchased.

FOREIGN TRAVEL

People going abroad on business or for pleasure who do not wish to carry large amounts of money with them can obtain *travellers' cheques* which can be cashed at banks in overseas countries.

BANKER'S DRAFTS

Customers of banks sometimes have to make payments to persons to whom they are unknown and who, because of this, will not accept a cheque in payment. A *draft*, which is really a cheque signed by the bank manager and drawn on the bank itself, can be used instead. This is acceptable to the person to whom the payment is to be made because it is the *bank's cheque,* and it is the bank which is promising to make the payment.

CREDIT CARDS

For a number of years persons living in the United States of America have been able to use credit cards supplied by a well-known international credit organization called the *American Express Company.* Indeed, this facility is made available by the same company all over the world, including Great Britain. In recent years they have been introduced by British concerns including Barclays Bank with their *Barclaycard.* Person who are considered sufficiently creditworthy can obtain a credit card, and certain shops, garages, hotels, etc., who operate the scheme, will provide them with goods and services up to a previously agreed amount of money. The feature of this service is that items can be purchased at any time during the month, and the total amount of their expenditure during the month is deducted from their bank account at the end of the month in question.

Credit cards have become very popular in this country, as they have in fact, all over the world. Some people argue that in future years the *cheque* as a method of payment will become out-of-date and that most persons will use the credit card system. Traders benefit from this system, because even though they have to pay a small discount to the credit card company, they are provided with a guarantee by them that all amounts owing by customers using the service will be paid.

CHEQUE CARDS

Cheque cards were introduced into this country a number of years ago, and are rather different from credit cards. A practical problem that sometimes arises with the use of cheques, is that if a person is unknown to a trader, or perhaps on holiday at home or overseas, his cheque may not be accepted. To overcome this problem, the customer, by arrangement with his bank, can be provided with a special card which certifies that his cheque can be accepted with safety, and that the bank will guarantee that payment will be made. The card will state the maximum amount of money the bank will guarantee, and this is, of course, a safeguard for the trader who accepts a person's cheque. Cheque cards are an extremely useful banking service, and becoming increasingly popular today.

BANK MONEY TRANSFER SERVICES

The commercial banks call their various methods of transferring money *Bank Money Transfer Services*. In addition to the methods of making payment already mentioned, they operate a scheme known as *direct debiting*. This method is very similar to the standing order service because it is very useful for persons making regular periodical payments of fixed amounts of money. The difference between the two methods is that under the *direct debiting* scheme the creditor (the person to whom money is owed) claims the payment, subject to the payer's agreement. The Post Office Giro scheme also offers this method of making payment of bills, and it should prove to be a tremendous help to firms and institutions who need to collect amounts of money at regular intervals from their customers.

EXPERT ADVICE AND FINANCIAL BACKING

There are many problems that customers can take to their bank manager. Advice may be needed on matters such as income tax, the investment of savings, or on more personal financial problems. Whatever the problem, the customer is assured of a quick and efficient service.

The British banks have an international reputation second to none and have branches in many different parts of the world. The financial backing they give to business concerns and to private individuals plays an extremely large part in ensuring that many difficult financial problems are solved, and they play a leading role in the "world of commerce."

BANK MERGERS

As in "Big Business" generally there is a tendency for concerns to take over other firms, or to join together, and become more efficient in their trading activities. We usually call this a *merger*. In recent years a number of the commercial banks have merged. An example is the merger between the National Provincial and Westminster banks. Barclays and Martins have also merged in the same way.

The Bank of England

The Bank of England is the central bank of this country, and in 1946 was nationalized by the Government of that time. It is a very powerful institution and acts as the agent for the Government in its matters of financial policy. Each week the "Court" of the Bank of England, which is really a committee responsible for its policy, meets to decide what the official Bank of England rate of interest will be (the *bank rate*), and when, as occasionally happens, the bank rate is altered, all the commercial banks of this country bring their own interest rates into line. As we can now see, should the Government decide to make money *dearer* and *harder to borrow*, the bank rate is increased. Should the opposite effect be desired (i.e. the reduction of interest rates generally), the bank rate is reduced.

The Bank of England is the only bank in England allowed to issue *bank-notes*, and a very careful watch is kept on the quantity being issued. The result of having too many bank-notes in circulation throughout the country would be that the prices of goods would rise and our money would be worth much less. Shortly after the First World War, this did happen in Germany: too many marks were issued and, as a consequence, there was a grave financial crisis in the country, with prices of many commodities, such as bread, rocketing sky high.

The Bank of England suggests the policy to be adopted by all the commercial banks and has a great influence on national financial affairs.

Questions

1. Describe the services that the commercial banks provide for—

   (i) the private individual,
   (ii) the business man.

2. Name the main commercial banks. How do they differ from savings banks?

3. Describe the various methods of borrowing money available to customers of the commercial banks.

4. Explain the difference between the personal loan and the bank loan. How does the bank loan differ from an overdraft? Which method does the business man use if he is short of money for paying current business expenses?

5. Name the *three* parties to a cheque.

6. Describe the work of the London Clearing House, using an example to illustrate your answer.

7. Write briefly on the Bank of England and its importance to the Government.

8. What are the advantages for the business man if he opens a current account with a commercial or joint-stock bank?

9. Distinguish between a current account and a deposit account at a joint-stock bank. What other facilities are offered by banks to a business man? (*Middlesex Reg. Exam. Board.*)

10. (i) What is the name of the central bank of England?

    (ii) Name three services provided by commercial banks for the business man.

    (iii) What do customers investing their money in deposit accounts receive from banks?

Practical work

1. You are commencing in business on your own account. Make a list of all the banking services you will require.

2. Draft a bank statement. Insert specimen entries showing the state of the account.

3. Draw a street plan of your town, showing the situation of the leading banks.

4. You require a personal loan from your bank. Make a note of all the points you will put to your bank manager regarding the proposed loan.

13 Making Payments, and Post Office Services

When we do our shopping or pay household bills such as rent, electricity, and gas, the money that we use often takes the form of *cash*. This may be quite convenient when large sums of money are not involved, and it is simply a question of handing the money over to another person. It is rather different, however, if it becomes necessary to pay money to a firm or person situated a long distance away, when considerations such as safety and convenience have to be taken into account.

We know from our chapter on the services of the commercial banks, that the cheque system offers an alternative to making payment by cash. In addition to the two already mentioned, there are other methods of making payment which are in extensive use today, each of them having its own particular merits.

Paying In Cash

Cash consist of coins and bank-notes; it is really a form of *token* which is accepted by everybody and which can therefore be used for the settlement of debts. Today coins are made of metals which are of little value in themselves, and bank-notes are merely pieces of paper; their value lies in what they will purchase for us.

If the strict letter of the law is to be obeyed, *only cash is legally acceptable* when making payments, and the term *legal tender* is used to describe those forms of money which can be legally offered when paying for goods and services. This means that there are restrictions on the *quantity of coins* that can be used as a means of settling debts, as under—

> *Cupro-nickel* (*silver*)—coins up to and including 10p up to a maximum of £5; 50p up to a maximum of £10.
>
> *Bronze* (*copper*)—up to a maximum of 20p.

In practice, of course, although a person might not be very pleased if he was paid a debt of £5 all in pennies, and would be perfectly entitled

100

to refuse such a payment, most people find that there are no real problems, and money is exchanged which is not strictly speaking in the form of legal tender.

Bank-notes can be used in making payment, up to any amount, but officially the bank-notes of the Scottish and Northern Ireland Banks are legal tender only in those countries, although, in practice, they are usually quite acceptable in England.

Paying By Cheque

Although only cash is legal tender, most people will accept cheques in settlement of debts, because a cheque does in fact *represent* cash.

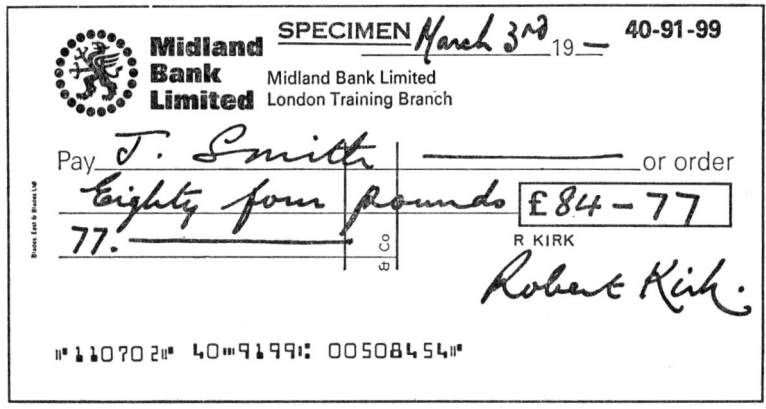

Courtesy of the Midland Bank Limited

Fig. 14. A Crossed Cheque

If the cheque in Figure 14 is examined closely it will be found that two lines have been drawn across its face. This is called *crossing* the cheque. The effect of crossing a cheque is that it must be paid into a banking account, and this is a safety device, since, should a cheque fall into the wrong hands, it cannot be *cashed* at a bank.

An *uncrossed cheque*, termed an "open cheque," can, however, be cashed at the branch of the bank on which it is drawn, and although this means that there is not the same margin of safety as when a crossed cheque is used, it is sometimes considered desirable to omit the crossing so that the person receiving the cheque can go to the bank and obtain cash for the amount stated. The uncrossed cheque is sometimes

101

used by employers when paying their employees' salaries, as some employees may not have banking accounts.

DIFFERENT TYPES OF CHEQUE CROSSINGS
Crossing (*a*) shown below is all that is needed to ensure that the person receiving it pays it into his bank account. The inclusion of the words "& Co." is normal practice, but has no legal significance.

A cheque crossed "A/c payee only," as shown in (*b*), can only be paid into the banking account of the person to whom it is made payable (the payee). This is a further safety measure that can be taken when making payment by cheque.

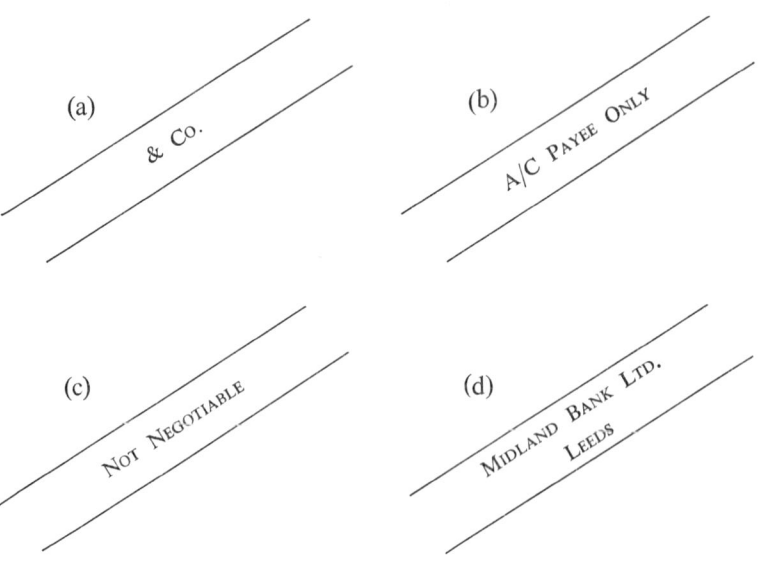

Cheques are normally what are known as "negotiable instruments." It is possible for a person receiving a cheque to sign his name on the back (termed "endorsing"), and then pass it on to another person to whom he wishes to make payment. This is called *negotiating* a cheque. Provided he gave value for it and took it in good faith the person receiving the cheque has a legal right to it, even though it is afterwards discovered that the person giving the cheque had no right to it and that some other person was the rightful owner.

102

Although it would appear from the crossing illustrated in (*c*) that the words really mean what they say, and that the cheque cannot be endorsed and then given to another person, it is not so. The crossing "not negotiable" means that a person receiving a cheque crossed in this manner receives no better legal right to it than had the person from whom he received it. In other words, if the cheque was received from a person who had no legal right to it, it would, legally, still be the property of the previous, rightful, holder. This method of crossing a cheque is an extra precaution in case it should be stolen.

A further precaution is to write in the crossing the name and address of a bank branch, as in (*d*). This ensures that the cheque can only be paid into an account at that particular bank. Many mail order firms request their customers to cross cheques in this way when making payment, to ensure that, should the cheque fall into wrong hands, it will be of little value to the holder.

Post Office Methods of Payment

GIRO SYSTEM

The Giro system commenced in October, 1968 with its headquarters at Bootle in Lancashire. This is a new banking service which offers facilities for transferring money, similar to those offered by the commercial banks. It is hoped that the Giro service will bring banking facilities to a much wider range of the public. It offers a quick and reliable service at a relatively low cost. Any person aged sixteen years and over can use this scheme which is operated with the help of all the branch post offices throughout the country.

Giro customers receive services similar to those operated by the commercial banks. One should remember, however, that basically the Post Office Giro is a *money transfer* service, and does not offer *all* the facilities offered by the commercial banks. In 1970, in conjunction with Mercantile Credit Co. Ltd., a specialist finance institution, the Post Office Giro began to offer persons with an adequate credit worth, *personal loans* up to an agreed amount.

The Post Office Giro service has expanded quite rapidly since it was first introduced, and many large companies and other organizations are now using the facilities available. The Giro service is particularly useful for large companies in their collection and banking of large amounts of cash from many different sources.

103

POSTAL ORDERS

Postal orders can be obtained for amounts ranging from a few pence up to £5 in value. Postal orders may be crossed which makes it necessary for them to be paid into a bank account.

Fig. 15. A Postal Order

MONEY ORDERS

For amounts up to £50 money orders can be purchased, but a special form has to be filled in and handed over the post office counter, stating the value of the money order required, the name of the person to whom it is to be made payable, and the name of the post office where it should be cashed. Because the money order can only be cashed at the post office stated, by a person who must be able to disclose from whom he received it, it is a safer method of making payment than the postal order. On both postal orders and money orders, stamp duty or *poundage* has to be paid according to the value of the order being purchased. Should it be necessary to make a payment very quickly, a *telegraphic money order* can be sent, the reverse side of the form used when applying for an ordinary money order being completed with the necessary details. An extra charge is made to cover the cost of sending the telegram. A money order may be crossed if desired.

REGISTERED POST

This is a method of sending cash through the post in a special envelope supplied by the Post Office. A charge is made for this service which will depend on the amount of cash being sent in this way. It is really a form

104

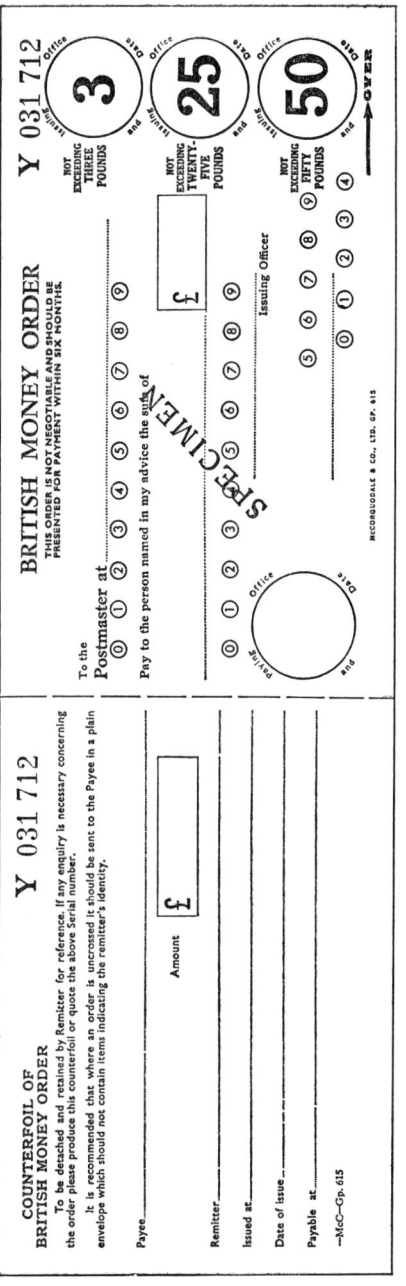

Fig. 16. A Money Order

Reproduced by Permission of The Post Office

of insurance cover provided by the Post Office, so that, in the event of any loss whilst the envelope is in the post, compensation can be claimed. It is also possible to register (insure) the contents of parcels being sent through the post.

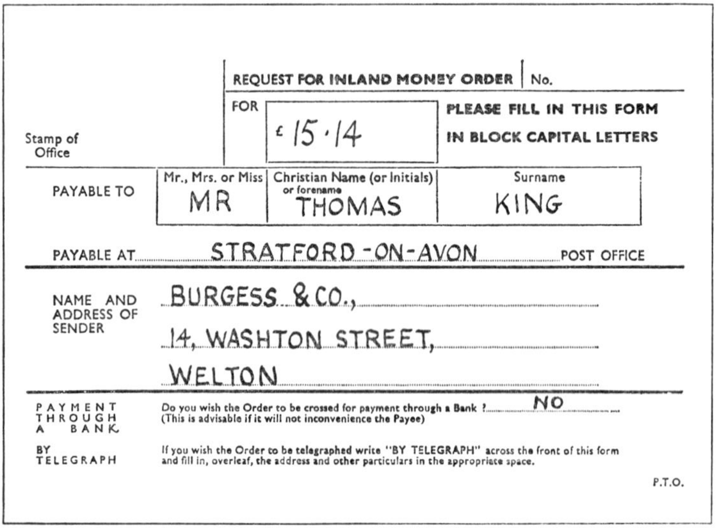

	REQUEST FOR INLAND MONEY ORDER	No.	
	FOR	PLEASE FILL IN THIS FORM	
Stamp of Office	£ 15·14	IN BLOCK CAPITAL LETTERS	

	Mr., Mrs. or Miss	Christian Name (or Initials) or forename	Surname
PAYABLE TO	MR	THOMAS	KING

PAYABLE AT ....STRATFORD-ON-AVON........ POST OFFICE

NAME AND ADDRESS OF SENDER ..BURGESS & CO.,........

..14, WASHTON STREET,........

..WELTON........

PAYMENT THROUGH A BANK — Do you wish the Order to be crossed for payment through a Bank? ....NO........ (This is advisable if it will not inconvenience the Payee)

BY TELEGRAPH — If you wish the Order to be telegraphed write "BY TELEGRAPH" across the front of this form and fill in, overleaf, the address and other particulars in the appropriate space.

P.T.O.

Fig. 17. An Application Form for a Money Order

Other Post Office Services

The Post Office is a State-owned concern which, in addition to the services already mentioned, provides a means of *communication* between people living, not only in this country, but in many different parts of the world. All private individuals find these services of immense benefit, and the business man, too, is provided with facilities which are very necessary if he is to keep in touch with both his suppliers and customers.

LETTER AND PARCEL POST

This service is of extreme value and makes it possible for people to communicate with each other at a very small cost.

A two-tier letter and parcel post system is operated. Persons wanting quick delivery of their letters and parcels must buy stamps in accordance with the rates for *first-class* post. A lower charge is made for *second-class* letters and parcels but delivery usually takes at least one day

106

longer, especially at peak-post times such as Christmas. If you want to ensure prompt delivery of your post it is usually advisable to pay the rates appropriate for first-class post.

RECORDED DELIVERY

This service provides, at a small cost, the sender of letters with the security of knowing that the person receiving the letter must acknowledge receipt, by signing a form, before the postman will make the delivery. For a small additional charge the Post Office will notify the sender of the letter that delivery has been made.

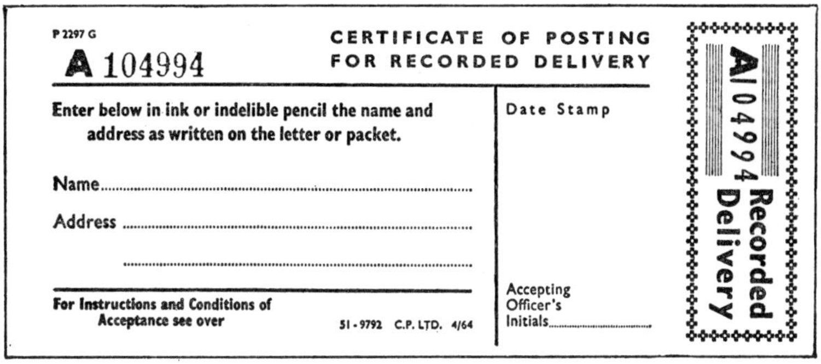
P 2297 G

A 104994

CERTIFICATE OF POSTING
FOR RECORDED DELIVERY

Enter below in ink or indelible pencil the name and address as written on the letter or packet.

Name..

Address.....................................

....

For Instructions and Conditions of Acceptance see over

51-9792 C.P. LTD. 4/64

Date Stamp

Accepting Officer's Initials..................

A104994 Recorded Delivery

Reproduced by Permission of The Post Office

Fig. 18. A Recorded Delivery Form

POST OFFICE BOX NUMBERS

Persons or firms not wishing to have mail delivered to their home or place of business can, on payment of an annual fee, have all post held by the Post Office for them.

EXPRESS DELIVERY

For a small charge, a letter can be dispatched immediately without having to wait for sorting, and at the receiving end it will be sent out by the next delivery.

CASH ON DELIVERY (C.O.D.)

This service is particularly useful when goods are ordered through the post and it is not desired to make payment in advance. The purchaser pays the postman when delivery is made.

BUSINESS REPLY CARDS AND ENVELOPES

This is an arrangement whereby a firm can send prospective customers a postcard or envelope, prepaid for a reply. A licence must first be obtained from the Post Office and the postcards and envelopes must conform to a special (or standard) design. This service is very beneficial to the business man because he is able to offer prospective customers the use of the post at his expense.

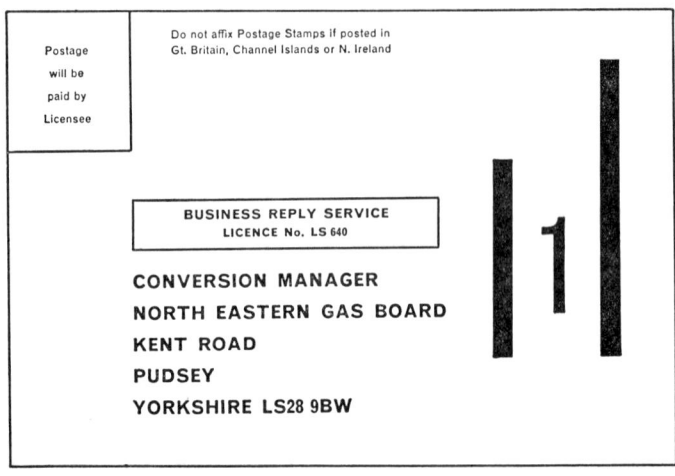

Postage
will be
paid by
Licensee

Do not affix Postage Stamps if posted in
Gt. Britain, Channel Islands or N. Ireland

BUSINESS REPLY SERVICE
LICENCE No. LS 640

CONVERSION MANAGER

NORTH EASTERN GAS BOARD

KENT ROAD

PUDSEY

YORKSHIRE LS28 9BW

Courtesy of North Eastern Gas Board

Fig. 19. A Business Reply Card

FRANKING OF LETTERS

Firms and persons whose practice it is to send out large quantities of letters can obtain a *franking machine,* which prints a stamp on the envelope, the machine recording automatically the number of times it is used. This service saves a great deal of time in affixing stamps to envelopes. Should a franking machine not be in use, and it be desired to send out a large number of letters, the Post Office can arrange to frank the letters on behalf of the sender.

TELEGRAMS AND CABLEGRAMS

When it is desired to send messages quickly, a telegram can be sent and the charge is based on the number of words in the message. Cablegrams can be sent to persons living in countries overseas, the charge being made in the same way. Many firms, on payment of a fee to the Post

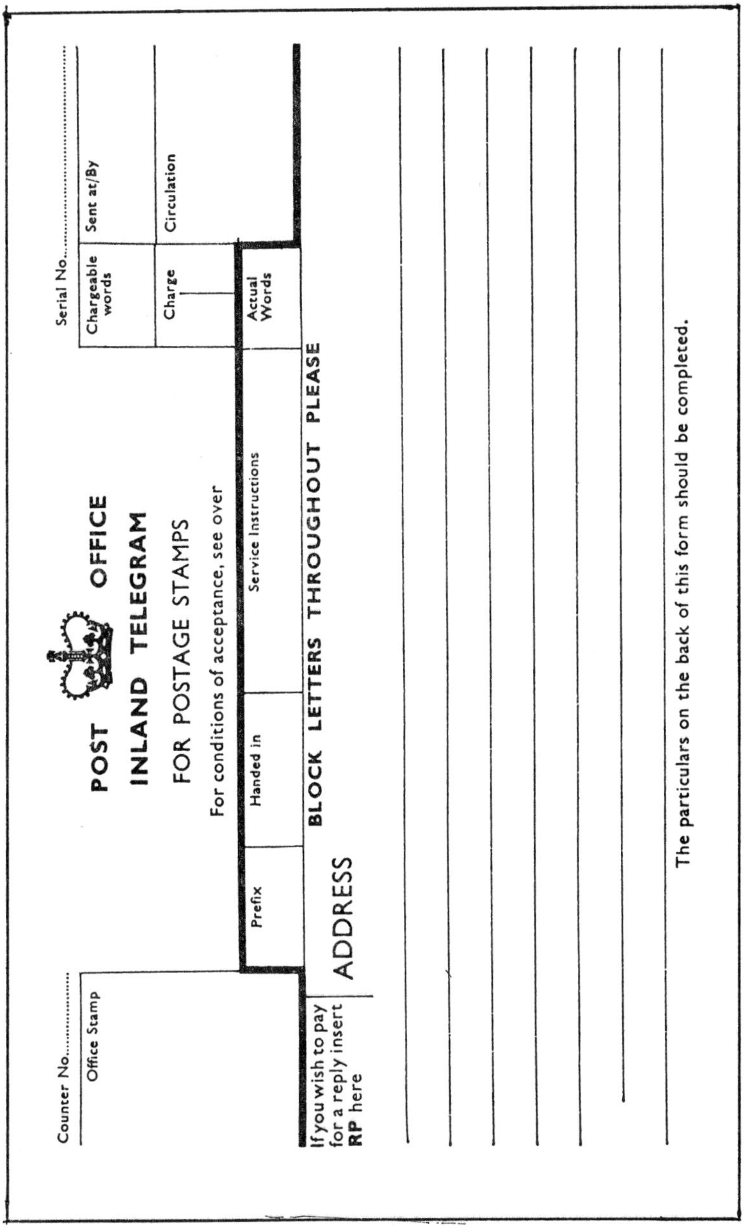
Counter No.............

Office Stamp

POST OFFICE

INLAND TELEGRAM

FOR POSTAGE STAMPS

For conditions of acceptance, see over

Serial No.............................

Chargeable words	Sent at/By
Charge	Circulation

Prefix	Handed in	Service Instructions	Actual Words

If you wish to pay for a reply insert **RP** here

ADDRESS

BLOCK LETTERS THROUGHOUT PLEASE

The particulars on the back of this form should be completed.

Reproduced by Permission of The Post Office

Fig. 20. The Form Used when Sending a Telegram

Office, use an abbreviated telegraphic address, which reduces the cost for persons sending messages to them.

THE TELEPHONE

The use of the telephone has been a tremendous boon to business men and private individuals in that it enables people to speak to each other over both long and short distances. In this age, when speed is often so vital, and messages have to be received promptly, the telephone often means the difference between gaining and losing an order, and sometimes even between life and death.

THE TELEX SERVICE

The telex service is really an extension of the telephone service, messages being sent by an operator who uses a machine, called a teleprinter, similar in appearance to a typewriter. At the receiving end, the message is automatically printed onto paper and so forms a permanent record of the message. The usefulness of this system is that, whereas telephone messages may be misheard, the actual printing of the message gives a high degree of accuracy. Many large firms have installed teleprinters, because they realize that, although the telephone in itself is a very speedy method of communication, the actual printing of the message at the receiving end saves time and makes for an accurate recording of the message. The telex service is also cheaper than the telephone, provided there is a sufficient volume of messages.

Questions

1. Explain the meaning of legal tender.
2. Why are cheques usually acceptable, even though they are not really legal tender?
3. What is the difference between an open cheque and a crossed cheque? Why is it safer to use crossed cheques?
4. Explain the meaning of a cheque crossed "A/c payee only."
5. What does it mean when we say that a cheque is "negotiable"?
6. What services does the Post Office provide for the business man?
7. List the various methods of making payments which are most useful to the business man. Write briefly on each one.
8. Discuss the value of Post Office services to the community.

110

9. What methods of making payment would *you* use for the following?

   (i) Payment of 5*p* for a small booklet about a holiday resort town.

   (ii) The sending of 50*p* to a relative as a birthday present.

   (iii) The purchase of goods from a firm unknown to you, and situated a good distance from your own town.

   (iv) The settlement of a debt to a person residing in another town who stipulates that he must have *cash* in settlement.

   (v) The payment of a debt of £50 to a firm.

10. Clive Brooks sent a cheque crossed "not negotiable" through the post to Harold Watson. It was stolen by an unknown person who gave it to Flash Cars Ltd., as a deposit on a motor-car. Discuss the implications involved, stating who has the right to the cheque.

11. Of what value are the telegraph and telephone services to the individual and to commerce?

12. How are payments made by cheque? How does this method differ from a payment made by credit transfer?

13.   (i) What is the amount of legal tender for bronze coins?

   (ii) Who owns the Post Office?

   (iii) Name three Post Office services.

   (iv) Who is the payee of a cheque?

   (v) What does C.O.D. mean?

Practical Work

1. Obtain application forms for a money order and a telegram. Insert specimen entries and place in your notebook.

2. Find out from a post office the current rates for—

   (i) inland letters,

   (ii) parcels,

   (iii) postcards,

   (iv) printed papers.

3. Draw a cheque and complete specimen entries, making a note underneath of the names of the drawer, drawee and payee.

4. Compile a scrap book on Post Office services, obtaining as many examples as possible.

14 Buying Goods

Buying goods is often a simple act. It is so if we make payment for our purchases immediately, as in the case of our normal day-to-day shopping. There are other occasions, however, when we may need a little time before being able to pay for the goods, and the shopkeeper allows us to take them home and pay at a later date.

When we make immediate payment for our purchases, it is known as a *cash transaction*. When, however, we are allowed to delay our payment for a while, we term it a *credit transaction*. Many persons now take advantage of this system of "buying now and paying later," particularly when purchasing items such as household furniture, washing machines and the like. Certain shops in your own area may even encourage this practice because it enables them to make sales which otherwise would not be possible.

Cash Discount

In order to encourage customers to make payment for their wants at the time of purchase, certain shopkeepers offer *cash discounts*. For instance, if a record player priced at £18 is being purchased, a shopkeeper may offer, as an encouragement to pay immediate cash, $2\frac{1}{2}$ per cent discount. The actual price to be paid is arrived at as follows—

	£
Cost of record player	18·00
Less cash discount of $2\frac{1}{2}$ per cent	0·45
Price paid	17·55

Even if payment is delayed for a short time, the shopkeeper may still grant a discount, especially if the customer is known to him. The actual amount of cash discount offered to customers for immediate or prompt settlement varies from shop to shop. It may be only $2\frac{1}{2}$ per cent at one shop but as high as 10 per cent at another. Because of this variety in discounts from one shop to another, a customer wishing to purchase a large item, such as a washing machine or carpeting, would be well advised to check on the amount of cash discount given by the various shopkeepers and, provided quality is the same, to buy from the shop offering the best discount. It will not always follow, however, that this is the *best buy* for there are other considerations, such as after-sales service, which are often equally important.

In just the same way that we as individuals are sometimes given cash discounts when making our purchases, business concerns trading with one another encourage the prompt settling of debts between themselves by offering cash discounts. This helps to ensure a speeding up in the process of settling debts, and business concerns are able to finance the buying of fresh stocks of goods and materials more easily than would otherwise be possible.

Credit and Credit Worth

Try to visualize the enormous amounts of money that are needed by business concerns: money for the purchasing of raw materials that will eventually be used in the manufacture of their products; cash for the payment of wages each week to employees, and for all the other items of expense. We may appreciate just how difficult it often is for them to pay immediate cash. Thus it is the usual practice for business concerns to allow one another a period of time before actual payment is required. The length of time, or *period of credit* as it is known, varies according to the circumstances. In some cases a month may be allowed, in others a longer period may be given. Credit facilities are of considerable import-ance to the business world, because it must be borne in mind that business concerns have many expenses to meet before they sell the goods they produce, and if payment of these expenses can be delayed for a time, it helps to relieve the financial burden very considerably.

When persons or firms wish to purchase goods or services on credit, the seller has to be satisfied that the customer will be able to pay. It is therefore usual in the business world for a prospective purchaser requir-ing time in which to pay to supply the seller with references from his bankers or other business concerns confirming his ability to pay. Alternatively, a specialist firm of *status inquirers* can be employed by the sellers, such as Stubb's or Kemp's, who will, for a fee, undertake to establish the *credit worth* of the prospective purchaser. The credit worth of private individuals often has to be established by shopkeepers and

113

they sometimes employ representatives who make inquiries in the vicinity of the customer's home regarding his ability to repay debts. Shops selling goods on hire purchase often make use of these methods in order to ascertain a prospective customer's reliability.

Trade Discount

There is another form of discount given by one trader to another and this is known as *trade discount*. Retailers, for example, receive this discount from manufacturers and wholesalers, and it is often the difference between the amount of money they pay for the goods when purchasing and the price at which they sell the goods to the consumer (the customer). This difference, after deduction of all his expenses, represents the shopkeeper's profit. The example below illustrates trade discount.

GOODS PURCHASED BY A RETAILER FROM A WHOLESALER

		£
6 tape recorders at £30 each		180
12 record players at £20 each		240
	Total	420
Less trade discount of 15 per cent		63
Price paid by retailer		357

The percentage trade discount allowed by one trader to another varies according to the type of trade engaged in. Whereas a shopkeeper selling furniture may receive a trade discount of 40 per cent, a shopkeeper selling provisions may receive only 10 per cent. Although in certain trades this form of discount may appear to be unduly high, the expense of running a business considerably reduces the amount of profit the trader makes.

Questions

1. Explain—
   (i) cash discount,
   (ii) trade discount.

2. M. Spratt Ltd. purchased goods to the value of £150 from Electric Machinery Co. Ltd. Trade discount allowed amounted to 20 per cent. M. Spratt Ltd. were allowed 5 per cent cash discount when paying their account. Calculate (showing your workings in full)—

    (i) the amount of trade discount received,

    (ii) the amount of cash discount received.

3. What is meant by a credit transaction?

4. Why is it necessary for *firms* to allow their customers periods of credit?

5. A new customer has placed a large order with you. What methods could you employ in order to ascertain his credit worth?

6. Why is trade discount normally higher than cash discount?

Practical work

1. When shopping, observe if any shops are offering cash discounts to customers paying cash, and calculate how much can be saved on particular items when such discount is given.

2. If you know a shopkeeper, see if you can find out from him what proportion of his sales are—

    (i) credit transactions,

    (ii) cash transactions.

3. Prepare a diagram which shows the information received in 2 above.

4. Prepare a talk on the reasons for there being a necessity for *firms* to receive periods of credit in their business transactions with one another.

15 Making Sales

All businesses, large and small, are interested in knowing at frequent intervals how many sales they have made, and the value in pounds and pence of these sales. They also need to know various other facts and figures so that they can compare one period with another, and so ascertain whether or not trading is being carried on successfully.

The Turnover of a Business

If, in a particular year, a shopkeeper sold goods to a total value of £5,000, it is said that his sales were £5,000. This same value is often given an alternative name and called *turnover*. In effect, turnover for a particular period of time, whether it is one week, one month, or one year, is simply the sales made by the business for that particular period of time.

The Cost of Sales

Most business concerns also need to know the difference between what they have themselves paid for the goods and the amount received on their sale. The difference between the two is not all profit, because it must be borne in mind that a business has many expenses or overheads, such as wages for assistants, rent and rates, heating and lighting, etc. The amount of money paid by a business for the goods it sells is termed the *cost price* of the goods, and is also known as the *cost of sales*.

Stock Valuation

It is unusual for a business to sell immediately the goods that are purchased for re-sale. At the end of a particular financial period (which is usually one year) a quantity of goods may still be left on the shelves, or in the case of a manufacturer a certain amount of raw materials may remain unused. These goods and materials remaining unsold or unused are referred to as the *stocks* on hand at the end of the particular year. The end of the financial year is always a very busy time for the owners and employees of a business concern, because the stock

116

held by the firm must be valued. This is necessary because unless the value of stock is known, the profits for the year cannot be calculated. It is also necessary as a check against losses due to theft or some other reason.

Shopkeepers often value their stocks at the selling price (the price at which they are sold). Other types of business value their stocks at cost price, although the practice does in fact vary in the retail trade according to the requirements of the individual concern.

Calculation of the Average Stock of a Business

Many business concerns, particularly shops, find it necessary to determine the value of the average stock held over a period, usually a year. The usual practice is to add the value of the stock on hand at the beginning of the year to the value of the stock held at the end of the same year, and to find the average by dividing the total obtained by two. For example—

	£
Stock valuation, 1st January, 19.	1,500
Stock valuation, 31st December, 19.	1,300
Total	2,800

Average stock is therefore—

$$\frac{£2,800}{2} = £1,400$$

Rate of Turnover

If the turnover of a business for a particular period is known, and in addition the value of the average stock held for that same period, it is possible to calculate what is known as the *rate of turnover* (or stockturn) for the business, by dividing the turnover by the average stock. For example—

Year Ending 31st December 19.

	£
Turnover (total sales)	10,000
Average stock	
(at selling price)	1,000

The rate of turnover or stockturn is—

$$\frac{£10,000}{£\ 1,000} \text{ i.e. } \textit{ten times.}$$

117

The rate of turnover is the *rate at which stocks are being sold*. In the above example the stock has been valued at selling price, and it is therefore quite in order to divide turnover, which is the grand total of all goods sold, by a stock figure based on selling prices. If, however, the business had valued its stocks at cost price, it would have been necessary to calculate the cost price of the goods sold during the period, and call this the turnover for the business.

The calculation of the rate of turnover (or the stockturn) of the business is an extremely useful one for shopkeepers and wholesalers, because once it is known it can be compared with figures obtained in previous periods to discover whether the business is selling an increasing or decreasing quantity of goods. In any form of business *stocks must be kept moving*, and the quicker the rate of turnover, or speed at which stocks are sold, the greater the profits should be.

All businesses divide their trading periods into what are known as financial years, for example 1st January to 31st December of the same year, and whilst it is important to make all the calculations mentioned at the end of each trading year, many business concerns do in fact do this at more frequent intervals.

The rate of turnover varies a good deal between different trades. Whereas a greengrocer or general store normally enjoys a high rate of turnover because of the frequent demand for such goods as foodstuffs, shops selling furniture and similar products, for which there is a smaller demand in terms of quantity, have a lower rate of turnover. A business having a high rate of turnover will normally make only a small profit margin on each product sold, whereas a business with a low rate will expect a higher profit margin on each sale.

The Profits (or Financial Rewards) that a Business Makes

GROSS PROFIT

If the cost price of the goods sold during a particular period is deducted from the total value of sales made during the same period, the difference so calculated represents the *gross profit* made by the business. For example—

Year Ending 31st March 19.

	£
Total sales—	8,000
Less cost price of goods sold—	6,000
Gross profit	2,000

NET PROFIT
Gross profit is not, however, the *true profit* made by the business during
a period. All the expenses associated with running the undertaking
have to be deducted before the true, or *net profit* as it is known, can be
ascertained. The following example will illustrate this point—

Year Ending 31st March 19.

	£
Total sales—	8,000
Less cost price of goods sold—	6,000
Gross profit—	2,000

Other expenses incurred
as follows—

	£	
Rent and rates	250	
Wages and salaries	500	
Office expenses	50	
Advertising	100	
Insurance	25	
Delivery expenses	50	
Sundries, including postage, printing, etc.	25	
		1,000
Net profit		1,000

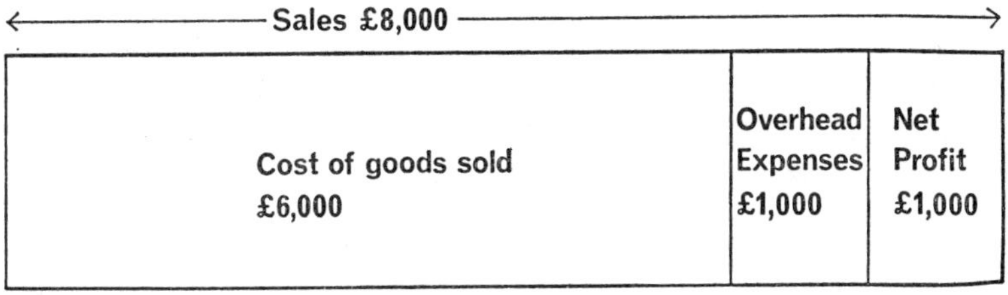

←——————— Sales £8,000 ———————→

Cost of goods sold £6,000	Overhead Expenses £1,000	Net Profit £1,000

Fig. 21. How the Money Received for Sales is Spent

The net profit made by the business during the year belongs to the
owner. He may take it all out of the business so that he and his family
may live on it, but he must, of course, pay what is due in income tax.
It must be remembered that the owner of the business has not been
drawing wages each week in the same way that an employee of the
firm has, and the net profit made is his financial reward.

119

COMPARISON OF PROFITS

Many business men like to compare the gross and net profits made in one particular year with those made in previous years in order to ascertain whether or not the profits are being maintained at a satisfactory level. One method of doing this is to calculate the proportion that gross and net profits bear to sales. For example—

Year Ending 31st December 19.

	£
Value of sales made—	8,000
Gross profit—	2,000
Net profit—	1,000

The percentage *gross profit* to sales is—

$$\frac{£2,000}{£8,000} \times \frac{100}{1} = 25 \text{ per cent}$$

The percentage *net profit* to sales is—

$$\frac{£1,000}{£8,000} \times \frac{100}{1} = 12\frac{1}{2} \text{ per cent}$$

If, in one year, the percentage of net profit to sales is less than that of the previous year or years, it may indicate that the expenses of running the business are increasing. The solution would be either to reduce the expenses as much as possible or to increase the selling prices of products. A decrease in the percentage of gross profit to sales value might indicate that the selling prices of products are too low.

There are many other calculations that can be made in order to determine whether a business is prospering, and it is now realized by business men that, unless the financial affairs of the concern can be examined in this way at frequent intervals, action that could have been taken in order to adjust any decline in the business may be unduly delayed.

Questions

1. Explain—

(i) turnover,
(ii) rate of turnover (or stockturn).

2. How is the average stock of a business calculated?

3. Explain the importance of knowing the rate of turnover of a business.

4. The following is the stock position of a business—

1st January, 19. —stock valued at £3,000 (selling price).
31st December (same year)—stock valued at £4,000 (selling price).

   (i) Calculate the average stock.
   (ii) If turnover for the same period amounted to £17,500, what is the rate of turnover (or stockturn) of the business?

5. Explain the difference between gross and net profit.

6. Calculate, from the following information, gross and net profits, and percentages of gross and net profits to sales—

Period Ending 31*st March* 19.

	£
Sales	15,000
Cost price of goods sold	9,000
Expenses of running the business	3,000

7. What steps can a business man take—

   (i) if the gross profit is too low?
   (ii) if the net profit is too low?

8. (i) What remains after overhead expenses are deducted from gross profit?
   (ii) What does cost price mean?

Practical work

1. Draw up a financial statement for a concern, which shows that profits are declining because of high running expenses. Suggest ways and means of putting the matter right.

2. Prepare a chart (e.g. a bar chart) which shows a firm's sales, and the manner in which money received for sales is spent.

3. List the type of overhead expenses you think a departmental store and a unit (small) shopkeeper incur, and then make a comparison between any differences you observe.

16 Documents: their Use in Business

The buying and selling of all the many goods and services that are available today involves a great deal of paper work, and certain business documents have come into being which put into writing the relationship that exists between the seller and the purchaser of goods and services. Although many firms use forms etc., of their own particular design and style of printing, these documents normally conform to a standard.

These business documents are a means of communication between the customer and the supplier, and set out in writing the different aspects of the transactions they enter into with one another. In their simplest form they are really *business letters*, each one having its own particular purpose.

The Familiar Business Documents in Use

THE LETTER OF INQUIRY
This is the letter written by a person or firm to a prospective supplier, asking whether certain goods or services can be supplied and the price. A request for delivery dates is often incorporated in this letter.

THE QUOTATION
The supplier receiving the letter of inquiry will reply by means of a letter called a quotation, stating at what price the goods or services can be supplied (i.e. quoting) and, possibly, a date for delivery and any terms and conditions subject to which the goods will be sold.

THE OFFICIAL ORDER
If the terms quoted are suited to the person or firm making the inquiry, it is usual for him to send to the supplier a letter called the official order, which confirms that the terms quoted by the supplier are acceptable, and requests delivery of the goods.

Note: There are occasions when a firm requiring goods or services

122

sends letters of inquiry to a number of suppliers and then does business with the one offering the best terms.

THE ADVICE NOTE

The supplier, prior to delivering the goods ordered by the customer, often sends an advice note through the post, advising the customer that the goods have been sent off to him and what method of transport has been used. It will include a description of the goods.

THE DELIVERY NOTE

This normally contains the same information as given in the advice note and is usually sent with the goods so that the customer can check, on receipt of the goods, that the correct quantity has been received. Often, a copy of the delivery note is signed by the customer as an acknowledgement of receipt of the goods.

Note: Some firms use the following documents—(*a*) packing note, (*b*) contents note, (*c*) dispatch note—which are all in fact forms of delivery note.

THE INVOICE

This document is the formal *bill*, or request, from the supplier, asking the customer to pay the amount of money due for the goods supplied. It gives a description of the goods, the quantity supplied, and the price being charged. Should the supplier be in the habit of offering special terms to customers, such as discounts, these will be shown on the invoice.

THE STATEMENT OF ACCOUNT

At the end of every month, the supplier of goods and services sends to each of his customers a *statement* showing any amount of money owed by the customer at the beginning of the month, the individual amounts owed for goods or services supplied during the month, as indicated on the invoices, less any amounts of cash paid by the customer during the same period and allowances for goods returned. The balance of cash owing at the month end is due to be paid to the supplier.

Other Business Documents and Terms

There are other business documents in use in addition to those already mentioned. Various other terms are also in general use throughout industry and commerce, and we should not presume that the documents and terms mentioned are the only ones that would be encountered. There are in this country many different kinds of firms engaged in many different trades, and each uses the documents and terms which are peculiar to its particular requirements.

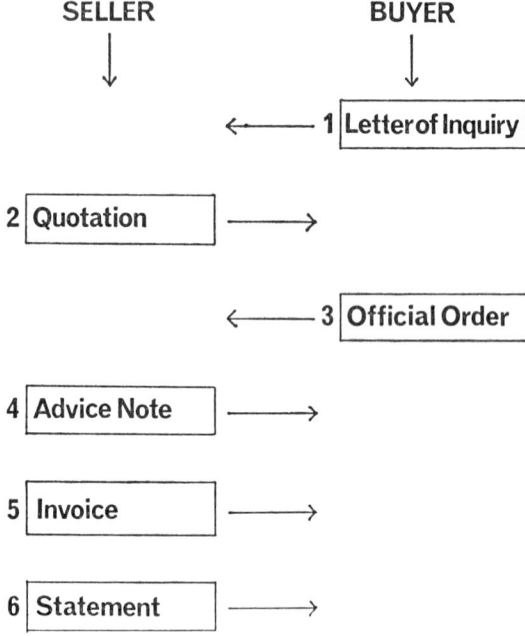

Fig. 22. Business Documents and their Sequence

THE CREDIT NOTE

This business document is normally printed in *red* to distinguish it from the invoice, and is regarded as confirmation by the supplier that, should for any reason goods have been returned by the customer, an allowance will be made which is deductable from the price of the goods as shown on the original invoice.

THE PRO FORMA INVOICE

The main use of this document arises when the seller of goods is uncertain of the buyer's ability to pay, or has not, perhaps, done business with him previously. It is really a way of requesting payment for the goods in advance.

124

THE DEBIT NOTE

This is sometimes used when the information on the original invoice is found to be incorrect, and the customer has been *undercharged.* Instead of cancelling the original invoice and sending an amended one (this is not always convenient), an extra invoice is sent, called a debit note, for the additional amount of money due. Many firms today do not use the term debit note, and refer to the document as an additional or supplementary invoice.

THE RECEIPT

When amounts are paid in settling an account for goods or services received, the seller acknowledges receipt of this money by sending a receipt. Prior to decimalization of currency in Great Britain in February, 1971 if the amount was £2 or over, the seller's signature would be written over a 2*d.* stamp. Students should now establish the current position for themselves.

When payment is made by cheque, it is now the usual practice to dispense with a receipt, unless it is especially asked for, although prior to the Cheques Act of 1957 receipts were normally required.

PRICE LISTS

Some firms, especially wholesalers, issue price lists to their customers which set out the descriptions and prices of many of the products kept in stock. A price list is very useful to a customer because it often gives detailed information on a whole range of goods, and the customer does not have to send a letter of inquiry as he knows the firm's terms of business. It is also convenient for the seller as he does not need to send a quotation to the customer.

CATALOGUES

Many firms send prospective customers catalogues which describe and often illustrate the type of goods being sold. They serve a purpose similar to that of the price list. Often a catalogue is sent to a customer in response to a particular inquiry. They are often attractively produced and illustrated in colour. Those sent out by mail order firms are usually like large glossy magazines.

ESTIMATES

When a firm receives an inquiry from a prospective customer, it sometimes has to spend a considerable amount of time in calculating or

125

estimating at what price the goods can be supplied. For instance a firm of shipbuilders, receiving an inquiry for the supply of a large vessel, will spend a considerable amount of time in working out how much will need to be charged to the ship-owner. The estimate will be sent to the prospective customer who will examine it and decide whether to place an order.

TENDERS

This is a term used in certain trades when a buyer requires estimates, often from a number of firms, of the cost of providing a particular product. The buyer invites suppliers to submit *tenders*, which are a form of quotation stating at what price the work can be undertaken. Many local authorities operate this system of tenders, for example when requiring a school or college to be built. Tenders for the same job may be submitted by a number of firms, and the buyer will accept the one which he thinks most suitable, having regard to price and quality, etc.

DOCUMENTS USED IN THE EXPORT TRADE

In the export trade business transactions are, of course, very much more complicated than in the home trade and, in addition to the documents we have already talked of, several others may be used, probably the most important being the *bill of lading*. The person or firm who is sending the goods abroad fills in the bill of lading (or instructs his shipping agent to do so) and sends it with his goods to the vessel. The master signs the bill of lading and returns it to the shipper (or his agent) who forwards it by registered post to the consignee (the person or firm to whom the shipment is being made). Until he produces the bill of lading the consignee will not be able to take the goods off the vessel.

Examples of Business Documents

The following examples of the main business documents will illustrate their use. If you examine each document carefully you will see that a specimen business transaction has taken place, in this instance between a *wholesaler* and a *retailer*. These specimen business documents are only examples of those that might be used by firms such as these, and it must be borne in mind that individual firms have a layout which best suits their particular purposes. For instance, a firm manufacturing steel will have an invoice with more columns, so that details of weight, etc., can be inserted.

TELEPHONE: 2121

N. MOORE & CO. LTD.

—Electrical Stockists—

48 QUEEN STREET, STOCKTON-ON-TEES, TEESSIDE.

Our ref: T M / L D   19 October, 19..
T. Bradley & Co. Ltd.,
King Street,
Leeds, 1.

Dear Sirs,

Please quote us for the following:

(*a*)   12 television receivers, reference 221 (Pye)

(*b*)   6 *de luxe* record players, reference 145 (Bush)

The goods are required as soon as possible. Would you therefore let us know your earliest delivery date.

Yours faithfully,
for N. Moore & Co. Ltd.,

Manager.

TELEPHONE 4261   QUOTATION   Ref: 101

T. BRADLEY & CO. LTD.

(*Electrical Wholesalers*)
KING STREET, LEEDS 1

21st October, 19..

N. Moore & Co. Ltd.,
48 Queen Street,
Stockton-on-Tees, Teesside.

Dear Sirs,

Thank you for your inquiry of 19th October, 19.. We are pleased to quote you as follows:—

12 television receivers, reference 221 (Pye) at £60 (SIXTY POUNDS) each.

6 *de luxe* record players, reference 145 (Bush) at £30 (THIRTY POUNDS) each.

All goods are subject to a trade discount of 30 per cent, and delivery could be made within seven days.

Yours faithfully,
for T. Bradley & Co. Ltd.,

Sales Manager.

TELEPHONE: 2121   23rd October, 19..

N. MOORE & CO. LTD.

—Electrical Stockists—

48 QUEEN STREET, STOCKTON-ON-TEES, TEESSIDE.

Ref: TM/LD

To: T. Bradley & Co. Ltd.,
     King Street,
     Leeds, 1.

Please Supply—

12 television receivers, reference 221 (Pye) at £60 (SIXTY POUNDS) each.

6 *de luxe* record players, reference 145 (Bush) at £30 (THIRTY POUNDS) each.

All subject to a trade discount of 30 per cent.

In accordance with your quotation of 21st October, 19.. reference 101.

                          For N. Moore & Co. Ltd.,

                                              (Manager)

ADVICE NOTE

T. BRADLEY & CO. LTD.

(*Electrical Wholesalers*)

KING STREET, LEEDS 1

TELEPHONE 4261   28th October, 19..

To: N. Moore & Co. Ltd.,
     48, Queen Street,
     Stockton-on-Tees, Teesside.

We have dispatched today—

12 television receivers, reference 221 (Pye)

6 *De luxe* record players, reference 145 (Bush)

Per: Our own transport.

                          For T. Bradley & Co. Ltd.

Invoice

No: 502

T. BRADLEY & CO. LTD.

(Electrical Wholesalers)
KING STREET, LEEDS 1

28th October 19..

N. Moore & Co. Ltd.,
48, Queen Street,
Stockton-on-Tees, Teesside.

Date	Quantity	Description	Price	Amount
19..				£
28 Oct.	12	television receivers, reference 221 (Pye)	£60 ea.	720·00
28 Oct.	6	*de luxe* record players, reference 145 (Bush)	£30 ea.	180·00
				900·00
		Less 30 per cent trade discount		270·00
				630·00

Terms: 2½% cash
discount One Month
E. & O.E.

Credit Note

T. BRADLEY & CO. LTD.

(Electrical Wholesalers)
KING STREET, LEEDS 1

TELEPHONE 4261   30th October, 19..
N. Moore & Co. Ltd.,
48, Queen Street,
Stockton-on-Tees, Teesside.

	£
By allowance in respect of—	
1 television receiver, reference 221 (Pye) returned owing to damage in transit.	60·00
Less 30 per cent trade discount	18·00
	42·00

Statement

T. BRADLEY & CO. LTD.

(*Electrical Wholesalers*)
KING STREET, LEEDS 1

TELEPHONE 4261   31st October, 19..
N. Moore & Co. Ltd.,
48, Queen Street,
Stockton-on-Tees, Teesside.
2½% One Month

Date	Invoice Number	Debit	Credit	Balance
19..		£	£	£
28 Oct.	Goods 502	630·00		630·00
30 Oct.	Goods returned		42·00	588·00

Note for Students Studying Book-keeping

1. As the invoices are received from suppliers, the information on them will be entered in the Purchases Day Book.

2. The information contained on the copies of invoices sent to customers will be entered in the Sales Day Book.

3. The information contained on credit notes received from suppliers will be entered in the Returns Outwards Book (or Purchases Returns Book).

4. The information contained on copies of credit notes sent to customers will be entered in the Returns Inwards Book (or Sales Returns Book).

Some Terms and Abbreviations in General Use

ex warehouse—the buyer must pay all costs after the goods have left the seller's warehouse.

ex works—the buyer must pay all costs after the goods have left the seller's works.

carr. fwd.—carriage forward.

carr. pd.—carriage paid.

130

Terms used in foreign trade

f.o.b.—free on board, the seller paying all costs up to the time the goods are placed on board the ship.

c.i.f.—costs, insurance, freight. The seller to pay cost of shipping and insurance as necessary.

franco.—all costs are paid by the seller.

f.a.t.—free alongside truck.

f.a.s.—free alongside ship.

Other general terms

cat.—catalogue.

c/n.—credit note.

c.o.d.—cash on delivery.

dept.—department.

disc.—discount.

div.—dividend.

E. & O.E.—errors and omissions excepted.

inv.—invoice.

Ltd.—limited.

M.O.—money order.

per pro.—on behalf of.

P.O.—postal order.

pro forma—taking the form of.

R/D—refer to drawer.

Tel.—telephone.

Questions

1. For what purposes are the following used?

    (i) quotation,
    (ii) advice note,
    (iii) invoice,
    (iv) statement of account,
    (v) credit note.

2. Explain the purpose of a debit note.

3. Explain the meaning of the following—

    (i) ex works,
    (ii) carr. pd.,

    (iii) E. & O.E.,

    (iv) pro forma,

    (v) R/D.

  4. Equipment Ltd. supply some machinery to Metal Fabricators Ltd. The machinery is delivered by Equipment Ltd.'s own transport. Mention all the documents used throughout the transaction.

  5. Write briefly on the purpose of business documents.

  6. (i) Name the document which is sent to the buyer notifying him of the charge for goods sold to him.

    (ii) When the seller of goods confirms that he is making an allowance to be set off the invoice price of goods what document does he send to the purchaser?

    (iii) What document does the seller send to the prospective purchaser in reply to the initial inquiry?

    (iv) If the seller has stated that he can supply goods and the terms are acceptable to the purchaser, what document will the purchaser send to the seller?

Practical Work

  1. Draft out four business documents to illustrate an imaginary business transaction, entering specimen details.

  2. Obtain *actual examples* of as many business documents as possible for inclusion in your notebook.

  3. Conduct a business transaction with a friend in your class, one of you being the seller and the other the purchaser. Draft your own documents, entering on each one the necessary details.

  4. Prepare a diagram which illustrates all the business documents in use.

17 Insurance

We are all familiar with the insurance agent, who calls on a great many families each week to collect premiums. Such agents as he are the representatives of a number of insurance companies which help us in providing for the future, and for the uncertainty that the future may hold for us. Insurance is really the pooling of the joint financial resources of many persons, so that in the event of any one of their number suffering a loss of any kind, he can be adequately compensated out of the joint funds which have been accumulated.

Insurance companies undertake about four-fifths of the insurance business in Great Britain and Lloyd's Corporation transacts the remaining one-fifth.

The Security That Insurance Gives Us

If we bring to mind the extent of insurance cover needed by our own family—financial protection in the event of damage to property through fire, or compensation in the event of losses as a result of burglary—its benefits will be apparent. The consequences for any family suffering such a loss as the destruction of their home through fire, without any form of insurance cover, are very serious indeed. Business men also need this aid, for there is always the risk of damage to their premises or stocks of goods and materials, or of having to pay compensation to employees who are injured as a result of an accident whilst at work.

Security, then, is the keynote of insurance, and it is the insurance companies which organize the pooling of our joint resources, so that the future can be faced without the worry of possible financial hardship. It is now possible to take out insurance cover against many different kinds of risks.

Some Types of Cover Available

MORTGAGE PROTECTION
For those buying their own house, it is now possible to make arrangements with an insurance company so that, in the event of the death

133

Many persons

Pool their resources through the Insurance Companies

who

Invest the money in Industry and Commerce

So that it earns Interest and Dividends

and Compensation is paid to persons

suffering a loss of any kind

from the joint pool of money accumulated

Fig. 23. How Insurance Works

before the end of the mortgage period of the person making the mortgage repayments, the insurance company will pay off any sum still owed to the building society. It is really a form of *life assurance*, the usual procedure being to make a small payment each year, or to make a lump sum payment at the outset. Whichever method is used, there is no doubt that this scheme offers a great deal of security to the families of persons buying their own homes.

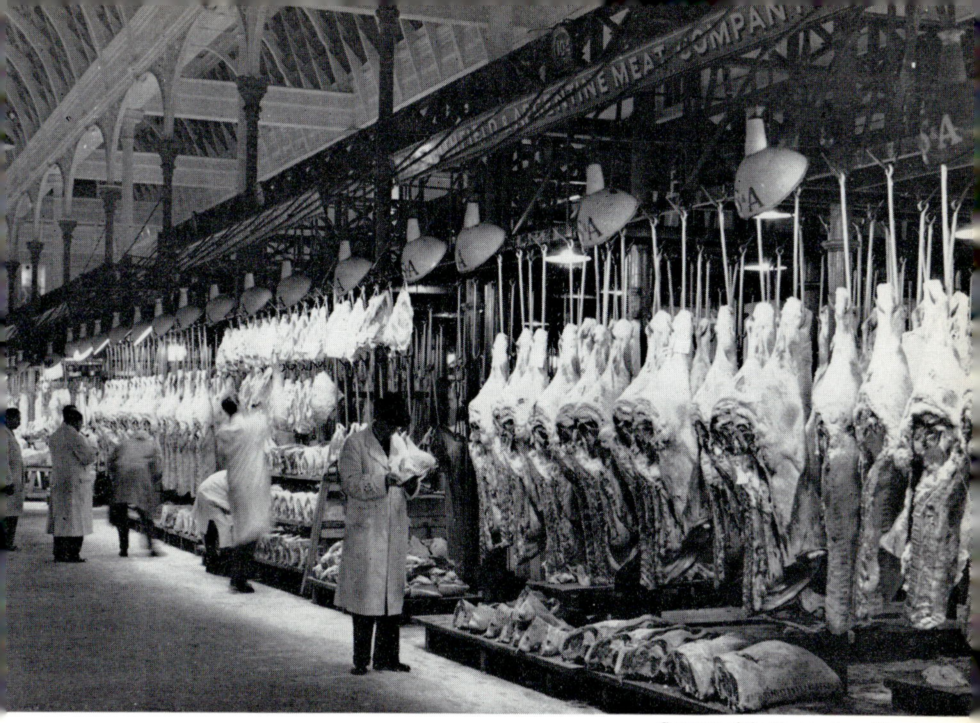

Courtesy of the Corporation of London

Plate 9. Smithfield Market

Plate 10. A risk that should be Insured Against

Courtesy of C. C. Ashton Esq., Kingsway, Rochdale

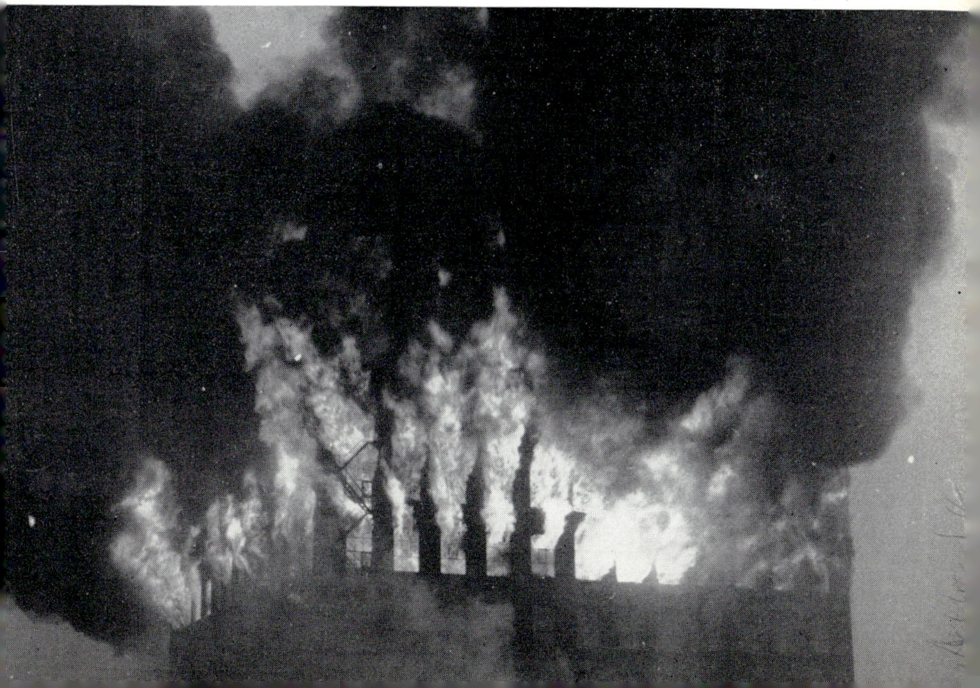

Courtesy of London Midland Region (B.R.)

Plate 11. An Express Freight Train

Plate 12. Stoke-on-Trent Rail Freight Terminal

Courtesy of London Midland Region (B.R.)

FIRE

This type of insurance cover needs little explanation, but it should be emphasized that there are still some people who neglect to insure their property against the possibility of damage caused through fire. A glance at the daily newspaper headlines all too often tells us of the outbreak of a fire causing immense destruction. In this country alone, fires account for damage amounting to millions of pounds each year.

THEFT

We all like to think of everyone in this country as being *honest*. Unfortunately there are still a large number of people who, at the expense of their fellow citizens, resort to crime. A visit to a court in your locality will provide sufficient evidence of the high number of crimes involving theft which are being committed each day. It is therefore a wise person who insures his possessions against burglary and theft.

MOTOR VEHICLE INSURANCE

The roads today are more crowded than ever, and there is every likelihood that the situation will become increasingly worse. This particular risk against which insurance companies offer us cover is therefore a very important one. We read every month of the appalling number of accidents occurring on our overcrowded roads, causing injury and sometimes death to the persons involved, and damage to vehicles. Before any person can drive a vehicle the law insists that an insurance cover must be taken out against "third party risks," so that, in the event of an accident, compensation may be paid to any person who suffers injury or loss. This type of cover is extremely important to firms owning fleets of vans and lorries which are on the road each day.

DAMAGE TO GOODS WHILST IN TRANSIT

If we bring to mind the very large quantities of goods of all descriptions which are transported both to inland destinations and to places abroad, and the great risk involved, it will be apparent to us that without there being some form of insurance cover available, many private persons and business men would think twice before allowing their goods to be transported over long distances.

HOUSEHOLD PROTECTION

Many insurance companies offer a *householders' policy*, which in general covers all the contents of a home against various types of risk, including

135

fire, burglary, burst pipes, glass breakage, flooding and gale damage. Premiums paid are usually very small considering the extent of risk involved.

CASH IN TRANSIT

How often have you entered the post office with a letter or a parcel and seen the clerk behind the counter writing out a form of receipt for a customer who has asked for a parcel or a packet containing cash to be registered? This post office service is a very useful one, and is a *form of insurance*, which gives protection should a parcel with its contents be damaged or lost.

There is another side to this story, as many people in business all too often find out to their cost. Cash in transit to and from the bank (the weekly wages of employees of the business, for example) or post office must also be safeguarded. There is a very serious risk of a hold-up or an armed robbery, and therefore it is the usual practice for all firms to take out a policy with an insurance company to protect themselves against such an occurrence.

PERSONAL ACCIDENT AND SICKNESS

For the man who wishes to ensure that his family does not suffer hardship should he be involved in an accident or be off work through illness, insurance companies offer a personal accident and sickness policy which guarantees a weekly or monthly payment of cash for the period of the illness or disablement.

PLATE GLASS (SHOP WINDOWS)

Plate glass is a very special glass used by shopkeepers for their shop fronts. It is expensive to install, and there is a considerable risk of its being shattered as a result of some unfortunate accident. Most shopkeepers take out this kind of insurance as a precaution, because the replacement of a plate glass window is a very costly matter.

EMPLOYERS' LIABILITY AND THIRD PARTY

How often do you walk down the High Street and see workmen climbing up scaffolding and ladders, busy in the building of a block of offices or shops? These workmen are in fact taking, at times, quite considerable risks, even though many safety precautions are in existence.

If an employee has an accident whilst at work as a result of the negligence of the firm or of another employee, the firm might have to pay him compensation. The premium is worked out as a percentage of the firm's wages bill, but the greater the risk involved the higher will be the premium. For example, a firm employing steel erectors, who often work at great heights, will pay higher premiums than a firm which employs only clerical workers.

Third party insurance is also very necessary for persons in business since, should a third party (i.e. someone who is *not* an employee) suffer injury or loss because of the firm's negligence, the firm might have to compensate that person.

LIFE ASSURANCE

There is another form of insurance, which will no doubt be familiar to you, called *life assurance*. (Notice the difference in the spelling.) Many people take out this form of cover so that, in the event of the death of the person insured, a lump sum will be paid to the next-of-kin. Apart from the main consideration, which is to provide financial security, making payments under a life assurance policy can be a form of long-term saving, and the premiums payable are allowable for income tax relief.

Life assurance can take the form of either *whole-life* or *endowment* policies, the difference between the two being that, whereas in the former case a lump sum is payable only on the death of the person insured, in the case of the latter a sum of money is payable by the insurance company either at the end of an agreed period (called the maturity date) or at death, whichever occurs first.

It is important that we distinguish between *insurance* and *assurance*. The difference is that whereas an insurance policy is taken out against risks which are *not bound to happen* as, for example, the risk of fire or accident, an assurance policy is taken out as cover against an event which *must happen sooner or later* (i.e. death).

RISKS BUSINESS MEN CANNOT INSURE AGAINST

Insurance does not grant any protection to business men who suffer losses because of their own inefficiencies and bad business sense. A business man cannot insure against the following risks—

    (*a*) decrease in the value of stocks of goods and materials held by the firm;

    (*b*) any loss of profits because of a decrease in value of stocks held;

    (*c*) his own bankruptcy.

Commerce and the World Outside

Marine Insurance and Lloyd's

Marine insurance has for long been a necessity for ship owners, not only in this country but in many other parts of the world, and it is to the insurance concerns of Great Britain that many maritime nations look when they wish to insure their ships and valuable cargoes against loss whilst at sea. If marine insurance were not made available, it is probable that ship owners and merchants would be reluctant to operate as the risks of loss and damage would be so great. Trade would therefore suffer.

LLOYD'S

The Corporation of Lloyd's is an international market for various types of insurance, but in particular *marine* insurance. It is also the world centre for a host of information. Lloyd's is situated in the heart of London where insurers (known as underwriters because they underwrite risks) accept an immense amount of marine business. Lloyd's itself is not a company which does business with persons or firms wishing to insure their vessels and cargoes, but is the market place where the members (the underwriters) meet and transact their insurance business.

Very stringent regulations have to be complied with before any person can become a Lloyd's underwriter, it being essential that they have at their disposal a large private fortune, which, if necessary, can be paid out to persons or firms suffering marine losses. Since the beginning of 1970, women have been allowed for the first time to become members of Lloyd's.

The underwriters themselves do not all meet each day in the huge underwriting room in Lloyd's new building, but form themselves into groups known as syndicates, and each syndicate appoints one underwriter to accept business on its behalf; in other words to act as an agent. As there are some 5,800 underwriting members we can perhaps appreciate why such a system has to be used. The underwriters are not necessarily specialists in insurance matters—they often follow occupations in other walks of life. They may be writers or film actors, for example, or just rich people. What is important is that they are persons of character with very sound financial resources, who use these resources to insure the ship owners and merchants of the world against losses.

The impressive underwriting room at Lloyd's, 340 ft. long by 120 ft. wide and surrounded on all sides by a gallery, is probably the largest air-conditioned room in Europe. Lloyd's is a British institution of
138

which we should be very proud, and it is through the joint resources of its many underwriters that the ships of all nations can plough the seas,

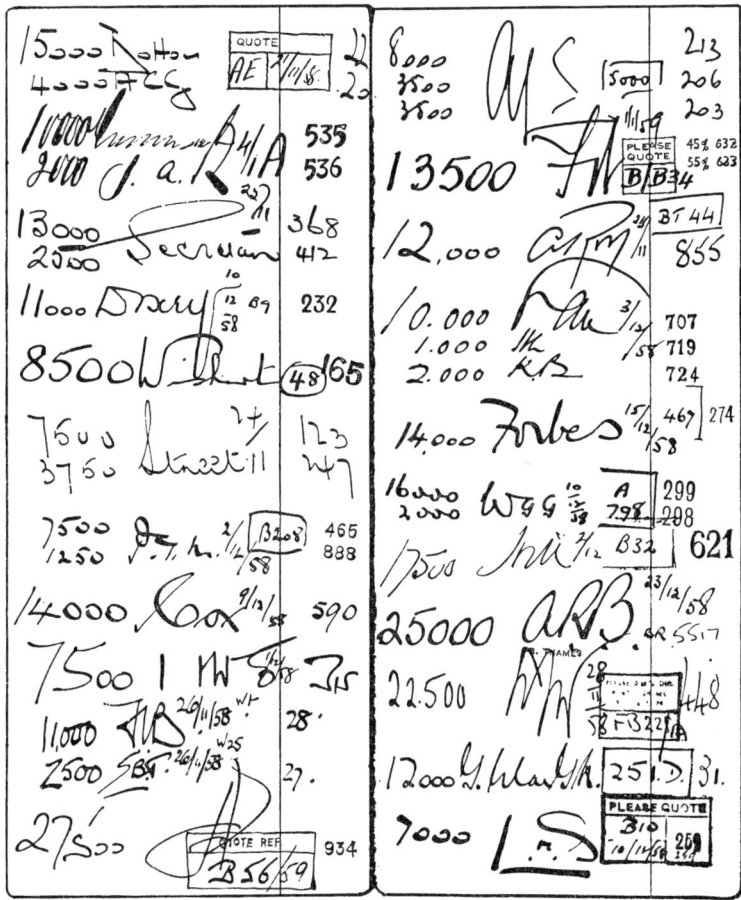

Fig. 24. Part of a Broker's Slip (*showing the initials of the underwriters and the amount of the risk they have accepted on behalf of their syndicates*)

the shipowners happy in the knowledge that, should any mishap occur, the underwriters of Lloyd's will compensate them for any losses incurred.

A booklet describing the history and activities of Lloyd's is available on request from the Corporation of Lloyd's, Lime Street, London, EC3M 7HA.

THE MEANING OF UNDERWRITING AND AN EXAMPLE

Underwriting is really an *undertaking* or a *guarantee* to compensate those who suffer some form of loss, and the chief snag with undertaking to grant insurance cover in the world of shipping is that no one person has sufficient financial resources to compensate those suffering very heavy losses. If we bring to mind that ships are worth a great deal of money, as for instance liners such as the *Queen Elizabeth II* and that the loss whilst at sea of such vessels would amount to millions of pounds, we can better appreciate why no one person can agree to give adequate cover.

Lloyd's underwriters work in groups which we now know are called syndicates, and it is thus possible for a large number of people to agree jointly to grant insurance cover. The following will serve as an illustration—

The White Star Shipping Line wishes to insure its vessel, s.s. *Clarendon*, against possible loss whilst at sea. The value of the vessel is £1,000,000. In our example, let us suppose that fifty syndicates agree jointly to insure the vessel and pool their resources as follows:

Sum to be insured £1,000,000	
Vessel: *s.s. Clarendon*	
Number of syndicates	£
25 (comprising 750 members) agree to grant cover of £20,000 each	500,000
15 (comprising 600 members) agree to grant cover of £16,000 each	240,000
10 (comprising 400 members) agree to grant cover of £26,000 each	260,000
Total insurance cover is	1,000,000

All the underwriters involved in insuring our ship, s.s. *Clarendon*, sign their names on a slip of paper, thus binding not only themselves but also the other members of the syndicate.

All the insurances that Lloyd's underwriters accept are brought to them by firms of Lloyd's brokers who represent the shipowners and any other clients. When the whole insurance has been completed the broker makes out the policy and attaches a list of underwriting members involved.

Motor Insurance Co. Ltd.

Private Car Insurance

Name of Proposer ....

Address ....

Business or Profession ....

Address at which Car is garaged ....

Make of Car .... Type of Body............

Year of Manufacture .... Registered Number ......

Proposer's Estimate of Present Value £................

Cubic Capacity .... Seating Capacity ....

Date of Purchase by Proposer ....Price Paid £........
Type of Cover Required—whether Comprehensive, Third
　　　　　　　　Party, Fire and/or Theft, or Third Party

....

Rating Area .... Amount of Premium £
　　　　　　　　　　　　　 Less Reductions

　　　　　　　　　　　　　 ....

　　　　　　　　　　　　　 ....

　　　　　　　　　　　　　 ....————

　　　　　　　　　　　　　 Amount Due:　　————

Policy to Operate from ....
The Following Questions to be Answered:

Have you any infirmity of any kind? If so state particulars

....

How long has driving licence been held? ....
I/We undertake that the car or cars will not be driven by any
person who has previously been refused any vehicle insurance.

Date .... Proposer's Signature........

Some Insurance Terms

There are certain *terms* used in insurance matters which we should know and understand as they are in common use.

Cover—the risk which is being covered, such as fire, theft, death.

Policy—the agreement between the insurance company or underwriters and the person or firm taking out the cover. The policy states on what terms the insurance is being granted and contains all the relevant conditions, which will depend on the type of cover taken out.

Premium—the sum of money payable by the policy-holder to the insurance company or underwriters for the protection being given. It varies according to the nature of the risk and the value of the property insured: the greater the risk and value, the higher will be the premium.

Renewal date—the date on which the premium falls due each year.

The Proposal—the form filled in by the person wishing to take the insurance cover. It is the basis of the contract. All relevant details have to be shown as can be seen if the example on p. 141 is studied. No proposal is required for marine insurance.

Utmost Good Faith—at the time of completing the proposal form, it is expected that the person taking out the insurance, or assurance, will acquaint the insurer with all the true facts, and any risk the insurer accepts is based on what he believes to be the true facts. From the insured person's point of view, he also has a right to be provided by the insurer with all relevant information.

The Insured—the person taking out a policy of insurance.

The Assured—the person taking out a life or endowment policy.

Insurable Interest—it is a condition that individuals or firms must not insure against any risk which does not directly affect them. The person or firm taking out the policy must have an interest in the thing insured. For example, whilst it is permissible for a man to insure his own property against fire or burglary, he must not insure the property of a neighbour or friend unless he has some special interest in it.

Other Forms of Insurance, and National Insurance

There are many other types of insurance cover available, both for business men and private persons. Almost anything may be insured against provided the person taking out the policy has an interest in the property he wishes to insure. It would be useful if you were to prepare a list of as many different forms of insurance cover you can think of, separating them into those useful for the business man and those necessary for the private person.

NATIONAL INSURANCE

Each week all employers, employees and self-employed persons have to pay a sum of money to the Government to help in the provision of pensions for retired persons, of sick and unemployment benefit for those in need, and for the medical services we receive.

Employees have an amount deducted from their wages by their employers, who purchase National Insurance stamps from a post office for affixing to the National Insurance card kept by the firm for each of its employees. Self-employed persons purchase their own stamps from a post office. The money obtained in this way is then handed over to the Government.

National Insurance is a form of *compulsory social insurance*. A contribution is made by the Government to the pool of National Insurance funds.

Questions

1. Explain the difference between *insurance* and *assurance*.
2. What is meant by "the pooling of resources"?
3. Briefly describe the various types of insurance cover available—
   (i) for the private individual,
   (ii) for the business man.
4. What are meant by the following terms?
   (i) Policy,
   (ii) Proposal,
   (iii) Premium,
   (iv) Cover.

5. Write briefly on Lloyd's and the part the underwriters play in assisting the world shipping lines.
6. Why does the business man take out insurance cover?
7. You have a small retail business, employing three assistants in the shop and a van driver who delivers for you. List the types of risk against which you would insure.

8. Describe three of the business risks against which a prudent wholesaler should insure and say how he would effect the insurances.

(Middlesex Reg. Exam. Board.)

9. What are the chief risks that the owners of a small engineering factory might insure against?

10. (i) Name three different types of insurance cover.

(ii) Name the type of insurance policy a bank would accept as security for a loan.

(iii) What is the purpose of insurance?

(iv) To what organization do underwriters belong?

(v) Name *one* risk a business man cannot insure against.

Practical work

1. Obtain a copy of an insurance or assurance proposal form for inclusion in your notebook.

2. Prepare a diagram which shows the different forms of insurance cover available.

3. Prepare a talk on the reasons why everybody should take out insurance and assurance cover.

18 Transport

Travel plays an important part in our daily lives. All of us at one time or another need transport, whether it be to take us to school, to work, or on our annual summer holiday. There are many factors which have to be taken into account before we decide what method of transport is best suited to our own particular purposes. It is more than probable that the bus or coach is used to take us to school or to the factory. For holidays in this country we have a choice of coach, train, or perhaps the family car. It is rather more difficult when the question of holidays abroad crops up. Factors such as the length of holiday and the speed with which we need to arrive at our destination, all play an important part in our decision to use road, rail, sea, or air transport. Nor must it be forgotten that personal comfort is also a consideration for many people.

Planning a journey

Travel is for many people an adventure, and it is as well to make adequate preparations for a journey, and not to leave things until the last minute. A visit to a *travel agency* is often worth while because travel agents are experts who specialize in all aspects of travel and not only in booking seats on organized tours. However, should the traveller wish to make his own arrangements, a visit to the railway station or motor-coach booking agent will be necessary. Timetables will have to be consulted in order to ascertain whether there is a train or coach running at the required time, and if the journey can be made direct or whether changes will be necessary *en route*. All the information should be carefully noted down and full allowance made for getting to the railway or motor-coach station on time. Local bus service times may also be needed if there is not to be any last minute hitch.

So journeys must be planned very carefully and should, if possible, take into account the following factors—

1. the distance;
2. how long the journey will take;

3. whether any changes *en route* will be involved;
4. comfort;
5. whether or not the journey is an urgent one;
6. the cost involved.

The passenger who has made *careful arrangements* will travel long distances with much less worry than one who has left things to chance— and it is exactly the same with people in business. They also must organize their whole transport and travel requirements with care, taking into account their particular needs.

Timetables sometimes seem to read like foreign languages to many people. This is because they are probably not used to handling them, and it is very useful experience to practise using rail and coach timetables.

The Importance of Transport to the World of Commerce

We probably all realize just what the effects would be for each one of us if all the various transport services ceased to function. The railways, the municipal and private bus companies, the shipping lines, and the airlines provide the means whereby passengers can be carried over both short and long distances, and their services are essential in the modern world.

Although the carrying of passengers is an extremely important service, the transporting of goods and materials over varying distances is also absolutely vital to us. Transport, then, is a *function of commerce* which helps to ensure that industry is provided with all the materials needed in the manufacture of goods, and that once the goods have been made, they can be sent to whoever requires them.

Through the years, the growth of industry has been helped a great deal as a direct result of the enormous expansion of transport. We know from our reading so far that in the early days factories often had to be situated near to the sources of power (e.g. coal) and raw materials, and that townships grew around these factories. The difficulties of transporting materials and goods was a problem which restricted the location of industries to particular areas of the country, and this meant that, whilst some parts of the country had many industrial developments, other areas were almost completely rural.

The inventions that have taken place in the world of transport since those early days have contributed to a very large extent to the general
146

prosperity of the nation, and have made it possible for industries to be situated in many different parts of the country, so spreading more evenly the number of jobs available. Although the distance which goods and materials have to be transported to and from a factory plays a large part in adding to the cost of a product, how beneficial it is for us to be able to enjoy the use of all these products, sometimes brought to us from many different countries.

Railways

After the Second World War the railway companies of this country were taken over by the Government and became a *State-owned concern*. During the war very little had been done in improving the system apart from ensuring that munitions and troops could be moved from one place to another in as short a space of time as possible. A great deal of money was needed to renew many items of equipment and stock and generally to modernize the railways. Even today, much still remains to be done in providing express goods trains which can transport goods and materials quickly. As in industry, new methods and techniques are being introduced in order that the railways can become more efficient and better able to cope with the increasing volume of goods and materials.

As a result of the Beeching Report in 1963, some lines which were considered to be unprofitable have now been closed and there has been a greater concentration on providing a railway system which, with the use of *express freight carriers*, can offer industry a speedy and reliable service.

ADVANTAGES OF RAIL TRANSPORT

1. It is usually cheaper for the transporting of heavy and bulky goods.

2. It may be speedier for goods being transported over long distances.

3. Some factories have their own *rail sidings*, and goods can be transported directly to and from the factory itself.

4. There are many links with the ports, making it easier to move goods to and from ships.

DISADVANTAGES OF RAIL TRANSPORT

1. The amount charged for delivery of small consignments is often higher than the charge made by road haulage concerns.

147

2. There may be delays in making delivery, as a complete train load may have to be made up before the goods are moved.

3. Further delays may be caused in the loading and unloading of goods from the rail wagons.

Although most goods and materials are carried by what are termed *goods services* or *goods trains*, smaller parcels can be carried, at a higher rate, by *passenger trains*, which provide a speedier service.

Road Transport

There are many road haulage concerns in this country today, some of them, such as British Road Services, a State-owned concern, being very large. The extension of the motorways has done a great deal to make the carriage of goods by road a speedy and efficient method of transportation. It is perhaps inevitable, though, that in the future more goods than at present will have to be carried by rail, as the roads are becoming increasingly overloaded with goods vehicles and private cars. There is a great deal of competition for business between the railways and road haulage concerns.

Many firms operate their own fleets of motor vehicles, which not only helps them to reduce carriage costs, but enables them to make deliveries of goods to customers very promptly.

ADVANTAGES OF ROAD TRANSPORT

1. Can often transport less bulky goods considerably more cheaply than by rail.

2. Is usually speedier for shorter journeys.

3. Can provide a door-to-door service.

DISADVANTAGE OF ROAD TRANSPORT

May be dearer for the transporting of bulky goods and materials.

Canals

Although today our canals are not used extensively, they do offer an alternative form of transport in certain areas for bulky goods, such as coal. As a method of transportation the canal system is very slow, but is cheap and reliable.

Whether canals will emerge in the future as a suitable alternative to other methods of transport remains to be seen, but some people are of the opinion that as the roads in this country become even more over-crowded, money should be spent on the canals to widen them and bring them up to date, so that they can assist in relieving the congestion on the roads.

Shipping

For many centuries Great Britain has been a powerful shipping nation. This has been so because of its geographical location which has meant that many of its foodstuffs and raw materials for industry have had to be carried across the seas. The increased trade between the nations of the world is made possible by the use of ships, including the large oil tankers and ore carriers, which sail the oceans of the world carrying their cargoes between different ports.

Even today there is still a great deal of adventure in the world of shipping. A visit to ports such as London and Liverpool will indicate the tremendous amount of activity that is constantly taking place in ensuring that people all over the world are helped in the movement of vast quantities of goods and materials to places where they are needed. The hazards of the high seas are still a challenge to the men who sail in our ships, but a good deal has been done in helping to make their job safer and more comfortable by the building of vessels costing millions of pounds, which incorporate the best of modern equipment and improved quarters for the crew.

COASTAL STEAMERS

These vessels sail the coastal waters around Great Britain carrying their cargoes, which are usually bulky materials such as coal, between the various ports. They provide a cheap and efficient method of transportation for very bulky goods which otherwise would have to be carried across the country by rail or road.

TRAMP VESSELS

These are *cargo carrying* vessels which sail to all parts of the world with many different kinds of cargo. They do not usually sail according to a definite timetable, but can be hired by private arrangement to take a consignment such as ore, grain, wheat, and timber to its destination. Cargoes of coal are still carried in the coastal waters around Great Britain, and even manufacturers of large pieces of machinery are now occasionally using sea transport when convenient.

Commerce and the World Outside

The Baltic Exchange is a central meeting place in London for owners of tramp ships and merchants requiring goods and materials to be transported to different parts of the world. Much information is provided at this exchange on the activities of tramp vessels throughout the world, and terms can be agreed, between shipowners and persons needing transport, on costs and the ports to be visited.

Tramp vessels are often away from their home ports for long periods of time, sometimes for two to three years or more, getting work where they can.

CARGO LINERS

These are vessels which carry mainly cargo, but which also have a few cabins for passengers. They usually keep to definite routes and schedules and carry a variety of goods, including meat, grain and oil. For the person who wishes to travel overseas and who has plenty of time to do so, they are an excellent alternative to the normal passenger liners. The passengers have the thrill of seeing the cargoes being unloaded at the different ports, and the cost for the passengers is usually less than it would be on a passenger liner.

TANKERS

These vessels are used for carrying large quantities of commodities such as oil and chemicals. They are specially constructed for this particular purpose, their large tanks holding enormous quantities. Commodities such as oil are of great importance to the industry of this country, and increasing numbers of tankers are now being built for the carrying of bulk liquids.

Today, even larger tankers are being built. This means that many of our ports are not large enough to cope with such huge vessels. A relatively new development is the building of *outports* such as Milford Haven, where the dock facilities are extended outwards so that the tankers can be berthed. These outports also have refining facilities, so that the oil can be piped direct to the refinery.

PASSENGER LINERS

A visit to a port such as Southampton is always a thrill for people of all ages. It is a wonderful sight to see the great luxury passenger liners such as the *Queen Elizabeth II* riding at anchor in port. These vessels keep to regular routes and timetables and carry small quantities of certain types of cargo. The shipping lines of this country are famous throughout the

Courtesy of the Public Works Department, City of Birmingham

Plate 13. The Bull Ring, Birmingham

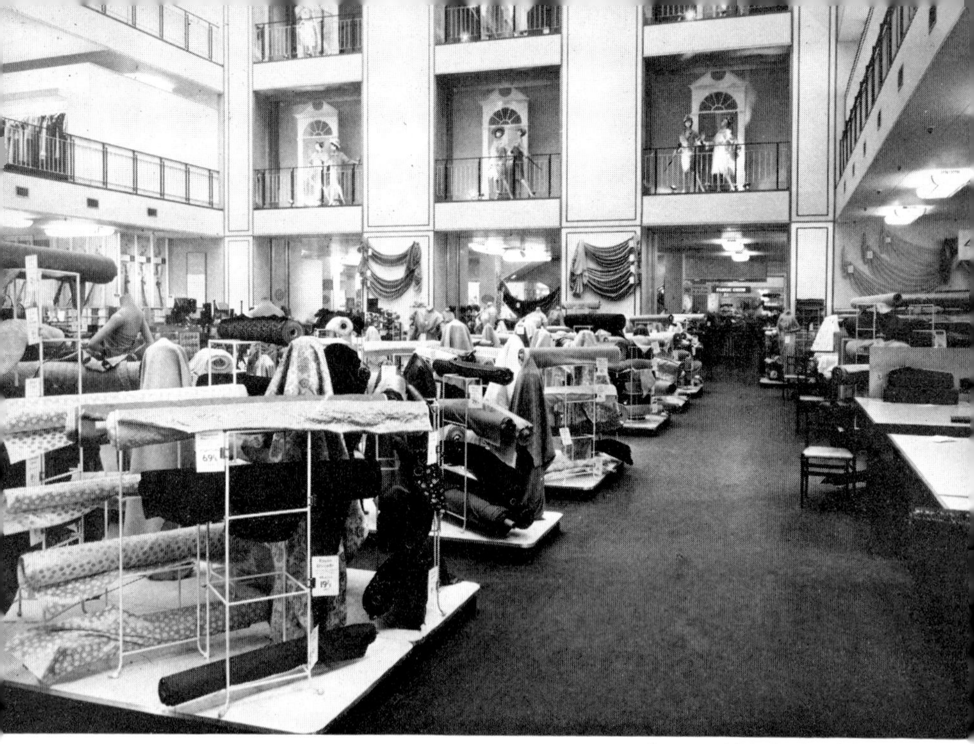

Courtesy of John Lewis and Company Ltd.

Plate 14. A Departmental Store

Plate 15. A Modern Supermarket

Courtesy of GEM Supercentres Ltd.

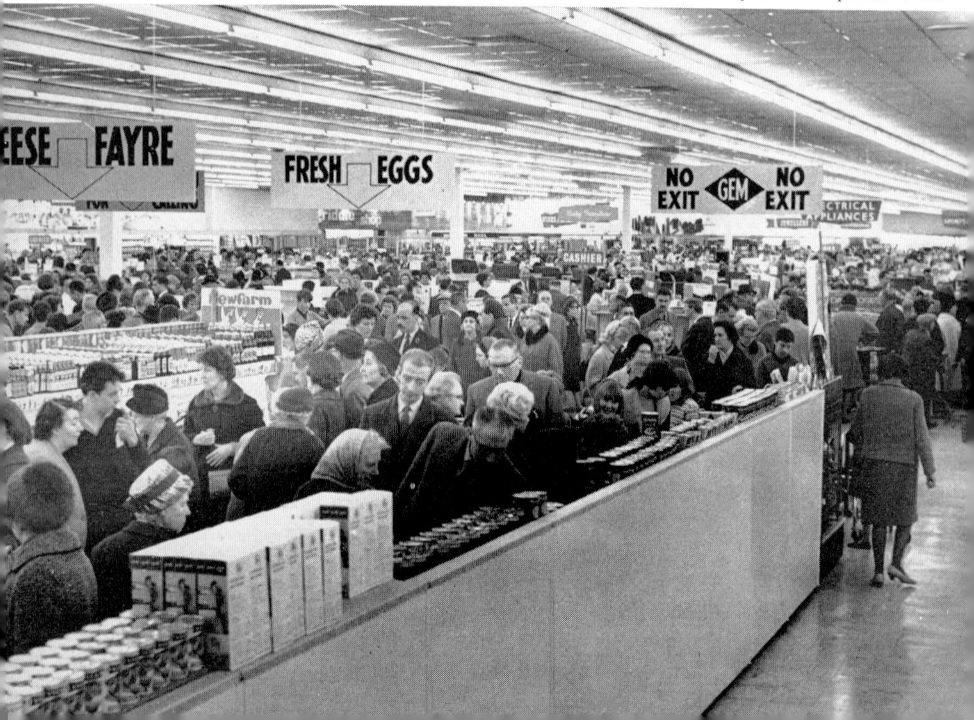

world and include among their number such famous names as "Cunard" and "P. and O." It is possible to obtain permits from the head offices of shipping lines which enable you to go aboard and see for yourself the high standard they set in providing for the comfort of the passengers who travel in these liners.

REFRIGERATED VESSELS
Many ships have now installed special refrigerated holds, which keep commodities, such as meat, fresh for very long journeys. They make it possible for us to sit down on Sunday to a plate of New Zealand lamb, which has been carried across the world to this country in special containers to ensure that the meat is kept absolutely fresh.

Ports

The ports of this country play an important part in trade by ensuring that goods and materials of all types can be loaded onto and discharged from vessels calling there. There is always a tremendous amount of activity at the seaports of this country, as at ports elsewhere, and a walk along the quayside will provide interesting evidence of this. Giant cranes are busy throughout the day, loading and unloading valuable cargoes, which are then often stored until required in large warehouses in the vicinity, sometimes to be processed prior to distribution. This country imports and exports hundreds of millions of pounds' worth of goods and materials each month, and it is vital that we have enough ports with the necessary facilities for handling these goods. Each port must also have good road and rail facilities leading to and from it, so that the various commodities, including perishable foodstuffs, can be transported quickly and efficiently to their destinations. Examine the maps (Figs. 25, 26) and you will see the network of roads and railways linking the Port of London with other areas of the country.

PORT OF LONDON
Visitors to London would find it interesting to pay a visit to one of the great London docks to see the harbour facilities for themselves. Ships of many different types are to be seen. At the Royal Albert Dock there are special arrangements for the handling of *bananas*. The Millwall Dock specializes in the handling of *grain*, which is sucked from the holds of vessels by special pneumatic elevators, before being passed into a central granary. The East India Dock used to handle many goods

151

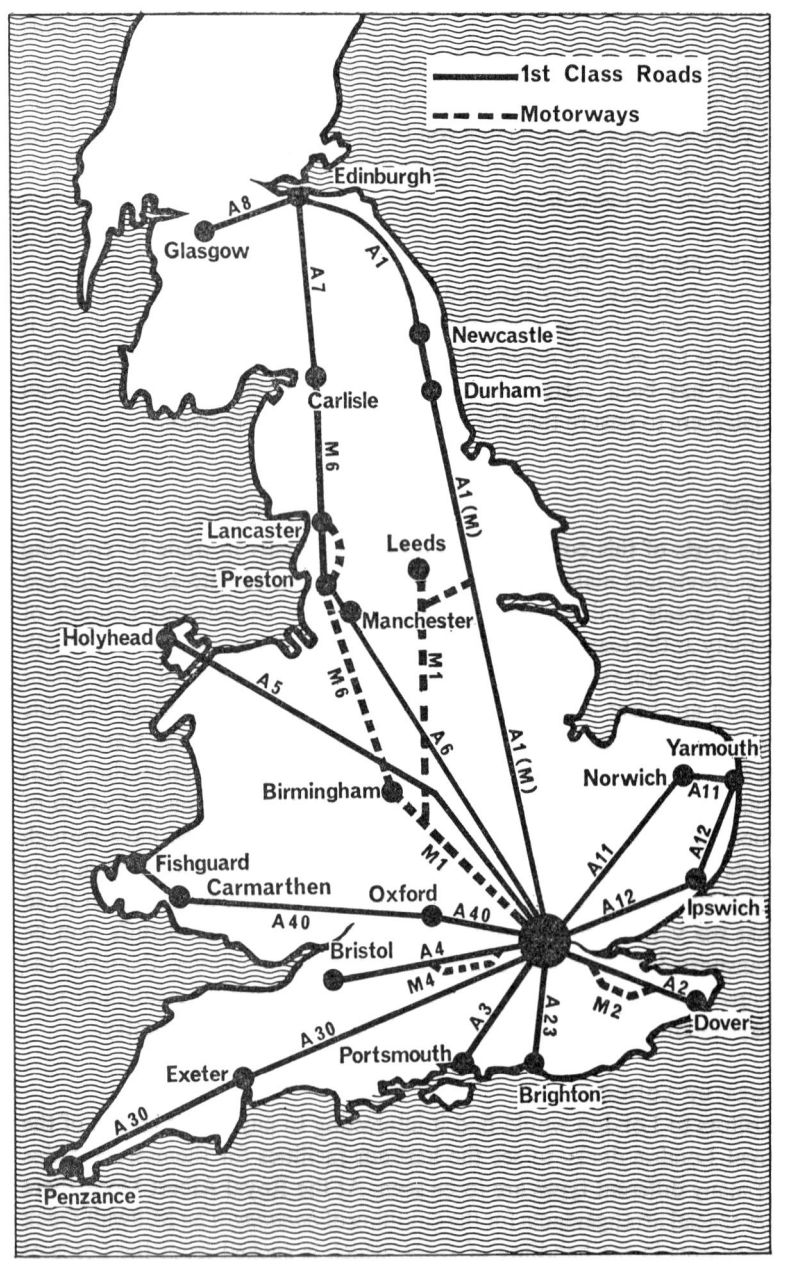

Fig. 25. Network of Certain Main Roads Radiating from London

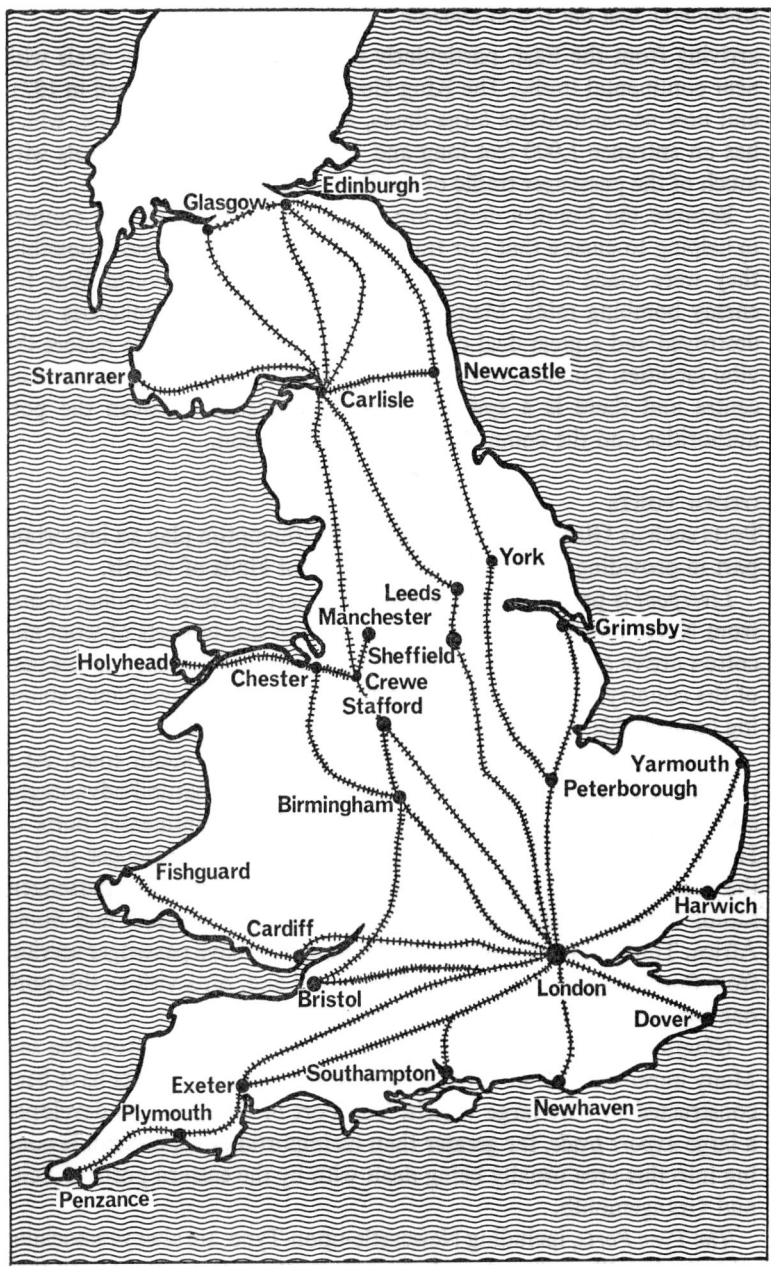

Fig. 26. Main Railway Lines Radiating from London

arriving from the East, particularly tea and silks, but now deals with near continental traffic. The King George V Dock was opened in 1921, and now accommodates large liners, as does the Tilbury Dock, which has an entrance 1,000 feet long and 110 feet wide and now deals with much of the passenger traffic of the Port of London.

Because the London docks are of such importance to this country in helping to ensure that our trade with other nations is made possible, they were made a special target during the Second World War for enemy bombing raids. Many installations and giant warehouses were destroyed and a great deal of work had to be carried out to restore the vital facilities. London, our capital city, is a very important commercial centre and there is a spirit of close co-operation between the port authorities and the commercial centres of London.

OTHER PORTS

Ports such as Glasgow, Liverpool, and Southampton play an important part in providing facilities for many different kinds of vessels.

Liverpool is particularly important as a port for vessels sailing to and from North and South America, and most of our imports of wool and cotton arrive at Liverpool. There is a great deal of industry in this part of the country, and it is important that a seaport of Liverpool's standing be available for handling the many ships' cargoes.

Southampton is the chief commercial port on the south coast. As a port it has a good geographical position and many natural advantages, and it is within easy reach of London and the continental ports of Havre and Cherbourg. Southampton is the leading passenger port in the country, dealing with about half the total of ocean-going passengers sailing between Britain and the United States of America and South Africa. Thirty of the world's main shipping lines have passenger services from Southampton to all parts of the world and, on a visit to this port, one can see the large passenger-carrying liners.

Glasgow is situated on the River Clyde some 22 miles from the sea. Many improvements have been made to the river, and docks have been constructed to take large vessels. The Port of Glasgow has developed a large *export trade*, far greater than its importing one, foodstuffs coming into this area usually being dealt with by the eastern ports of Leith and Grangemouth.

The Tyne Ports, including Newcastle-upon-Tyne, are always associated with the handling of coal, and one can see the many colliers with their cargoes of coal being loaded ready for transporting to various places.

154

Sunderland is known throughout the world for its shipbuilding activities.

Manchester is one of the largest ports in the country and is important for the handling of large quantities of cotton imported for the Lancashire cotton industry. This inland port is connected to the sea by the Manchester Ship Canal, which stretches from the Mersey to Manchester and is thirty-six miles in length. The canal is the most important one in this country and is large enough to enable ocean-going vessels to use it.

Container Developments

In recent years an important development within the field of transport has been the increasing use made of containers. It is found that by packing goods in containers (virtually large boxes) goods can be handled much more conveniently and speedily.

Road haulage concerns and British Rail are making increasing use of containers for the carriage of goods. Although proving extremely useful in home trade, it is in the shipment of goods abroad that the value of containers is particularly appreciated, and a number of *container ships* have now been built for carrying containers. Certain ports have to be specially equipped for handling these giant containers, at a cost of millions of pounds, but in the long term the sender of goods may find his carriage charges lower as a result of the use of containers. A useful *project* would be to find out as much as possible about containers, and how their use in the exporting of goods overseas benefits manufacturers in this country.

Air Transport

The main advantage of this form of transport is the speed at which passengers, mail and goods can be carried to all parts of the world, and in this *jet age* it is possible to breakfast in one country and lunch in another country a vast distance away on the same day.

There is, of course, a restriction on the amount and size of goods that can be carried by aircraft, but it is possible today to fly overseas for a holiday, your car being transported in the same plane. Increasing use is being made of this method of travel, and today the convenience of a speedy and comfortable journey to places near and far is a boon not only to business men, but to many thousands of people travelling to their holiday destinations. As a method of transport it is still not cheap, but as the airways improve in their efficiency, and use bigger aircraft capable of carrying larger numbers of people and more goods, costs are being reduced. The giant Jumbo jets have made an enormous impact in the passenger transport field, and as the size of aircraft is increased for the carrying of goods, carriage charges should be reduced.

Questions

1. Choose the best means of transporting the following—
    (i) Cut flowers from the Channel Islands to Covent Garden, London.
    (ii) Gravel from Liverpool to Manchester.
    (iii) An urgent medicine from London to Italy.
    (iv) A race-horse running at Redcar on Saturday, and in Ireland on Monday.
    (v) A consignment of motor-cars from Great Britain to the United States of America.

2. Compare road, rail, and sea transport as aids to industry.

3. Describe the facilities you would expect to be provided in a modern port. Why is it essential that cargoes should be loaded and unloaded without delay? (*Middlesex Reg. Exam. Board.*)

4. What are the reasons for the large increase in recent years in the amount of goods transported by air? To what extent do you think that air transport is likely to become a serious competitor of other means of transport? (*Middlesex Reg. Exam. Board.*)

5. List the advantages of road transport as compared with rail. In what ways can rail transport compete with road haulage concerns?

6. What do you think is the answer to the problem of there being too many vehicles on the roads of this country?

7. Write briefly on the main seaports of this country.

8. Write a brief account of the main shipping lines of Great Britain.

9. Explain the differences between tramp vessels, cargo liners and passenger liners.

10. Write briefly on the work of the Baltic Exchange.

11. (i) Name two kinds of passenger transport.
    (ii) What would be the most important consideration for a person in deciding to use *air* as a method of transport for a small, valuable package?

(iii) Name the different types of vessels which transport goods and passengers across the seas.

(iv) Name three ports in Great Britain.

Practical work

1. Plan a timetable for a passenger liner calling at various ports on its journey.

2. Plan a holiday in this country, and draw up a schedule of train and bus times for you to reach your destination. Plan your return journey in the same way.

3. Draw a map of your area, marking all main train and bus routes. Show main roads also.

4. Draw a plan of a major seaport in Great Britain. Write briefly on the amenities of this port.

5. Inquire of local factories in your own area as to the different products made, and

(i) how they transport goods sold; and

(ii) how goods and materials they receive are transported to them.

19 The Wholesaler

When we walk into a shop and buy our various needs, we should realize that our purchases have had to be manufactured in a factory, situated either in this country or perhaps in a country overseas. We may then consider how those goods came to be transferred from the manufacturer to the retailer. The distribution of the large number of goods we require is an essential aspect of *commerce*, and it is the *wholesaler*, acting in his capacity as the *middleman* between the manufacturer and the retailer, who plays the extremely important part of ensuring that, through him, the manufacturer, the retailer, and the consumer have their own particular needs satisfied.

For a vast range of goods of one kind and another the normal procedure is for the manufacturer to sell his products to firms of wholesalers, who in turn sell to shopkeepers. Quite naturally, the wholesaler must be rewarded for the part he plays in ensuring that the consumer receives the goods he needs, and this reward (or profit) is obtained by charging the shopkeeper a higher price for the goods than the wholesaler himself paid to the manufacturer.

Why the Wholesaler is Needed

Some people express the view that the wholesaler is an unnecessary part of the process of distributing goods, and that prices paid by the consumer would be lower if the manufacturer supplied the shopkeeper direct, thus cutting out the wholesaler's profit margin. The other point of view is that, even if the wholesaler were eliminated, it would still be necessary for the manufacturer to do the work of the wholesaler, and this would increase the manufacturer's costs.

HOW HE HELPS THE MANUFACTURER

One of the chief difficulties for the manufacturer is that, in order to produce goods at the cheapest possible price, a steady rate of production has to take place throughout the year. Manufacturers, having spent a great deal of money in equipping their factories with modern machinery, need to have them in constant use. Apart from this, no employer wants to be constantly paying off his employees, and starting them in work again when demand for his products increases, as it does for various goods at certain times of the year. Products such as electric fires, television sets, and record players are usually only in large demand at certain times of the year. This creates problems for the manufacturers of these types of products, because

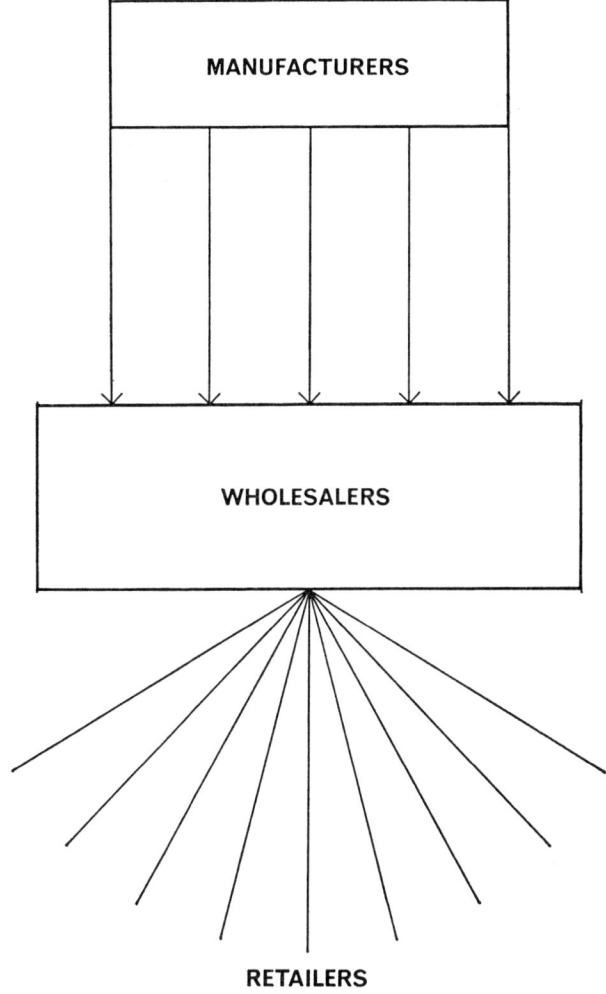

Fig. 27. The Chain of Distribution

they would find it very difficult always to manufacture the right quantity of goods at the precise time they were wanted by the consumer. The wholesaler relieves the manufacturer of certain problems by providing services which include—

1. Taking large quantities of goods off the manufacturer's hands and storing them until required by the shopkeeper.

2. Supplying the manufacturer with information on possible future demand for products.

The storing of goods until required by the consumer costs a good deal of money. Warehouses are needed for the accommodation of the goods and the wholesaler often provides this facility. This is very beneficial to the manufacturer since storage of goods in suitable premises costs money and, because the wholesaler buys in large quantities (in bulk), the manufacturer does not have so much of his money tied up in financing large stocks of goods.

HOW HE HELPS THE RETAILER

The shopkeeper cannot usually afford to have a lot of money invested in large stocks of many different products, and would not usually have room for them. So he relies on the wholesaler who, having bought from the manufacturer in large quantities, sells to the shopkeeper in smaller quantities as he requires the goods. Some very large retail organizations, such as supermarkets, are able to buy direct from manufacturers because of their large financial resources, but as they have to store the goods until required by the customer, they cannot always follow their usual practice of cutting prices, because they need to be compensated for the time and money they have spent in storing the goods.

In addition to the problems already mentioned there is the geographical one. If a shopkeeper had to order his wants direct from a manufacturer situated in an entirely different part of the country, supplies would take longer in reaching him. It is very convenient for both the manufacturer and the shopkeeper to be able to rely on a chain of wholesalers situated in all areas of the country. The cost to the manufacturer of sending a large quantity of goods to a number of wholesalers is considerably less than it would be if small quantities of assorted goods had to be sent to thousands of shopkeepers. Also, should the shopkeeper find his stocks of a particular commodity running low, it is a simple matter for him to telephone or write to the wholesaler in his area, ordering fresh supplies. Although a number of manufacturers deal directly with the shopkeeper, the customer does not benefit particularly, as the manufacturer has to perform the work that would otherwise be done by the wholesaler and his costs rise because of this.

A Wholesaler's Organization

A typical example of a wholesaler's organization might be—
1. A warehouse, together with the necessary staff.
2. Showrooms (if necessary), for displaying manufacturers' products.
3. Offices—responsible for the clerical work involved.
4. A fleet of vans for making deliveries to shopkeepers.
5. Sales representatives to call on shopkeepers to ascertain their requirements and introduce new lines.

The distribution of catalogues and price lists to the shopkeeper with information on the goods kept in stock, and the provision of technical information on the products, are also important functions of the wholesaler.

The Wholesaler and Costs

The wholesaler makes only a small profit on each item he sells, far less, in fact, than does the retailer. He relies on selling larger quantities at a time.

A practical example of how costs for a manufacturer may be reduced if he works through a wholesaler will perhaps help us to understand the importance of the wholesaler's work—

Example A. A factory manufacturing knitwear garments is selling direct to shopkeepers from its headquarters in Nottingham—

Number of shopkeepers throughout the country to whom garments are sold—2,500

Each month, therefore, the following documents may be used by the manufacturer—
2,500 acknowledgements of orders,
2,500 invoices,
2,500 statements of account.

Plus all the extra labour and expense involved in dealing with many different customers (e.g. representatives, fleet of vans, large warehouse).

Example B. The same factory selling only through wholesalers—

Number of wholesalers to whom garments are sold—   25
Documents necessary each month—
25 acknowledgements of orders
25 invoices
25 statements of account

In Example A, the factory would need a *large staff of clerical workers* to deal with all the acknowledgements of orders, invoices and statements of account. A *large number of representatives* would have to be employed to call on all the shopkeepers, and it is likely that a *fleet of vans* would be kept to make the many deliveries. A *big warehouse* would be needed for storage of the garments. Obviously, then, the expenses of running the business this way would be high.

In Example B, on the other hand, costs would be much lower because only a *small staff* of clerks and representatives would be necessary. *Two or three vans* could probably cope with all the deliveries, and there would be *no need for a large warehouse.*

If in one year the manufacturer sold 100,000 garments, the average reduction he would be able to make on the price of each garment by selling through a wholesaler might amount to 50p. From the manufacturer's point of view it would be easier for him to let the wholesaler handle the distribution of the garments. His own profits would probably be higher, and the public would pay no more for their garments because the wholesaler's costs and profits would not exceed this 50p per garment. They might, in fact, be considerably less.

Wholesale Markets

Certain commodities are sold in special markets where producers, wholesalers and retailers can meet and do their buying and selling. Most cities and towns have *wholesale markets* where different commodities are bought and sold. Because many of these commodities, vegetables and fruit for instance, are perishable, transactions between the different traders must be effected quickly, and wholesale markets carry out an extremely important function by enabling this to be done.

These markets are best visited at an early hour (around 0500 hrs.), when they are a hive of activity, with merchants and retailers buying their produce, ready for distribution to many different parts of the area.

There are in London a number of very famous wholesale markets, including—

> Covent Garden (fruit and vegetables)
> Billingsgate (fish)
> Smithfield (meat)

Note: Wholesale markets should not be confused with the smaller open and covered markets, situated in many towns, which sell produce to members of the public.

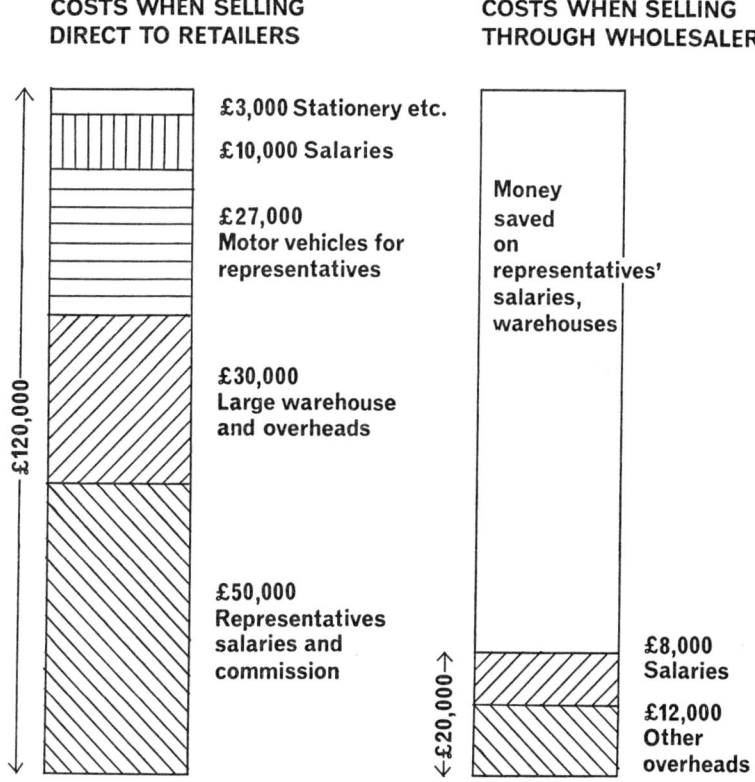

COSTS WHEN SELLING DIRECT TO RETAILERS

£3,000 Stationery etc.

£10,000 Salaries

£27,000 Motor vehicles for representatives

£30,000 Large warehouse and overheads

£50,000 Representatives salaries and commission

£120,000

COSTS WHEN SELLING THROUGH WHOLESALER

Money saved on representatives' salaries, warehouses

£8,000 Salaries

£12,000 Other overheads

£20,000

Fig. 28. Comparison of Costs for Different Methods of Distribution

163

Questions

1. Discuss the work of the wholesaler.

2. Explain the importance of the wholesaler in the channels of distribution in *either* the grocery *or* the greengrocery trade.

3. What are the advantages and disadvantages of a retail shop purchasing stock for resale direct from the manufacturers?

4. Why is the wholesaler so important in the drapery trade?

5. It is asserted that the wholesale trader renders services to manufacturers on the one hand and to retailers on the other. What are these services and in what way do they result in benefit to the ordinary member of the public purchasing goods? (*Middlesex Reg. Exam. Board.*)

6. Why is the wholesaler often spoken of as the middleman?

7. A party of commerce students were taken on a visit to a wholesale textile warehouse. After they had been shown round, questions were invited and one student asked this question:

"Whenever I go into a shop to buy clothes or material, the price seems to be higher than it was last time. All you seem to do here is to collect things from manufacturers and pass them on at a higher price. Wouldn't it be cheaper for us and simpler for the retailer if the wholesaler were left out and retailers dealt directly with manufacturers?"

What reply do you think this student might receive from the wholesaler? Your answer should take the form of a reasoned explanation of the wholesaler's position in the textile industry. (*Metropolitan Reg. Exam. Board.*)

8. Why do the manufacturer's costs sometimes increase if he deals directly with the retailer?

9. Write briefly on wholesale markets, mentioning some important ones in London.

10. (i) What is the name sometimes given to the wholesaler?

    (ii) Name two functions the wholesaler performs for the manufacturer.

    (iii) What is the name of the place where a wholesaler stores his goods?

    (iv) What is the allowance given by wholesalers to retailers?

Practical work

1. Prepare a talk on the work of the wholesaler, defending him against the type of person who says: "Cut the middleman out."

2. Prepare a diagram illustrating the work of the wholesaler.

3. Prepare a chart showing the organization of the wholesaler's warehouse.

4. Make a list of local factories producing products for the consumer, and find out whether or not they use the services of the wholesaler.

20 Shops and Other Retail Outlets

Events have moved very quickly in the retail trade in recent years, and we know from our shopping habits that we now have a considerable choice in the matter of the type of shop to which we can go in purchasing our own wants. During the course of a year we probably visit a number of shops, all different in their own way. Perhaps the supermarket is visited on a Saturday, and we can serve ourselves by selecting the various provisions needed for the week-end. At Christmas time it is pleasant, if at times a little hectic, to be able to walk round the gaily-decorated departmental stores where an enormous choice of gifts is available for selection.

The shopkeeper is the final link in a chain of events which commences with the raw materials being purchased by the manufacturer, then converted into products of all descriptions, stored by the wholesaler, and later made available to the consumer by the shopkeeper. There are some instances of certain manufacturers selling their products direct to the consumer, but most shoppers still prefer—

1. a variety of choice,
2. the freedom to see and examine the goods before making the purchase,
3. the convenience of a shop situated in the vicinity.

The shopkeeper provides the customer with these very important services by making his purchases from the wholesaler and manufacturer, and then selling to the consumer at a higher price, thereby making his profit. And even though we may occasionally purchase items direct from the manufacturer, the bulk of our buying is done through the shopkeeper. Also, of course, the shopkeeper is helping the manufacturer by establishing an outlet for the goods he is producing.

The Small Shopkeeper (The Unit Shop)

There is in this country a very large number of small shops, many of them situated in the outlying districts of cities and towns. Typical of this type of shop are the general dealer, the greengrocer, and the sweet shop, which we call the confectioner. They are owned by the shopkeepers themselves, and give a very high standard of personal service to the customer. They are usually open for much longer hours than the larger shops situated in the centre of the town, and the shopkeepers often find time for a friendly chat with the customer, who is usually in the habit of shopping there regularly. The small shopkeeper's prices may at times be a little higher than those of the larger, self-service and supermarket establishments, as he purchases his stock from the wholesalers in smaller quantities than they do, and so receives smaller discounts. For many shoppers, however, the personal and convenient service he provides more than makes up for the slightly higher prices sometimes charged.

The Departmental Store

Most towns now have at least one departmental store, the larger towns and cities having a number of this kind of shop. It is the type of shop we visit if we wish to purchase a large item such as a piece of furniture, or if we want a large variety from which to choose. Departmental stores are really a *number of shops*, all contained under the same roof, which are termed departments. The smaller stores may have up to twenty different departments, the larger ones such as Harrods and Selfridges in London containing hundreds of departments, where it is possible to purchase anything from a pin to the entire furnishings for a home.

The departmental store is usually a spacious shop, often carpeted throughout, and one has that feeling of comfort and luxury when walking through the different departments, including those selling items such as sports goods, toys, cosmetics, clothing, records, and furnishings. The window displays are usually very eye-catching, and the goods for sale are so laid out that often there is very little persuasion needed on the part of the sales assistant for the customer to make a purchase. On entering the store, the customer finds he is able to purchase almost any item he needs, and most stores now even have self-service food departments offering a good choice.

Apart from providing the shopper with the opportunity of purchasing the goods of his choice, the departmental store offers services such as restaurants, hairdressing salons, facilities for theatre bookings, post office services, and rest rooms. The object of the store is to attract the

167

customer into the shop, very often by extensive advertising in the local newspaper, or by offering certain goods at low prices in order to tempt the customer into making additional purchases. Most stores offer the customer hire-purchase facilities so that payment for large items can be spread over a long period of time, and also provide credit terms whereby the customer opens an account with the store, one bill for a number of purchases being sent each month to the customer.

Each department in the store has at its head a person known as the *buyer*, who organizes the work of the sales assistants and generally manages the department. The buyer, as his name implies, also assumes the responsibility for the purchasing of the department's stocks of goods. His decisions on the type and quality of goods to be purchased for the department are made after he has estimated what the customers' requirements will be. To a large extent, therefore, the profits made by a department are a reflection on the good judgement of the buyer. This particular aspect of his job often proves extremely difficult, as in the case of ladies' fashions, where tastes and preferences vary a good deal from year to year.

The organization behind a departmental store will vary according to the size of the shop, but in the larger ones the staff employed would include—

Department buyers
Sales assistants
Accountants
Clerical workers
Carpenters and joiners
Electricians

There is, in addition to the normal business of selling goods, a great deal of "behind the scenes" work in making display units, ensuring good lighting, and dealing with the clerical work involved. It is the responsibility of the *general manager* to ensure that the store is run in an efficient manner and to provide for the needs of its customers.

The costs of operating departmental stores are very high. The land on which they are situated, often in the busy town centres, is expensive to buy. The costs of providing attractive window displays and the services already mentioned are also high, and in order to pay these expenses and provide adequate profits for the owners, prices charged by the stores are sometimes higher than those of other shops.

168

THE PLACING OF DEPARTMENTS

It is possible to walk into many different departmental stores and find that there is a very similar layout in each store. Try this sometimes for yourself when you are shopping.

What is the first thing you notice when you enter the main door on the ground floor? All the departments selling such articles as ladies' nylons, wool, cosmetics, books, stationery, etc., are all near to hand. This is because most people will not bother to walk up stairs, or use lifts and escalators to other floors, if they want only comparatively small items. Should a customer be shopping for a large item such as a washing machine, television set, or perhaps a suite of furniture, he will probably be prepared to spend quite a long time in looking around before coming to a decision on what is to be purchased. He will even be prepared to go to the top floor if the items he is looking for are on view in that particular department.

It is usual, therefore, to find the departments situated in a pattern as indicated below.

LAYOUT OF DEPARTMENTAL STORE

Basement	kitchenware, gardening tools, crockery, sports and travel goods, domestic appliances.
Ground floor	stationery, books, cosmetics, foodstuffs.
1st floor	millinery, fashions, shoes, children's wear.
2nd floor	soft furnishings, television sets.
3rd floor	furniture, carpets.
4th floor	restaurants, hairdressing salon.
5th floor	offices, staff facilities, etc.

Different stores do, of course, situate their departments on different floors, and this example is only intended to indicate on a broad basis the pattern which is established.

It is a good idea to plan the layout of a departmental store for yourself, using your own ideas on how you think a store should be planned, and why.

The Multiple Shop

There are a large number of multiple shop organizations, some examples being—

169

Commerce and the World Outside

Marks and Spencer
Woolworth's
Boots (Chemists)
Sainsbury's (Groceries)
W. H. Smith and Son (Newsagents and Booksellers)
Saxone (Shoes)
Fine Fare (Supermarkets)
Burton's (Tailors)

Some multiple shops such as Woolworth's are also called *chain stores*, but there is really little difference as they are similar types of shops. The chain store is really a multiple which sells a *variety* of goods. The multiple shop organization is a business which has a number of branch shops, sometimes situated in all parts of the country. Usually the external appearance and window design of each branch are alike.

A branch manager is responsible for supervising the work of the sales assistants in his particular shop, and in ensuring that he always has adequate stocks of goods. In addition he will see that the takings are paid into the bank each day.

The branch shops are supervised by a *head office*. All the purchasing of goods to be resold by the branch shops is made in very large quantities by expert buyers who have to see that plentiful supplies of goods are available for dispatch to the branches. In addition to the head office, there will be at least one *central warehouse* where the goods are kept in store until required by the branch shops. *Area inspectors* or *supervisors* are employed who visit all the branches in their district at regular intervals, to check on stocks of goods held by each shop and to ensure that the branch manager and his assistants are performing their duties correctly. Many multiples own their own fleets of vans, so that quick deliveries can be made to the branches.

Goods sold by these shops are often cheaper than those of the small trader, as, by purchasing goods in bulk from the manufacturers, large discounts may be obtained, enabling the multiple shop to pass some of the benefit on to the customer. Some of these concerns own their own factories, where they manufacture products which are then sold in their branch shops.

It is the multiples which often set the fashion in the retail trade, and which were responsible for the introduction of self-service shops and supermarkets in this country. There is a great deal of competition between them and the small traders and although small shopkeepers

170

do complain that these giants of the retail trade are a threat to their livelihood when they start price-cutting wars, it is an opinion expressed by some people that healthy competition often leads to an efficient and prosperous retail trade.

The Co-operative Society

The *co-operative societies* are retail organizations with which we are all familiar, as they have shops situated in all towns and cities throughout the country. During the nineteenth century, a group of weavers living in Rochdale, who were not satisfied with the services of the existing shops, formed their own shop together with other people interested in their scheme. Sufficient money was raised by this group of people to start what became the first of many hundreds of retail co-operative societies.

Most parts of the country now have a local co-operative retail society with branch shops in the various districts. Many of the goods sold in these shops are obtained from the Co-operative Wholesale Society, which has large warehouses in Manchester, and in addition, factories where a great variety of products are made for sale in the shops of the co-operative societies.

It is the shoppers themselves who own the co-operative societies. They become members by purchasing a share or a number of shares, costing £1 each, in their local society, up to a maximum of 1,000 shares. Each half-year members are paid a dividend, according to the amount of money they have spent at co-operative shops in the previous six months. The idea behind the co-operative movement is that the profits made by the shops should be returned to the members, who are, of course, the customers. The larger the profits made, the higher the rate of dividend declared. An example of a dividend received might be—

A customer spends £50 during the half-year.
Dividend declared is 5p in the pound.
Amount of dividend received by the customer would be 5p multiplied by 50 which equals £2·50.

The members of the individual co-operative retail societies elect each year a board of directors who are responsible for managing the activities of their society. The directors are elected from the ranks of the members themselves and often consist of housewives, and men with other full-time jobs. One criticism of co-operative retail societies is that the directors are not always experienced in the work of running a shop, and that they devote only part of their time to the duties entailed in being a director. But there are permanent officials and other staff who are full-time employees, and whilst it is the board of directors which lays down the policy to be adopted by the society, the full-time officials work in the shops and are responsible for carrying out the normal trading activities.

In recent years a number of retail co-operative societies have had financial problems. In an effort to make the co-operative movement more competitive with other shops a large number of retail societies have merged with each other, and there is now a total of approximately fifty retail societies throughout the country. It is hoped that these measures will result in a more efficient national organization. Many persons connected with the co-operative movement would eventually like to see *one* giant retail society for the whole of England. An increasing number of retail societies are now issuing customers with "Divi" stamps instead of declaring dividends. At the end of each half-year customers have the option of obtaining cash in exchange for the stamps, or if desired, exchanging them for goods of a slightly higher value.

The co-operative movement has developed other establishments which are in addition to its retail activities. The Nationwide Building Society and the Co-operative Insurance Society play a large part in providing members of the public with homes and security.

The co-operative movement has developed very extensively since its early days, and though it is often criticized, there is no doubt that it provides important and useful services to a very large section of the community.

Other Forms of Retailing

Although shops form a very large proportion of the total retail trade in this country, there are other types of retailing which play an important part in helping to provide us with our wants.

MARKETS

Many towns have *covered public markets* where stallholders sell a large variety of goods, particularly fruit and vegetables, at prices often lower than those of shopkeepers, although the quality sometimes is not as good. Also there are still certain towns where *open markets* are held on one or two days of the week.

DOOR-TO-DOOR SALESMEN

There are a number of firms who prefer to sell their products direct to the public and who employ salesmen to call at houses, inviting householders to inspect their products and then make a purchase. Although both the wholesaler and the retailer are eliminated, products sold in this way are not usually any cheaper, as the salesmen have to be paid a salary and commission for their work.

MACHINE VENDING

Automatic machines, providing a whole range of goods, including chocolate, mineral waters, milk and films, offer a very useful service to the public, especially when the shops are closed (they are often to be found adjacent to the shopkeeper's premises for this reason). The machines are rather expensive to install so many of them are rented by shopkeepers from firms who specialize in this kind of retailing.

MOBILE SHOPS

Many persons, particularly those living in outlying districts, find the visits of *mobile shops* of great benefit, and the housewife who is too busy to make a call on the conventional shopkeeper can often rely on regular supplies of provisions, bread, fruit and vegetables, and meat being delivered to her own doorstep.

DIRECT SELLING

Firms who employ door-to-door salesmen are using direct selling methods of retailing, but there are other concerns which, by extensive advertising on television and in the national and local newspapers, are able to sell their products direct to the consumer. Prices are not usually cheaper than those charged by shopkeepers, because delivery charges and the cost of advertising their products are high.

Concerns selling their products in this way will often tell us that by eliminating the wholesaler and the retailer they can afford to sell to the customer at lower prices, but this is not always so and the customer must be wary of the claims that are made.

MAIL ORDER

Mail order concerns provide a popular method of shopping. Householders, acting as agents for the firms, loan catalogues to their friends, which illustrate and describe a whole range of goods for sale. Customers make their choice of goods in the comfort of their homes, and pay for

173

their purchases by weekly instalments, which are collected by the agent.

Mail order firms are now firmly established in this country and include such concerns as Littlewood's, Gratton's, and Kay's. One reason for their success is that customers are allowed at least twenty weeks in which to pay for their purchases, instalments being spread over that period. The agents receive a commission from the mail order firms on the purchases made by customers and this encourages them to show the attractive catalogues to all their friends.

Mail order is a form of direct selling, and as the cost of printing catalogues and stationery and providing for agents' commission, is very high, the prices charged to customers are usually much the same as those of conventional shops.

THE DISCOUNT STORE

In many ways the discount store and the supermarket have a good deal in common with each other. They are both self-service establishments, but whereas the supermarket has many attractive display stands and sets out to sell itself to the customer, the discount house often looks like a converted warehouse, and tries to keep all its expenses as low as possible by doing without such things as display units, attractive lighting, and so on. Customers shopping at the discount store will find that there are large discounts offered on items of household equipment and other goods, and it is possible to obtain bargains. There are certain disadvantages, however, in that the customer himself must take the goods away as no delivery service is provided, and there is often no after-sales service should the articles purchased need repairing.

Discount stores originated in the United States, and, although there are not many of them in this country at the present time, there is no doubt that they will become more popular. On the whole shopkeepers are not very pleased with the growth of discount stores, because they do the shopkeeper a good deal of harm by offering goods such as television sets, washing machines, refrigerators, etc., at much lower prices. What the customer has to decide is whether the advantage of cheaper goods compensates for the lack of after-sales service, delivery and shop demonstration of the product.

An obstacle preventing the more rapid development of these warehouse-shops in this country is the shortage of land for building premises, but as a result of the abolition of resale price maintenance which means that the manufacturers must not fix the selling prices of

174

their products, they will probably become more popular and will vie with other types of shops for your custom.

Manufacturers with Their Own Retail Outlets

Some manufacturers do not use the services of the retailer and the wholesaler, but provide their own *outlets* (shops). Examples of this kind of organization are Burton's (tailors) and Boots (chemists). Many multiples manufacture their own products and then sell them through their own shops. The manufacturer must of course, bear all the expenses involved in providing his own shops, and usually only the large manufacturers can afford to distribute their products in this way.

Many bakers provide their own shops, and often have a fleet of vans for making regular deliveries to customers. Breweries own many public houses, and sell their own brand of beer on the premises. Oil firms such as Esso, British Petroleum and Cleveland own petrol-filling stations and appoint managers to look after them. Often privately owned garages agree to sell only one brand of petrol, and in return they are helped by the oil company with which they have contracted. This help may take the form of installing servicing equipment, maintenance of the premises, and the provision of smart overalls for the petrol pump attendants.

Questions

1. What kind of shops are Marks and Spencer's stores? How do they differ from departmental stores?

2. Figures show that the small shopkeeper is losing an increasing amount of trade to the large multiple groups. What do you think are the reasons for this?

3. (i) If a manufacturer decided to produce clothes which only appealed to a few people of "way-out" taste, what channels of distribution might he use to sell his product? Give reasons for the methods you mention.

   (ii) Another manufacturer decided to go all out to produce clothes which the majority of people would be likely to buy. What would be a suitable marketing method for these? Give reasons for the methods you choose.

  (iii) Which of the two do you think would give the customer better value for money? Give reasons for your answer.

(Metropolitan Reg. Exam. Board.)

4. Why is it possible for so many different types of shops to continue in business?

5. Describe the services of the departmental store.

6. Describe the organization of a multiple shop group.

7. Why do many retail concerns dislike the activities of co-operative societies?

8. Write briefly on the different forms of retailing today.

9. Do direct selling methods offer any advantages to the consumer?

10. Write briefly on manufacturers selling through their own retail outlets. Does this offer any advantages to the consumer?

11. What are the advantages to the consumer in shopping at a supermarket?

12. (i) Name three departments often to be found in a departmental store.

   (ii) Name two types of shop.

   (iii) Give the names of two national multiple shop concerns.

   (iv) Give one reason for the popularity of supermarkets.

   (v) What is a *unit shop*?

   (vi) Name two methods of retailing not conducted through a shop.

Practical work

1. Draft a form suitable for use in a survey of the shopping habits of the public.

2. Conduct a survey in your local shopping centre, and try to establish the personal preferences of shoppers as to type of shop.

3. Discuss the results of your shopping survey. Do these results indicate the pattern of shops required for the future?

4. List twelve commodities, e.g. butter, tea, tinned-fruit. Then visit—

   (i) a supermarket,

   (ii) a small shop,

   (iii) the food department of a departmental store.

Make a comparison of the prices charged for each commodity, and the total amounts charged.

5. Draw a plan of your local shopping centre, marking on the plan the different types of shops, e.g. supermarkets, departmental stores, unit shops. Write briefly explaining why so many different kinds of shops can exist so near to one another.

21 Developments in the Retail Trade

The Siting of Shops

We have seen that there are many different kinds of shops in existence today. Some of them are controlled by very large concerns, others are small unit shops. In the shopping centres, there is a tendency for shops selling the same type of goods to group themselves close to one another, and if we find Woolworth's or Littlewoods, we know that Marks and Spencer is not very far away. These large *chain stores* are a big attraction to most shoppers and smaller shops often set up in business nearby so that they too will get a share of the sales that are made.

Supermarkets and Super Departmental Stores

The retail trade of today is "big business" and, as well as the more conventional kinds of shops, there are increasing numbers of self-service shops and supermarkets, which help to make shopping easier for the customer. Goods are attractively displayed on stands, and in some of the larger supermarkets soft background music is played to help the shopper feel more relaxed and able to enjoy his shopping. The techniques of self-service and soft music are really part of a scheme to try to induce the shopper to buy more goods than he originally intended. Although fewer sales assistants are needed in this kind of shop, there is a good deal of "behind the scenes" work in weighing and packing the goods. A new kind of *super departmental store* is to be found in a number of towns. The departments, which sell goods similar to those to be found in the conventional departmental stores, are all placed on the ground floor so that the job of shopping is made easier for the customer. This type of shop, an American idea, provides spacious car parks, which are adjacent to the shop itself to encourage the car-shopper to drive in.

Wholesaling Groups

Competition between the many different kinds of shops is steadily increasing. Some of them offer trading stamps with every purchase,

177

which can eventually be exchanged for gifts. Certain *wholesaling groups*, such as V.G., Mace, and Spar, have made arrangements with some of the smaller shopkeepers, who have agreed to purchase all their stocks of goods from them. This allows the wholesaler to buy in very large quantities and the larger discounts received by the wholesaler from the manufacturer allow him to resell to the shopkeeper at a lower price. Because of this, the small shopkeeper is able to compete with the larger stores for the consumers' trade and is able to make reasonable profits.

Cash and Carry

Many small shopkeepers use the facilities provided by wholesale warehouses, collecting the goods themselves with their own transport. This saves the wholesaler distribution costs. Because of this the retailer is given good discounts on the goods purchased.

Trading Stamps

Many shopkeepers now issue trading stamps such as *Green Shield* and *Pink* stamps, to their customers at the time of making purchases. From the shopkeeper's point of view the giving of trading stamps is an incentive to customers to shop regularly with him; from the customer's point of view it represents a saving because the stamps can be exchanged for "free gifts."

The trading stamp scheme is operated by the shopkeeper purchasing the stamps from the trading stamp firm and issuing them to the customer free according to the amount spent by him at the shop. The gifts which the customer eventually receives are provided by the trading stamp firm out of the money it has received from shopkeepers in exchange for the stamps.

Many garages offer trading stamps as an incentive to motorists to buy their petrol from them.

The many critics of trading stamp schemes point out that it would be better for the shopkeepers to reduce the prices of the goods they sell rather than offer gifts after so many pounds' worth of purchases have been made. The shopper (the consumer) must decide for himself the respective virtues and drawbacks of such schemes; whether it is better to obtain free gifts or to look around instead to see if other shops are selling the same products at lower prices.

Consumer Protection

Because there are so many different kinds of shops in existence today, the consumer has an excellent range of choice when making his purchases, but shoppers should compare the goods offered by different retailers, particularly when purchasing large items, to ensure that they are *getting good value for money.* But it would be unwise always to judge a shop on its prices only. It must be borne in mind that quality and after-sales service are equally important. Over the past few years a number of bodies have come into existence whose job it is to guide the consumer and to see that he gets a *fair deal.*

THE CONSUMER COUNCIL

This is a committee which watches over the interests of the millions of shoppers in this country. They take a keen interest in the activities of manufacturers, wholesalers and shopkeepers, and try to ensure that the services they provide meet the shopper's needs. If the Council thinks that the consumer is not getting a fair deal when purchasing particular products, it will make representations and see that, if a product is unsafe to use, not of a good enough quality, or too expensively priced, the faults are corrected. In 1970 the Government announced that it was to stop making a grant to this Council, and whether its work continues now remains to be seen.

THE CONSUMERS' ASSOCIATION

The Consumers' Association, with headquarters in London, has in recent years helped the shopping public a great deal. It publishes, each month, a magazine called *Which?* setting out the respective advantages and disadvantages of various products and indicating which products are the best buys. Each month a number of articles are selected for testing. Quality, safety, design, cost, etc., are all taken into account, and the results, obtained after putting different manufacturers' products through tests, are published in the Association's magazine.

It has become a very well known organization, and some of the tests conducted have been shown on television. As an association for consumer protection it has a good deal of influence with manufacturers, who often put right the faults of certain products which have been tested and found to be faulty in some respects. There is a saying that you only get what you pay for. In other words, if you buy articles very cheaply, you cannot expect to get the best quality. What the Consumers'

Association does is to take *all* factors into account, including the price, and state what, in their opinion, will be the consumer's best buy.

Annual subscriptions are paid by the members of the Consumers' Association, in return for which they receive, each month, a copy of *Which?*.

THE BRITISH STANDARDS INSTITUTION

This organization has done a great deal in recent years in ensuring that manufacturers produce goods of good quality and design which conform to a general *pattern* or *standard*. The Institution tries to ensure that all manufacturers producing a particular class of product make them to the same design or pattern, because this not only assists in making the manufacturing process cheaper, with lower prices for the shopping public generally, but it also helps to keep up the quality of the products and to ensure that they are produced with due regard for the safety of the public who will use them. An instance of their work is in the field of oil heaters. Some years ago it was found that certain manufacturers were producing dangerous heaters which were liable to set themselves on fire quite easily. Since that time the Institution has helped a great deal in seeing that only safe oil heaters are sold to the public.

Articles which pass the test of the British Standards Institution are allowed to bear the imprint of a kite, and the shopper should make a special point of looking for this mark when buying goods. Unfortunately, the Institution advises only on products made in this country, and there are still many articles imported from abroad which do not come up to their high standards of quality and safety.

CONSUMER PROTECTION PROVIDED BY THE GOVERNMENT AND LOCAL AUTHORITIES

There are various *Acts of Parliament* including the Sale of Goods Act, 1893, the Weights and Measures Acts, 1878–1963, the Food and Drugs Act, 1938, the Consumer Protection Act, 1961, the Advertisements (Hire-Purchase) Act, 1959, the Hire-Purchase Acts, 1938–1964, and the Trade Descriptions Act, 1968, all of which endeavour to protect the consumer in some way, e.g. from products which are unsafe to use, detrimental to health, or generally against the best interests of the shopping public. Under the Weights and Measures Acts, for example, local authorities have power to appoint special inspectors, who visit business premises and try to ensure that customers are given correct weight when buying vegetables, fruit, groceries, etc.; other inspectors have the job of ensuring that a good standard of cleanliness is maintained by shop-keepers and bakeries. How often do you read in your local newspaper of some person being prosecuted for selling items of foodstuffs containing mould for example?

These various Acts are rather too technical for this book, so we shall not examine them in detail; it is sufficient to say that there are many Acts of Parliament, such as the ones mentioned, which protect the consumer.

If you have any particular problem, a visit to your local *Citizens' Advice Bureau* which is there to assist people with their shopping and other domestic problems, will be well worth while. The staff there are always willing to help.

THE TRADE DESCRIPTIONS ACT, 1968

This Act of Parliament provides the consumer with much greater protection than hitherto. Its main purpose is to ensure that the shop-keeper tells the truth about goods, prices, and services. In the past when shops held sales, the customer was often misled by price tickets which implied genuine reductions, when this was not really the case. The Trade Descriptions Act now makes this illegal, and if shopkeepers *now* delete one price on the ticket, and show a smaller amount underneath, customers can generally assume that the reduction in the price of the article is a genuine one.

Two examples of price tickets may help us in understanding the position:

SALE was £3·50 now £2·75	*Special Offer* only £1·99
Example 1	Example 2

The second example is an illustration of a shop probably buying in goods at a special price purely for sale purposes. The goods are not in fact specially reduced.

181

GUARANTEES

Many manufacturers give the consumer a *guarantee* or undertaking that if within a limited time of purchase (often six or twelve months), the product should prove to be faulty and need repairing, any parts will be replaced free of charge. This undertaking is often printed on a card or piece of paper which is handed to the shopper by the shopkeeper, or packed with the goods.

In some cases the guarantee does not provide for labour charges, should a product need repairing within the time stated; consumers should therefore read the wording of the guarantee form very carefully to see if *only parts* will be replaced free of charge, or whether labour costs, too, are included in the guarantee.

If you read the local and national newspaper advertisements for different goods, you will sometimes find the wording "satisfaction guaranteed" or "money returned if not satisfied." This is another form of guarantee, which is aimed at persuading the customer to take the risk of sending for goods through the post. The customer knows that should the goods not be satisfactory or up to expectations, his money will be refunded on the return of the goods.

Resale Price Maintenance

For a number of years many manufacturers adopted a policy of *price maintenance*, which was the setting of fixed prices at which their products could be sold by the shopkeeper, who was not able to sell a product at a price different from that laid down by the manufacturer. A shopkeeper was unable to make any price cuts on goods that were subject to this condition, so the shopper was charged the same price for an article, no matter where he bought it. Manufacturers considered that this was a fair policy to adopt, as the shopper paid what was considered to be a reasonable price and the shopkeeper was assured of a fair profit.

Some shopkeepers resented this policy of price maintenance because they argued that the shopkeeper who was most *efficient* and could afford to cut prices was prevented from doing so. The shopper also suffered by not being able to buy at lower prices from the efficient shopkeeper, and the *inefficient* shopkeeper was being kept in business because of this policy. It should be remembered, of course, that the fixing of set prices for products did not allow shopkeepers to charge *more* for these goods than the price fixed by the manufacturer, and the

182

customer knew that no matter where he shopped, the price would always be the same.

Price maintenance was finally abolished by 1965, and retailers were allowed to sell at any price they chose, provision being made by the Government that if a manufacturer wished to continue a policy of price maintenance for his products, he would have to apply for special permission.

COMMERCIAL ASSOCIATIONS

Chambers of Commerce

Many of our towns and cities have local Chambers of Commerce. Membership is made up of the representatives of local firms engaged in industry and commerce. Their main purpose is to promote trade, and help their members with many of the problems faced in the manufacture and selling of goods at home and abroad. The individual Chambers of Commerce keep a watchful eye on events in their own particular areas and co-ordinate some of their work with other Chambers in the region. Probably the most well-known in this country is the London Chamber of Commerce.

Chambers of Trade

Many of our towns and cities have a local Chamber of Trade. Membership is made of representatives of the large shops, and the smaller shopkeepers. An important aim is to promote efficient trading in their own districts, and to do as much as possible to protect the interests of local retailers. Individual retailers with particular problems can make their views known through the local Chamber of Trade, and possibly seek advice, if required by them.

Questions

1. Why should the shopper beware of buying goods without giving the purchase a great deal of thought?

2. Write briefly on the advantages and disadvantages to the consumer of trading stamp schemes.

3. What protection does the consumer have today? Write briefly on the measures of protection mentioned.

4. If you buy a product with a "guarantee," does it cover you fully for all costs necessary in putting right a faulty article?

5. What was the purpose of resale price maintenance? What are the advantages and disadvantages to the consumer of resale price maintenance?

6. Briefly explain "value for money."

7. (i) Name two consumer protection associations.

   (ii) What type of shop attempts to persuade the shopper to buy impulsively?

   (iii) Name two wholesaling groups.

   (iv) Give two examples of a chain store.

Practical work

1. Prepare a talk bringing out the dangers of buying on impulse and without thought to cost.

2. Visit a supermarket and, after studying the shopping habits of the customers, make a list of the dangers of which the customer should be wary.

3. Form a group with certain of your friends in class. Select a product provided by one of your number and make a list of all the good and bad points of this particular product, from the consumer's point of view.

22 Advertising

Business concerns of all kinds spend a great deal of money each year on advertisements for their products, telling the public of their particular virtues and why they are considered to be the best buy. We are all exposed to advertising in one way or another, whether we are sitting at home watching the television, reading our daily newspaper, visiting the cinema or simply walking along the road. Many people say that if the money spent on advertising was used in helping to reduce the prices charged we should all benefit far more, but before we can really pass an opinion on this matter we should understand the *purposes* of advertising.

The Purposes of Advertising

Most of the products that we purchase today are sold under their trade names, and we term them *branded goods*. When we go into a shop and make a purchase, we do not ask, for instance, for a bar of chocolate: we state the name and type of chocolate we require. This naming or branding of goods makes it possible for the manufacturer to advertise the qualities of his product so that he can obtain as large a proportion as possible of the market, and he tries to create a following for his particular brand so that the consumer will continue to buy the product. The branding of goods allows the manufacturer to use *trade marks* on his products, which must not be copied by any of his competitors and which make it possible for the consumer to recognize easily which brand he is buying, as for instance, "Smith's Crisps."

It costs the manufacturer a great deal of money to equip his factory with all the machinery necessary for the production of goods, and he must try to sell as many of his products as possible so that these costs can be recovered, and a fair profit made for the people who have invested their money in the business. In addition, if, through advertising, sales of his products can be increased, the cost of producing each article will be reduced. The manufacturer therefore makes larger

185

profits, and may pass on some of the benefit to the consumer in the form of lower prices.

The following example will illustrate the effect of advertising on a manufacturer's sales—

SALES, PRICES, AND COSTS *before* EXTENSIVE ADVERTISING

SUPER WASHING MACHINE COMPANY LTD.
Monthly Sales to Wholesalers in Year 1

	£
1,000 washing machines sold at £50 each	50,000
Less cost of manufacturing machines	40,000
Total profit	10,000

SALES, PRICES, AND COSTS *after* EXTENSIVE ADVERTISING

SUPER WASHING MACHINE COMPANY LTD.
Monthly Sales to Wholesalers in Year 2

	£	£
1,500 washing machines sold at £50 each		75,000
Less cost of manufacturing machines	55,000	
(*Note:* some costs are fixed and will remain the same no matter how many machines are manufactured.)		
Additional advertising costs	5,000	
Total costs		60,000
Total profit		15,000

We can see that although the manufacturer has had to pay an extra £5,000 in advertising costs in the second year, the result has been an increase in sales and an *increase in total profits*. The manufacturer may feel that he can now afford to *reduce his selling price*—this means passing some of the benefit on to the consumer. As a result, his sales may increase even further as consumers learn of his price reductions.

The purposes of advertising are therefore—

1. To make the consumer aware that a particular product is available. This applies particularly to a *new* product.

2. To keep the name of a product in the mind of the public.

3. To try to stimulate demand even further (i.e. to obtain a larger share of the market for the product). This is sometimes done by designing new and more attractive wrappings.

BEFORE ADVERTISING

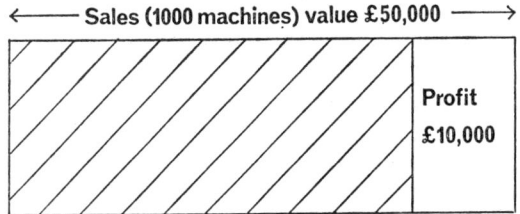

AFTER ADVERTISING

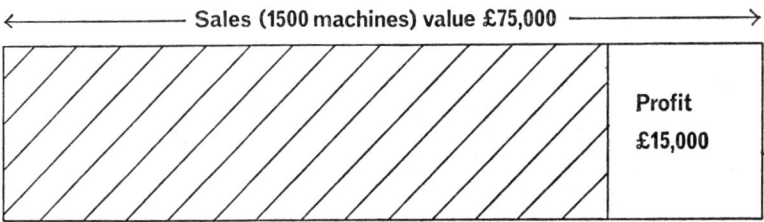

Fig. 29. Increase in Demand for Washing Machines

Methods of Advertising

There are many different methods of advertising in use today. Much depends on the size and type of business as to what method is used.

A large manufacturer of *consumer products*, wishing to stimulate a large-scale demand for his goods, might launch an advertising campaign through television, and national and local newspapers. The whole operation will be planned very carefully in conjunction with wholesalers and retailers. The television viewer will be subjected to the same

187

advertisement for this particular manufacturer's products on successive evenings, sometimes a number of times in the same evening. This form of advertising is called *saturation advertising* because the viewer is bombarded with repeats of particular advertisements. Some well-known examples are those for detergent powders, soap, and chocolate. Local and national newspapers will often have the same large display advertisements at the same time.

Smaller firms cannot usually afford to advertise on television, although some of the larger groups of departmental stores may run a series of short advertisements on local television stations, such as Tyne-Tees and Midland, announcing their annual sales. It is normally through the local newspaper and cinema advertisements that the smaller organization makes its services known to the public.

Other advertising media include *magazines* and *periodicals, billboards, posters, leaflets, commercial radio* and the *cinema*. Different products are advertised in different ways: the local self-service stores may distribute handbills informing the shopper of their price-cuts, whilst billboards are often used for advertisements for different brands of petrol and beer.

Radio Luxembourg is the largest source of commercial radio advertising in this country. Many products suitable for young people are advertised each evening, between programmes of "pop" music.

National newspapers and magazines, having circulations running into millions in some cases, carry a good deal of *display advertising*, large advertisements being placed in prominent positions in the paper or magazine. Periodicals such as *Woman* will carry many advertisements for women's clothing, cosmetics, and perhaps at Christmas time, gifts for men. Magazines catering for young people advertise a host of different products such as cosmetics, records, and record players. The class of products advertised in the national press varies according to the type of reader. There is very little point in advertising men's suits at £60 in the *Daily Express* if the majority of its readers earn under £30 per week. Local newspapers with a much smaller circulation—sometimes under 100,000—also carry large display advertisements, usually on behalf of shops in the area. In addition they have columns of *classified* advertisements such as births, marriages, deaths, situations vacant and so on. Naturally, this form of advertising is much cheaper than display advertising.

To summarize, then, the following methods of advertising are the most usual—

1. Commercial television;
2. Commercial radio;
3. National and local newspapers;
4. Magazines;
5. The cinema;
6. Posters and billboards;
7. Leaflets—distributed to households;
8. Shop-window displays.

Costs of Advertising

Manufacturers and others who wish to advertise on a national basis have to pay large sums of money to do so, whilst costs are much less for advertising in the local area only. Generally the greater the number of people who are likely to see the advertisement, the higher will be the cost. It follows that television advertising is the most expensive because programmes are being watched by millions of viewers. Television company advertising costs will vary according to the time of day the advertisement is to appear on the screen. For instance, an advertisement being shown at the height of the evening's viewing, when highly popular programmes are being televised, will cost far more than one appearing at tea-time or earlier in the day.

The following examples will give you some idea of variations in cost. An advertiser would pay well over £5,000/£6,000 for a full page advertisement in a popular national newspaper with a circulation of over 4,000,000, and read by approximately 12,000,000 people. A full page advertisement in a local evening newspaper, read by 100,000 persons, would cost somewhere in the region of £75/£100. Firms who advertise on television pay many thousands of pounds for an advertisement shown at peak viewing times, and lasting for perhaps 30 seconds.

Firms wishing to advertise their products usually engage a specialist *advertising agent*, who plans the advertising campaign, and receives a commission for his services.

Advertising and the Consumer

It is said that the advantage to the consumer of advertising is that, having been told the qualities of various products, he is therefore in the position of being able to judge which is the best one to buy. The potential customer must, however, be wary, for he may be unduly influenced by advertising and purchase articles which are not really needed, or which he cannot afford, or which may not in fact be the best quality he could buy for his money. How often we see the following type of advertisement on television—

BUY RESTORER HAIR CREAM
AND BE A
MAN ABOUT TOWN!

(*A glowing picture is painted of a young man who steps into his smart sports car, and then proceeds to collect his charming girl-friend.*)

The impression is given that by using a certain brand of hair cream, you, too, can have a smart car and a charming girl-friend, but does this advertisement really tell us very much about the qualities of the product? Here is another example—

BUY ONLY
DAZZLE LIPSTICK
IF YOU WANT TO BE
THE CENTRE OF ATTRACTION

Again, are we told in what way this particular brand of lipstick is superior to others? You will no doubt agree that a false impression is given by this advertisement too.

People who advertise are advised by experts on the techniques that have to be used if advertising is to be really successful. If we are not careful we tend to buy *on impulse*, without really thinking of the true facts. The tendency to buy on impulse in supermarkets has already been stressed.

It is always wise, particularly when planning to buy large articles such as items of furniture, washing machines, and television sets, to try not to be unduly swayed by high pressure attempts to get you to buy regardless of whether the product is really what you want, and indeed what your pocket can afford. Try to give yourself plenty of time to make a decision. The danger with advertising today is that it often sets out to make us dissatisfied with our present possessions, and to induce us to buy new ones. The shopper should always consider the virtues of respective products very carefully before buying, and not

190

always rely on the claims that are made by manufacturers when advertising their products.

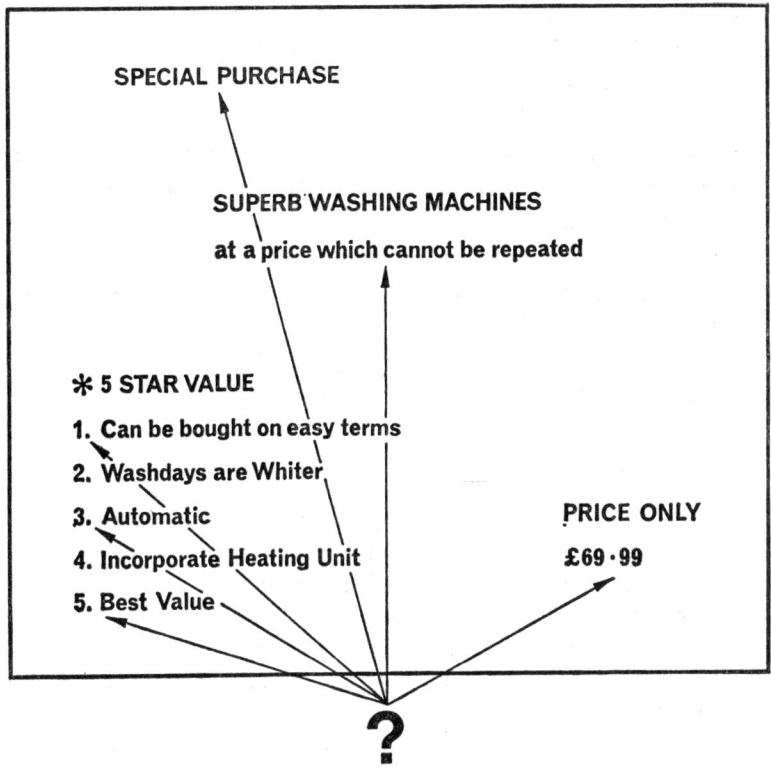

Fig. 30. The Dangers of Advertising

Should we believe everything we read?
Questions we should ask ourselves

1. What is meant by "special purchase"?
2. "Price which cannot be repeated."—How true is this statement?
3. Are the terms *easy*?
4. Is the machine *fully* automatic or not?
5. What does "best value" mean?
6. Is the price reasonable?
7. Is good after-sales service provided?

Questions

1. Explain the purposes of advertising.
2. Discuss the dangers to the consumer of advertising.
3. What are the advantages of advertising to—

    (i) The manufacturer?

    (ii) The consumer?

4. List eight methods used by suppliers to advertise their products and say which of these methods are most likely to be used by—

    (i) Manufacturers,

    (ii) Shopkeepers.

5. Why do manufacturers advertise their products? Why do they use brands (or trade marks)?

6. Why do manufacturers spend money on advertising, instead of reducing the prices of products they sell to us?

Practical work

1. Collect cuttings of advertisements for different products. Do they tell the whole story of the product, or not? Write briefly on any points you notice in the advertisements which appear to be of little value in assessing the worth of the products.

2. Prepare an advertisement for an imaginary product, which could be used to mislead the shopping public. Write brief notes on each misleading point.

3. Watch commercial television for one evening. Draft a statement showing the variety of products advertised.

4. Find out what your local evening newspaper charges for display advertising. Estimate, by looking through a Friday's edition of the newspaper, how much money has been spent by the advertisers.

23 Buying Now and Paying Later

Credit Sales

The problems in setting up a home are usually very formidable. The securing of adequate living accommodation in itself is not always an easy matter, and in addition a home needs to be furnished and made comfortable. There never seems to be sufficient money for everything, so many shops try to make things a little easier, particularly for young married couples, by offering their customers *credit facilities* (sometimes termed Deferred Payments) by means of which the shopper is given nine months or more to pay, by regular instalments, for the goods he has purchased. The manner in which shops operate credit facilities varies a good deal from shop to shop. Some allow the customer twenty weeks in which to pay for the goods purchased. Others allow longer periods of credit, but may compensate themselves by adding a small charge to the cash price of the goods. When this facility is allowed to the customer the transaction is termed a *credit sale.*

The normal credit sale, or deferred payments scheme, is operated by shopkeepers under a variety of different names. The usual monthly account arrangement as provided by departmental stores, and budget accounts are variations of the deferred payments scheme. Other examples of credit sales are the Barclay Card scheme operated by Barclays Bank, and the Diners' Card. It is a good idea to carry out some personal research and try to find out as much as possible about all these variations of the deferred payments plan, as provided by the shop-keepers in your own district.

Hire Purchase

Hire purchase, although a form of purchasing on credit, is different from the credit-sale arrangement, as the goods do not become the property of the purchaser until the price has been paid in full, whereas with a credit sale, even though the full amount has not been paid, the goods become the property of the buyer at the time of purchasing.

The distinction is that a person buying on hire purchase is legally only *hiring* the goods, and until the last payment is made they belong to the shopkeeper.

Subject to Government control, shops will often allow customers up to three years to pay for goods bought on hire-purchase terms, an *agreement* being signed by the hirer (the person buying the goods) by which he undertakes to keep the goods in satisfactory condition and to pay regular weekly or monthly instalments until the goods are finally paid for. It is most important that people buying goods on hire purchase do not re-sell them before they have completed paying for the goods, as legally they are still the property of the shopkeeper until final payment is made. Persons not complying with this requirement are liable to prison sentences.

THE ADVANTAGE OF HIRE PURCHASE — AND THE DANGERS
The advantage of buying goods on hire purchase is that it is possible for the buyer to enjoy the use of them before full payment is made, but there are certain dangers which should be considered before deciding to enter into such an agreement. They are—

1. It is not wise to buy too many articles on hire-purchase terms at any one time.

2. *Look well ahead.* Although you may have made calculations on paper which indicate that you can afford to keep up the necessary payments, in practice there are very few persons who are able to keep to their budgets.

3. It is difficult to forecast what the future holds for us, and remember that if the wage earner is off work through illness, difficulty may be encountered in making the payments.

4. Try to ensure that you are dealing with a reputable firm which will be considerate if at some time in the future you are unable to meet your commitments because of unforeseen financial difficulties.

The same considerations will also apply when making purchases on *credit-sale terms*.

LEGAL CONDITIONS
The following conditions will apply when hire-purchase agreements are made involving sums of *not more* than £2,000.

1. On purchasing goods, the customer may ask for a copy of the proposed agreement to take home to study.

2. If a hire-purchase agreement is signed at home, or indeed, at any other place *except a shop or showroom, or the office of a firm* granting hire-purchase facilities, a copy of the agreement must be left with the hirer, a second copy being sent through the post later. The hirer has the right to cancel the agreement made, provided he does so before the end of the fourth day after receiving the second copy of the agreement. If necessary this can be done through the post. Any amounts of money paid by the hirer must in this event be returned to him by the shop or firm.

3. If a customer defaults in making payments under a hire-purchase agreement, the shop or firm hiring the goods to the customer can, if less than one-third of the total amount payable has not been received, recover the goods from the customer. If more than one-third has been paid by the customer, the shop or firm can ask for a Court order to be made for recovery of the goods, or a ruling may be made requiring the customer to make payments as laid down by the Court.

4. A customer has the right to end a hire-purchase agreement. Details are given on the agreement itself, explaining how this can be done. In this event the customer must give the goods back to the shopkeeper, and, if the goods have not been kept in reasonable condition, he may be liable for any damage caused. In addition, any amounts of money that were owing to the shopkeeper because the customer was behind in payments would have to be paid by the customer.

The customer now has greater protection than he had in the past, but persons buying goods on hire purchase should always read the copy of the proposed agreement very carefully before signing their name to it. *On no account should a blank form be signed.*

In Scotland the owner of goods being hired must obtain a Court order before goods can be recovered, even if less than one-third of the purchase price has been paid.

CASH PRICE AND HIRE-PURCHASE PRICE

Although the provision of hire-purchase facilities is often a great help to many young married people, there are disadvantages, because the shop-keeper will want compensation for allowing the purchaser time in which to pay for the goods. He will therefore add to the cash price of the goods an amount of money in respect of *interest*, which is termed the

195

hire-purchase or *service charge*. The total amount of money to be paid by the customer is called the *hire-purchase price*.

Firms selling goods on hire purchase are required by law always to show the cash price of goods being displayed for sale in this way. There are no regulations fixing maximum hire-purchase interest charges. It is important, therefore, that customers should, before buying, ask for details of both the cash price of the goods and the hire-purchase price. This will indicate whether a reasonable amount of interest is being charged. If the customer considers that the interest charges are too high, he should then make inquiries at other shops, which may be able to provide better terms.

HOW THE HIRE-PURCHASE PRICE IS WORKED OUT

Purchase of Dining-room Suite on Hire Purchase

In this example the customer has been given two years in which to pay for the suite. The hire-purchase interest charge is five per cent for each year.

	£
Cash price of suite	50·00
Deduct	
deposit paid by the customer	10·00
Balance	40·00
Add hire-purchase charge	
$\dfrac{5}{100} \times \dfrac{£40}{1} \times \dfrac{2}{1} \;=\;$	4·00
	44·00
Add deposit paid by customer	10.00
Hire-purchase price	54·00

Note: As you can see, the hire-purchase price is the *cash price* plus the interest payable. In most transactions the customer pays a deposit and the hire-purchase charges are calculated on the balance remaining after the deposit paid has been deducted from the *cash price*.

Rentals

Many shops operate an alternative system to credit-sale and hire-purchase arrangements. An article is loaned to the customer in return for a weekly or monthly rental. Although the article never becomes the property of the customer, this system has the advantage that should the television set or washing machine on loan need repairing or not be functioning correctly, the shop from which it is rented will put it right at no extra charge. It is usual for the rental to be reduced slightly every six months.

Credit Trading Clubs

In recent years there has been a large increase in the amount of business done by firms which offer the shopping public yet another method of buying goods on an instalment basis. The *credit trading club* offers facilities similar in some ways to normal credit-sale agreements. The difference is that these "club traders" set up as agents and ask shop-keepers in their area to provide shoppers with goods on the production of a check by the shopper. This check, or "club" as it is sometimes termed, is signed by the shopkeeper, who also enters the value of the goods bought. At the time of making the purchase the shopper does not pay any cash to the shopkeeper, who is paid direct by the club trader.

The club trader receives a commission from the shopkeeper on the business done. This is because it is he who faces the risk of non-payment by the shopper, and not the shopkeeper himself.

TRADING CHECK

Divi-Traders			
3 Church Street, Hartlepool			
Please supply goods to .... of .... to a value of the balance shown. Opening credit £10.			
Name of Shop	*Amount Spent*	*Balance*	*Initials*
Mode Fashions Robinsons Ltd.	£ 4·00 2·00	£ 6·00 4·00	*D.B.* *L.W.T.*

Note: The layout of the check will vary from firm to firm.

197

In the first instance the shopper approaches the club trader or agent, and is provided with a check (or club) entitling him to make purchases at any of the shops which have agreed to participate in the scheme. These checks are granted up to varying amounts in value. The shopper agrees to pay the sum over a period, usually twenty weeks, in fixed instalments. In addition, for every £1 of credit granted, the shopper will have to pay the club trader a commission of 5p. *For example*, if Mrs. Booth approached "Divi-Traders" for a club amounting to £10 in value, 50p commission would be payable by Mrs. Booth, making the total repayment over twenty weeks £10·50.

The shopper is allowed to make his purchases from a variety of shops if desired, each shop making the appropriate entry on the check, and deducting the value of the purchases from the balance brought forward.

Many checks give a full list of shops participating in the club on the back of the check itself.

The chief snag with credit club trading is that some people secure a club from the agent or trader, full of good intentions of paying promptly the required amount each week, but then, perhaps because of illness in the family, the payments are not made, and the club trader is faced with losses.

Questions

1. Explain the differences between buying goods on hire purchase and making use of the credit-sale facilities offered by shopkeepers.

2. Explain the following and illustrate your answers with examples—

    (i) Cash price

    (ii) Hire-purchase price

3. A tape recorder was purchased from a shop on hire-purchase terms at a cash price of £35 with interest charges of 5 per cent per annum. Two years are allowed for payment. Taking into account that a deposit of £5 is paid—

    (i) what is the hire-purchase price?

    (ii) what is the amount of the weekly instalment (to the nearest penny)?

4. How does the granting of hire-purchase facilities by shops help the consumer?

5. What are the respective *advantages* and *disadvantages* of hire purchase for—

(i) the consumer?

(ii) the shopkeeper?

6. Discuss the dangers of buying goods on hire purchase.

7. Let us suppose you are buying a record player on hire purchase. When would you become its owner? To what points in the hire-purchase agreement would you pay especial attention before signing it?

8. What are credit trading clubs?

9. (i) Is cash price less or greater than hire-purchase price?

(ii) A person buying goods on hire purchase is called the . . .

(iii) What is the hire-purchase agreement?

(iv) What is the hire-purchase or service charge?

Practical work

1. Visit three shops in your own town. Ask if they have any leaflets on their hire-purchase terms and, if so, decide which shop offers the best terms.

2. Visit three shops in your own town. Ask for details of their credit-sale facilities, and inquire whether or not they charge interest. If so, make a comparison between the terms offered by the shops.

3. Select an article. Find out the relative costs if it were to be purchased on (*a*) hire-purchase or (*b*) credit-sale terms, over two years. Compare this with the cost over the same period if a personal loan were obtained from a local bank. Inquire whether the shopkeeper would give you a cash discount if cash were to be paid.

4. Plan your "dream home." Visit shops in your town and estimate what the cost of furnishing the home would be if—

(i) cash were paid,

(ii) hire purchase was necessary.

5. Visit shops in your town. Make comparisons between the cash price and the hire-purchase price of different articles.

6. Draw a diagram to illustrate the differences between cash price and hire-purchase price.

7. Prepare a talk on the advantages and dangers of hire purchase as far as the consumer is concerned.

Conclusion

The worlds of industry and commerce are constantly changing and progress is much more rapid nowadays than it has ever been. New techniques and the use of computers make ours the age of *automation*.

Everyone must be prepared to accept and adapt himself to these developments because there cannot be any real progress in the world unless there is *change*. Some countries are more aware of this need for change than others and it is they who have forged ahead in providing a better standard of living for their people.

It must be realized, too, that as a direct result of automation, people will have far more leisure time in the future; they must learn to use this wisely and profitably.

During their working lives, most men (and many women) will take their place in industry or commerce, or help in providing other *direct* services for the community (e.g. they will become doctors, nurses or teachers). Although we may sometimes think of these different fields as being quite separate from one another, they are in fact very closely connected, as we have seen in this book.

Remember, too, that all work is important to the community: the clerical worker has his part to play, as have the train driver, the shop assistant and the company director. Each man or woman, no matter what job he or she is engaged on, makes a valuable contribution to the community; we are all members of the "team."

Workbook

The material contained in this section should help pupils and students in their revision and consolidation of subject matter. It is hoped that teachers will find the material a useful aid, and the questions are divided into twenty-three sections based upon each chapter of the book. Increasing use is now being made of objective type tests, and this material is, of course, additional to the examination type questions, and practical work contained at the end of each chapter.

The answers to the questions set in this workbook section have been included in the book, and as teachers usually employ this form of testing in the classroom situation when supervision is possible, it is hoped that no practical difficulties will arise.

A practical snag, perhaps, with objective tests of the type included in the book is that in some instances alternative answers are possible. Wherever possible discretion should be used on these occasions, and students work marked accordingly.

It is suggested that pupils and students write their answers in a separate workbook of their own, or in an exercise book and NOT in the textbook. This means that the book can be shared between classes if desired and also retained for future use.

Chapter 1—The World Outside

PART 1. TEST YOUR PROGRESS

Complete the following statements by filling in the blanks.

1. The function of commerce is to promote the ——— of goods and services.
2. Commerce could be explained as trade and the —— —— ——.
3. Trade can be divided into two distinct sections, home trade, and ——— trade.
4. The aids to trade include, transport, banking, insurance and ———.

5. In this modern world of ours it would be true to say that virtually everybody is ———— upon many other persons for satisfaction of their needs.

Select the answer which you consider to be most appropriate.

1. A number of important commercial services are called:
   (*a*) business services, (*b*) aids to trade, (*c*) business units.

2. Trade is the word we use to describe:
   (*a*) exchange, (*b*) the manufacture of goods, (*c*) the growing of produce.

3. The term we use to describe the world of business is:
   (*a*) production, (*b*) services, (*c*) commerce.

4. Wholesalers and retailers are concerned with:
   (*a*) overseas trade, (*b*) home trade, (*c*) the transporting of goods.

5. An institution which provides many valuable financial services for the businessman is a:
   (*a*) bank, (*b*) building society, (*c*) wholesaler.

Chapter 2—Going to Work

Complete the following statements by filling in the blanks.

1. Persons such as doctors and dentists provide us with ———— services.

2. Persons following extractive and manufacturing occupations usually work in ————.

3. Bank clerks, shop assistants, and insurance agents are examples of ———— occupations.

4. Office workers are often described as —— ———— workers.

5. It would generally be true to say that all ———— are constructive.

Select the answer which you consider to be most appropriate.

1. A machine operator in a factory is an example of a:
   (*a*) commercial occupation, (*b*) extractive occupation, (*c*) manufacturing occupation.

2. A shop assistant can be said to:
(*a*) provide direct services, (*b*) follow a commercial occupation, (*c*) follow an extractive occupation.

3. The company secretary has the responsibility of supervising the following activities of a firm:
(*a*) the store-keepers, (*b*) the commercial activities, (*c*) the sales representatives.

4. It is said that all occupations can be classified into:
(*a*) two groups, (*b*) four groups, (*c*) six groups.

5. Commercial workers are persons who:
(*a*) only write or typewrite in their work, (*b*) work in the civil service, (*c*) work in commerce.

Chapter 3—The Help Industry Needs

PART 1. TEST YOUR PROGRESS

Complete the following statements by filling in the blanks.

1. It can be stated that ——— services the wheels of industry.

2. All products which are manufactured can be separated into consumer and ——— goods.

3. Through the medium of advertising sales of many ——— goods can be increased.

4. ——— is essential in ensuring that goods and materials are moved from one place to another.

5. Many persons and organizations use the services of the ——— banks who have branches in all parts of the country.

PART 2. WHICH ANSWER

Select the answer which you consider to be most appropriate.

1. An example of a consumer good would be:
(*a*) a drilling machine, (*b*) a ship, (*c*) a television set.

2. If modern machinery can be used in the manufacture of goods on a large scale, it is probable that prices will be:
(*a*) increased, (*b*) reduced, (*c*) remain the same.

3. Mechanization and the use of new techniques help to increase our:
(*a*) standard of living, (*b*) cost of living, (*c*) production expenses.

203

4. An alternative term which is sometimes used to describe shoppers is:
   (*a*) retailers, (*b*) wholesalers, (*c*) consumers.

5. Before any factory can produce, and eventually distribute its products it will require:
   (*a*) the services of commerce, (*b*) shop premises, (*c*) advertising services.

Chapter 4—Trade

PART 1. TEST YOUR PROGRESS

Complete the following statements by filling in the blanks.

1. A wage increase will only be of real value providing ——— do not increase in proportion.

2. Many years ago the exchange of articles and commodities between persons was called ———.

3. In this country during the eighteenth century when factories were first built we had the beginnings of the ——— ———.

4. Goods which we receive from other countries are referred to as ———. Goods which we sell to other countries are called ———.

5. The ——— — ——— represents the difference between this country's visible and invisible imports and exports.

PART 2. WHICH ANSWER

Select the answer which you consider to be most appropriate.

1. Certain goods which are imported from overseas are subject to a form of taxation known as:
   (*a*) income tax, (*b*) purchase tax, (*c*) customs duty.

2. Services which this country provides for overseas countries are known as:
   (*a*) imports and exports, (*b*) invisible exports, (*c*) warehouse facilities.

3. The difference between the amount of actual goods and commodities imported and exported by Great Britain is known as:
   (*a*) balance of trade, (*b*) balance of payments, (*c*) balance on hand.

4. Trade between different countries is called:
   (*a*) home trade, (*b*) international trade, (*c*) buying and selling.

5. Places for storing goods on which duty is payable are called:
(*a*) wholesalers' premises, (*b*) store houses, (*c*) bonded warehouses.

Chapter 5—Money

PART 1. TEST YOUR PROGRESS

Complete the following statements by filling in the blanks.

1. Money is a ——— of value which makes exchange between people possible.

2. Valuable metals such as —— and ——— were used by people in exchange of goods and services.

3. —— —— which are of little value in themselves provide a convenient form of money.

4. Before the invention of money ——— was the method used in exchanging goods.

5. Money is a —— which makes it possible for people to exchange goods and services.

PART 2. WHICH ANSWER

Select the answer which you consider to be most appropriate.

1. Money is sometimes described as a:
(*a*) valuable metal, (*b*) valuable possession, (*c*) measure of value.

2. Barter could be described as:
(*a*) swopping goods, (*b*) a form of money, (*c*) the exchange of gold and silver.

3. Trading between people may be referred to as:
(*a*) the selling of services, (*b*) exchange, (*c*) trade negotiations.

4. Wholesalers and retailers could be described as:
(*a*) traders, (*b*) businessmen, (*c*) factory owners.

5. Banknotes in themselves:
(*a*) have a high value, (*b*) have a high paper value, (*c*) are of little value.

Chapter 6—The Nation

PART 1. TEST YOUR PROGRESS

Complete the following statements by filling in the blanks.

1. The concentration of similar industries in one area is a form of ———.

2. In this modern age most people tend to ——— in their work rather than carry out a variety of tasks.

3. The manufacture of goods on a large scale is called —— ———.

4. Most firms incur a number of different types of ——— which have to be paid, regardless of the quantity of goods produced.

5. Mass production methods of ——— usually result in lower costs of production.

PART 2. WHICH ANSWER

Select the answer which you consider to be most appropriate.

1. Production on a large scale is often referred to as:
   (*a*) scale production, (*b*) high output, (*c*) mass production.

2. When persons concentrate on certain aspects only of a job it can be said that they:
   (*a*) economize, (*b*) specialize, (*c*) manage.

3. An alternative word which is used to describe the expenses of a business is:
   (*a*) costs, (*b*) values, (*c*) sales.

4. Products manufactured by a firm are often called:
   (*a*) components, (*b*) units of output, (*c*) goods produced.

5. The beginning of the factory age in Great Britain was the commencement of the:
   (*a*) industrial age, (*b*) machinery age, (*c*) industrial revolution.

Chapter 7—Services

PART 1. TEST YOUR PROGRESS

Complete the following statements by filling in the blanks.

1. The local Authority provides the community with many essential ———.

2. The —— system is a method by which local authorities raise the money which enables them to provide important local services.

3. National services are paid for by —— —— which is paid by many persons and organizations.

4. —— —— is really a form of sales tax which is charged on many articles we purchase.

5. Each year the Chancellor of the Exchequer prepares his ——— which sets out the methods by which he will raise the Government's revenue.

PART 2. WHICH ANSWER

Select the answer which you consider to be most appropriate.

1. Local taxation is known as:
   (*a*) income tax, (*b*) purchase tax, (*c*) rates.

2. An example of a national service is:
   (*a*) health service, (*b*) municipal bus service, (*c*) public library.

3. Purchase tax, and customs and excise duties are examples of:
   (*a*) direct taxation, (*b*) rates, (*c*) indirect taxation.

4. The system under which persons have income tax deducted from their weekly wages is known as:
   (*a*) Pay As You Earn, (*b*) cash on delivery, (*c*) payments in advance.

5. A special tax paid by limited companies is called:
   (*a*) profits tax, (*b*) corporation tax, (*c*) national tax.

Chapter 8—The Home

PART 1. TEST YOUR PROGRESS

Complete the following statements by filling in the blanks.

1. Persons who wish to buy a house with the help of a mortgage from a building society usually have to pay a ——— as the society will not usually grant a loan for the full cost of the house.

2. Before borrowers can have loans of money made available to them ——— need to deposit money with building societies.

3. Persons borrowing money from a building society are charged ———.

4. When purchasing a house a ——— must be engaged who will then be responsible for the legal details.

5. Persons wishing to sell their house often use the services of ——— ——— who receive a commission when the property is sold.

PART 2. WHICH ANSWER

Select the answer which you consider to be most appropriate.

1. The loan of money the building society advances to a borrower is called:
   (*a*) assurance, (*b*) mortgage, (*c*) deposit.

2. As their reward for investing their money in a building society an investor receives an amount of money which is known as:
   (*a*) fees, (*b*) dividends, (*c*) interest.

3. When persons pay amounts of money for the use of a flat or house which never becomes their own property this is called:
   (*a*) rent, (*b*) loan, (*c*) legal fees.

4. Borrowers usually repay building societies the amount of money they owe by:
   (*a*) fixed instalments, (*b*) periodical repayments, (*c*) yearly fees.

5. A proportion of the purchase price of a house which is usually paid by the borrower himself is the:
   (*a*) legal fees, (*b*) deposit, (*c*) interest.

Chapter 9—Budgeting

PART 1. TEST YOUR PROGRESS

Complete the following statements by filling in the blanks.

1. A good method of planning ahead is to ——— for future items of expense.

2. In budgeting one must make decisions on what the ——— are, and plan accordingly.

3. In planning a budget, we must take into account all of our —— and ——— for a given period.

4. The ——— Savings Movement provides us with a number of facilities for ———.

5. Organizations such as the commercial —— and the ——— societies provide facilities for saving.

208

PART 2. WHICH ANSWER

Select the answer which you consider to be most appropriate.

1. From the point of view of the investor, organizations such as the National Savings Movement, the National Savings Bank, and the Trustee Savings Bank are regarded as:
   (*a*) banks, (*b*) stable institutions, (*c*) risky undertakings.

2. Most persons cannot afford all that they want, and need, therefore, to arrange the order of their:
   (*a*) priorities, (*b*) expenses, (*c*) luxuries.

3. If an investor deposits his savings with the National Savings Bank he receives:
   (*a*) dividends, (*b*) commission, (*c*) interest.

4. Organizations which do not offer the investor a guaranteed return on his investment can be regarded as:
   (*a*) more stable investments, (*b*) less stable investments, (*c*) safe bets.

5. The estimating of future income, and how it is to be spent is a form of:
   (*a*) financing control, (*b*) investment, (*c*) budgeting.

Chapter 10—The Business

PART 1. TEST YOUR PROGRESS

Complete the following statements by filling in the blanks.

1. A popular type of business unit for professional persons such as doctors, solicitors, and accountants is the ———.

2. There are two forms of limited liability company, public and ———.

3. Persons who invest in limited companies are known as ———.

4. The ——— share carries a greater risk than other types of shares.

5. The calculation of the —— sometimes proves more informative than the rate of dividend payable.

6. Membership of the Stock Exchange is divided into stockbrokers and ———.

7. The National Coal Board is an example of a ——— industry.

8. The stockbroker makes his living by charging his clients a ——— based on the value of the share transactions he carries out for them.

209

PART 2. WHICH ANSWER

Select the answer which you consider to be most appropriate.

1. A form of business enterprise in which the liability of its owners is to some extent protected is a:
   (*a*) partnership, (*b*) sole trader, (*c*) limited company.

2. In most firms of partnership the maximum number of partners permissible is:
   (*a*) 5, (*b*) 20, (*c*) 30.

3. The maximum number of shareholders permitted in a private limited company, excluding past and present employees is:
   (*a*) 50, (*b*) 70, (*c*) 100.

4. The amount of money needed to set up in business is called:
   (*a*) shares, (*b*) finance, (*c*) capital.

5. The most common type of company share is the:
   (*a*) preference share, (*b*) ordinary share, (*c*) participating preference share.

6. An example of a nationalized concern is:
   (*a*) I.C.I., (*b*) G.E.C., (*c*) B.O.A.C.

7. A dealer in shares is called:
   (*a*) stockjobber, (*b*) stockbroker, (*c*) stocktaker.

8. When a stockjobber is asked the price of shares, he quotes:
   (*a*) one price, (*b*) two prices, (*c*) three prices.

Chapter 11—The Capital of the Business

PART 1. TEST YOUR PROGRESS

Complete the following statements by filling in the blanks.

1. A firm must raise sufficient ——— if it is to be in a position to finance its trading activities.

2. The amount of money invested in a business by the owner(s) is known as capital —— in the business.

3. ——— ——— is essential if a business is to be enabled to finance its day to day trading activities.

4. Items purchased out of the capital of the business, including such things as premises, fittings, and stocks of goods are known as ———.

5. The assets of the business are divided into two groups. One group representing assets which are to be retained for a long period of time is known as —— capital. The other group is known as —— capital.

PART 2. WHICH ANSWER

Select the answer which you consider to be most appropriate.

1. If the assets of the business are totalled, and the amount of the debtors deducted from this total, the resultant figure is known as:
   (*a*) capital owned, (*b*) working capital, (*c*) capital employed.

2. Those items (assets) used in the business, and which fluctuate from day to day are known as the:
   (*a*) fixed capital, (*b*) circulating capital, (*c*) working capital.

3. The circulating capital of the business less any amount due for repayment in the near future will provide us with the amount of:
   (*a*) capital employed, (*b*) fixed capital, (*c*) working capital.

4. The amount of money invested in a business by its owner(s) is known as:
   (*a*) capital owned, (*b*) capital employed, (*c*) working capital.

5. Persons owing money to a business are called:
   (*a*) creditors, (*b*) debtors, (*c*) liabilities.

Chapter 12—Banks—their Functions and Services

PART 1. TEST YOUR PROGRESS

Complete the following statements by filling in the blanks.

1. The Midland Bank is an example of a —— bank.

2. A person opening a deposit account at a bank is provided with a —— book.

3. A person with a current account often pays —— charges.

4. There are *three* parties involved in cheque transactions. They are drawer, drawee, and ——.

5. A customer of a commercial bank who would like a safe place for his money, but at the same time wishes to earn interest can open a —— account.

6. The purpose of the ——— —— is to ensure that persons and firms are able to make payments to one another by the use of cheques.

7. The bank ——— is a method by which a customer is allowed to overdraw on his ——— account at the bank.

8. Persons making regular periodical payments of fixed amounts of money can ask the bank to arrange to pay these amounts under the ——— —— service.

PART 2. WHICH ANSWER

Select the answer which you consider to be most appropriate.

1. Methods of payment offered by the commercial banks are known as: (*a*) payment services, (*b*) bank money transfer services, (*c*) cheque payment services.

2. Which of the following could be used as security when borrowing from a bank? (*a*) life assurance policy, (*b*) household comprehensive policy, (*c*) accident policy.

3. Customers with current accounts enter details of cheques and cash they are paying in to their current account on a: (*a*) statement, (*b*) credit transfer slip, (*c*) paying-in slip.

4. Which of the following banks have now merged with each other: (*a*) Lloyds and Midland, (*b*) Midland and Barclays, (*c*) National Provincial and Westminster.

5. The Bank of England is known as: (*a*) The Clearing Bank, (*b*) The Central Bank, (*c*) The International Bank.

6. When a customer with a current account is allowed to draw more money out of his bank account than he has in, he is said to have an: (*a*) overdraft, (*b*) personal loan, (*c*) standing order.

7. Businessmen and persons on holiday in overseas countries can use: (*a*) personal cheques, (*b*) crossed cheques, (*c*) travellers' cheques.

8. A rate of interest which usually affects many aspects of financial affairs in Great Britain is the: (*a*) bank rate, (*b*) money rate, (*c*) exchange rate.

Chapter 13—Making Payments and Post Office Services

PART 1. TEST YOUR PROGRESS

Complete the following statements by filling in the blanks.

1. A relatively new Post Office banking service is the —— ——
——.

2. Like customers of commercial banks with current accounts, persons
with P.O. Giro accounts may now obtain ——.

3. To ensure that a letter or parcel reaches its destination as quickly
as possible it should be sent by —— —— post.

4. When a person purchases goods from a mail order firm, and does
not wish to make payment in advance, he can use the Post Office
—— —— —— service.

5. A cheque crossed —— —— —— can only be paid into the
bank account of the person to whom the cheque is made payable.

PART 2. WHICH ANSWER

Select the answer which you consider to be most appropriate.

1. If you send a cheque to a creditor and wish him to be able to cash it
at a bank you should send him an:
(*a*) open cheque, (*b*) crossed cheque, (*c*) special cheque.

2. The term used to describe the amounts of cash which can legally be
used in settlement of a debt is:
(*a*) legal money, (*b*) legal tender, (*c*) legal money transfers.

3. A crossed postal order can only be:
(*a*) cashed at a post office, (*b*) paid into a bank account, (*c*) given to a
shopkeeper when paying for goods.

4. The cheapest method of ensuring that a person receives a letter by
signing a form acknowledging its delivery is to send the letter by:
(*a*) registered post, (*b*) first class post, (*c*) recorded delivery.

5. A cheque is known as:
(*a*) paper money, (*b*) banking document, (*c*) negotiable instrument.

213

Chapter 14—Buying Goods

Complete the following statements by filling in the blanks.

1. A —— —— encourages customers to pay their accounts promptly.
2. A person's —— — usually determines the amount of credit he will be allowed.
3. Wholesalers usually allow shopkeepers a —— ——.
4. A firm of —— —— can be employed to establish a person's credit worth or standing.

PART 2. WHICH ANSWER
Select the answer which you consider to be most appropriate.

1. An appropriate rate of cash discount would be:
   (a) $2\frac{1}{2}$–10 per cent, (b) 10–25 per cent, (c) 25–40 per cent.
2. Trade discount is usually given by:
   (a) mail order companies, (b) retailers, (c) wholesalers.
3. A person's credit worth is often determined by:
   (a) the value of his house, (b) the type of job he has, (c) the neighbourhood he lives in.
4. When we make immediate payment for our purchases it is known as:
   (a) a cash transaction, (b) a credit transaction, (c) an immediate transaction.

Chapter 15—Making Sales

PART 1. TEST YOUR PROGRESS
Complete the following statements by filling in the blanks.

1. —— is a term used to describe the sales of the business for its trading period.
2. One method of calculating —— — is to find the average of the value of a firm's stock at the beginning and the end of a trading period.
3. The term used to describe how quickly a firm is selling its stock of goods is —— — —— or, alternatively ——.

4. The difference between the price paid for goods during a particular period, and what they are sold for, represents a firm's —— profit.

5. The expenses incurred in operating a business are often referred to as the ——.

PART 2. WHICH ANSWER

Select the answer which you consider to be most appropriate.

1. The amount of money paid by a business for the goods it sells is often known as:
(*a*) cost of sales, (*b*) value of sales, (*c*) sales price.

2. Whilst certain retailers value their stock of goods at selling prices, others may value at:
(*a*) full price, (*b*) half price, (*c*) cost price.

3. A popular method of comparing the *true* profits made by a firm over a number of years is to calculate the:
(*a*) gross profit, (*b*) cost of sales, (*c*) percentage net profit to sales.

4. An alternative term used to describe the rate of turnover of a business is:
(*a*) stockturn, (*b*) average stock, (*c*) opening stock.

5. If, in a particular trading period it was found that the percentage net profit to sales was considerably lower than previous trading periods it may indicate that:
(*a*) the expenses of the business are increasing, (*b*) the expenses of the business are decreasing, (*c*) sales are increasing.

Chapter 16—Documents: their Use in Business

PART 1. TEST YOUR PROGRESS

Complete the following statements by filling in the blanks.

1. A firm receiving a letter of inquiry will usually provide a prospective customer with details of its prices and terms of business by sending a ——.

2. An —— is the formal bill for goods or services supplied.

3. A —— —— is the document which informs a buyer that he has been granted an allowance which can be deducted from the price of goods as shown on the ——.

215

4. Many firms send their customers an ——— — through the post, informing them that goods have been dispatched.

5. When a firm undercharges a customer because of mistake on the original invoice, it can remedy the error by sending a — — for the amount undercharged.

PART 2. WHICH ANSWER

Select the answer which you consider to be most appropriate.

1. Which term means that the buyer must pay all costs after the goods have left the seller's works?
   (*a*) ex warehouse, (*b*) ex works, (*c*) carr. fwd.

2. An alternative name for a supplementary invoice is:
   (*a*) credit note, (*b*) advice note, (*c*) debit note.

3. A method of requesting payment in advance for goods is to send a:
   (*a*) invoice, (*b*) pro forma invoice, (*c*) quotation.

4. A document sent by a firm to its customer, and which shows details of all amounts due, less any allowances and cash paid is called:
   (*a*) statement of account, (*b*) pro forma invoice, (*c*) receipt.

5. In certain trades when a buyer requires estimates of the cost of a specific job or product he may invite suppliers to submit:
   (*a*) catalogues, (*b*) price lists, (*c*) tenders.

Chapter 17—Insurance

PART 1. TEST YOUR PROGRESS

Complete the following statements by filling in the blanks.

1. ——— is taken out against a risk, or event which must happen sooner or later.

2. Persons buying their own house can take out a ——— ——— policy, so that in the event of death before the mortgage is repaid, any outstanding amount can be repaid by the insurance company.

3. The ——— — ——— is an international market for insurance. Its members are known as ———.

4. Insurance can be stated as the ——— of the joint financial resources of many persons and organizations.

216

5. The date on which insurance premiums fall due each year is known as the ——— ——.

Select the answer which you consider to be most appropriate.

1. A person taking out a life or endowment policy is known as the:
(*a*) assured, (*b*) insured, (*c*) householder.

2. Members of Lloyd's Corporation are called:
(*a*) insurance brokers, (*b*) underwriters, (*c*) insurance agents.

3. The type of insurance taken out by a firm against claims by employees for compensation as a result of an accident whilst at work is:
(*a*) employers' insurance, (*b*) employers' cover, (*c*) employers' liability.

4. The total number of underwriting members of Lloyd's is approximately:
(*a*) 3,500–4,000, (*b*) 5,500–6,000, (*c*) 7,500–8,000.

5. An insurance policy which covers the contents of the home against various types of risk is known as:
(*a*) home protection, (*b*) mortgage protection, (*c*) householders' policy.

Chapter 18—Transport

Complete the following statements by filling in the blanks.

1. A number of factories have their own rail ——— which make it easier to transport goods to and from the factory itself.

2. One important State-owned road haulage concern in Great Britain is ——— — ———.

3. ——— vessels sail to all parts of the ——— with many different kinds of cargo. They do not sail to any definite timetable.

4. Special ——— vessels are sometimes used for the carrying of containers. Such vessels are fitted with special facilities for handling these ———.

5. The ——— of London has many road and rail links for access to the various docks.

PART 2. WHICH ANSWER

Select the answer which you consider to be most appropriate.

1. The Beeching Report on the railway system in Great Britain was published in:
   (*a*) 1961, (*b*) 1963, (*c*) 1965.

2. Road transport concerns can usually carry less bulky goods:
   (*a*) dearer than by rail, (*b*) cheaper than by rail, (*c*) at approximately the same price as rail.

3. A central meeting place situated in London, for the chartering of tramp vessels is:
   (*a*) Lloyd's Corporation, (*b*) Royal Albert Dock, (*c*) The Baltic Exchange.

4. The leading passenger port in Great Britain is:
   (*a*) Southampton, (*b*) Liverpool, (*c*) London.

5. Vessels used for the carrying of oil and chemicals are called:
   (*a*) tankers, (*b*) container vessels, (*c*) cargo vessels.

Chapter 19—The Wholesaler

PART 1. TEST YOUR PROGRESS

Complete the following statements by filling in the blanks.

1. The wholesaler is sometimes referred to as the ———— because he buys from the manufacturer and sells to the retailer.

2. The chain of ———— is the term used for describing the processes which take place in ensuring that goods reach the consumer.

3. ———— is a prominent meat wholesale market in London.

4. One of the wholesaler's functions is to —— goods until they are required by the retailer.

5. It is often argued that it —— no more to use the wholesaler in the ———— of goods, than for the manufacturer to supply the retailer direct.

PART 2. WHICH ANSWER

Select the answer which you consider to be most appropriate.

1. The wholesaler usually makes:
   (*a*) unduly large profits on each item he sells, (*b*) large profits on each item he sells, (*c*) small profits on each item he sells.

218

2. Certain products such as electric fires have a large demand usually:
   (*a*) in the winter months, (*b*) in the summer months, (*c*) throughout the year.

3. An important wholesale market for fish which is situated in London is:
   (*a*) Covent Garden, (*b*) Billingsgate, (*c*) Smithfield.

4. Is the middleman a:
   (*a*) manufacturer? (*b*) wholesaler? (*c*) retailer?

5. The most important requirement for a firm of wholesalers is a:
   (*a*) offices, (*b*) showroom, (*c*) warehouse.

Chapter 20—Shops and Other Retail Outlets

PART 1. TEST YOUR PROGRESS

Complete the following statements by filling in the blanks.

1. The small shopkeeper's business is sometimes called a —— shop because it is the only one owned by him.

2. A —— —— can be described as a collection of shops, all under one roof.

3. —— —— concerns are increasing in popularity. Their catalogues are attractive, and the customer can select goods in the comfort of his own ——.

4. The —— retail societies hand back the profits to the shoppers in the form of —— and dividend stamps.

5. —— shops are controlled usually by a head office. In addition there will probably be a —— warehouse.

PART 2. WHICH ANSWER

Select the answer which you consider to be most appropriate.

1. W. H. Smith & Sons is an example of a:
   (*a*) variety chain store, (*b*) departmental store, (*c*) multiple shop.

2. The person in charge of a branch shop of a multiple organization is usually called the:
   (*a*) manager, (*b*) buyer, (*c*) supervisor.

3. The furniture department in a departmental store is usually situated:
   (*a*) in the basement, (*b*) on the first floor, (*c*) on the top floor.

4. Firms selling their products direct to the consumer charge prices which are usually:
   (*a*) lower than those of conventional shops, (*b*) higher than those of conventional shops, (*c*) the same as those of conventional shops.

5. A store which sells many items of household equipment at considerable reductions in price, but does not usually offer a delivery service, or shop demonstration, is called:
   (*a*) discount store, (*b*) self-service shop, (*c*) multiple shop.

Chapter 21—Developments in the Retail Trade

PART 1. TEST YOUR PROGRESS

Complete the following statements by filling in the blanks.

1. A self-service shop which has a relatively large floor area is called a ———.

2. Shopkeepers often issue ——— stamps as an incentive to customers to shop regularly with them.

3. The Trade ——— Act of 1968 provides much better protection for the consumer than hitherto.

4. ——— groups such as Spar, and Mace help the small retailer to compete more effectively with the supermarkets.

5. There are a number of bodies in existence today whose function is to try to ensure that the ——— gets a fair ———.

PART 2. WHICH ANSWER

Select the answer which you consider to be most appropriate.

1. An organization very much concerned with consumer protection and which publishes the magazine *Which?* is the:
   (*a*) Consumer Council, (*b*) Consumers' Association, (*c*) British Standards Institution.

2. The date of the present Hire Purchase Act is:
   (*a*) 1964, (*b*) 1966, (*c*) 1968.

3. R.P.M. is the abbreviation for:
   (*a*) resale price market, (*b*) resale price maintenance, (*c*) retail price maintenance.

4. An example of a large multiple supermarket organization in Great Britain is:
   (*a*) Saxone, (*b*) Boots (chemists), (*c*) Tesco.

5. A well-known trading stamp concern in Great Britain is:
   (*a*) Green Shield, (*b*) I.O. Stamps, (*c*) Check Stamps.

Chapter 22—Advertising

PART 1. TEST YOUR PROGRESS

Complete the following statements by filling in the blanks.

1. Goods sold under their trade names are called ——— —.

2. A successful advertising campaign usually results in increased —— of products.

3. The purpose of advertising is not only to ——— sales, but also to provide the consumer with ——— on the product.

4. ——— television is a popular form of ——— if the advertiser wishes to inform a large proportion of the public about his product.

5. Manufacturers often use trade —— on their products which make it possible for the consumer to recognize more easily the —— of product he is buying.

PART 2. WHICH ANSWER

Select the answer which you consider to be most appropriate.

1. The cost of one full page advertisement in a national daily such as the *Daily Express* is approximately:
   (*a*) £5,000/£6,000, (*b*) £8,000/£9,000, (*c*) £11,000/£12,000.

2. Saturation advertising means:
   (*a*) the repetition of the same advertisement in a short period of time, (*b*) occasional advertising of a product, (*c*) advertising of waterproof clothing.

3. Display advertising is:
   (*a*) a small advertisement in a newspaper's articles "For Sale" column, (*b*) a fairly large advertisement in a newspaper, (*c*) an advertisement with illustrations of a product.

4. An advertising agent is:

(*a*) a person who sells advertising space in a magazine, (*b*) a person who does the talking on a television commercial, (*c*) a specialist who plans advertising campaigns.

5. Is impulse buying:

(*a*) buying goods? (*b*) buying goods without much thought? (*c*) buying goods only after a good deal of thought?

Chapter 23—Buying Now and Paying Later

PART 1. TEST YOUR PROGRESS

Complete the following statements by filling in the blanks.

1. Hire Purchase is a form of buying on ——, the purchaser receiving a period of time in which to —— for the goods.

2. The hire purchase price is calculated by adding the amount of the interest charges to the —— price of the goods.

3. Under the —— payments scheme of buying goods on credit, the goods belong legally to the purchaser as soon as the goods are bought.

4. The credit —— club is a popular form of buying goods on ——, and the customer is usually offered a choice of shops in which to buy the goods.

5. It is usual for customers to pay a —— when buying goods on hire purchase.

PART 2. WHICH ANSWER

Select the answer which you consider to be most appropriate.

1. The provisions of the Hire Purchase Act apply only to agreements for sums of not more than:

(*a*) £1,000, (*b*) £2,000, (*c*) £3,000.

2. When goods are bought on hire purchase:

(*a*) until the last instalment is paid the purchaser does not legally own the goods, (*b*) after the first instalment is paid the goods legally belong to the purchaser, (*c*) the goods never become the legal property of the purchaser.

3. A hire-purchase agreement signed in the home:
(*a*) cannot afterwards be cancelled, (*b*) can be cancelled before the end of the fourth day, (*c*) can be cancelled before the end of the seventh day.

4. If *less* than one third of the total amount payable has been paid on goods bought on hire purchase, and the customer defaults in his payments, the shopkeeper:
(*a*) must ask a court for damages, (*b*) must ask a court for recovery of the goods, (*c*) can take back the goods without a court order.
Note: the correct answer does not apply to persons living in Scotland.

5. Under a rental agreement the customer:
(*a*) never owns the goods, (*b*) only owns the goods after one year, (*c*) only owns the goods after two years.

Answers

Chapter 1

1. exchange   2. aids to trade   3. overseas (foreign)
4. advertising   5. dependent

PART 2

1. (*b*)   2. (*a*)   3. (*c*)   4. (*b*)   5. (*a*)

Chapter 2

PART 1

1. direct   2. industry   3. commercial
4. white-collar   5. occupations

PART 2

1. (*c*)   2. (*b*)   3. (*b*)   4. (*b*)   5. (*c*)

Chapter 3

PART 1

1. commerce   2. producer   3. consumer
4. transport   5. commercial

PART 2

1. (*c*)   2. (*b*)   3. (*a*)   4. (*c*)   5. (*a*)

Chapter 4

PART 1

1. prices   2. barter   3. industrial revolution
4. imports, exports   5. balance of payments

PART 2

1. (*c*)   2. (*b*)   3. (*a*)   4. (*b*)   5. (*c*)

Chapter 5

PART 1

1. measure 2. gold, silver 3. bank notes
4. barter 5. token

PART 2

1. (*c*) 2. (*a*) 3. (*b*) 4. (*a*) 5. (*c*)

Chapter 6

PART 1

1. specialization 2. specialize 3. mass production
4. expenses 5. manufacture

PART 2

1. (*c*) 2. (*b*) 3. (*a*) 4. (*b*) 5. (*c*)

Chapter 7

PART 1

1. services 2. rates 3. income tax
4. purchase tax 5. budget

PART 2

1. (*c*) 2. (*a*) 3. (*c*) 4. (*a*) 5. (*b*)

Chapter 8

PART 1

1. deposit 2. investors 3. interest
4. solicitor 5. estate agents

PART 2

1. (*b*) 2. (*c*) 3. (*a*) 4. (*a*) 5. (*b*)

Chapter 9

PART 1

1. budget 2. priorities 3. income, expenditure
4. National, saving 5. banks, building

PART 2

1. (*b*) 2. (*a*) 3. (*c*) 4. (*b*) 5. (*c*)

Chapter 10

PART 1

1. partnership	**2.** private	**3.** shareholders
4. ordinary	**5.** yield	**6.** stockjobbers
7. nationalized	**8.** commission	

PART 2

1. (*c*) **2.** (*b*) **3.** (*a*) **4.** (*c*) **5.** (*b*) **6.** (*c*) **7.** (*a*) **8.** (*b*)

Chapter 11

PART 1

1. capital	**2.** owned	**3.** working capital
4. assets	**5.** fixed, circulating	

PART 2

1. (*c*) **2.** (*b*) **3.** (*c*) **4.** (*a*) **5.** (*b*)

Chapter 12

PART 1

1. commercial	**2.** bank	**3.** bank
4. payee	**5.** deposit (savings)	**6.** Clearing House
7. overdraft, current	**8.** standing order	

PART 2

1. (*b*) **2.** (*a*) **3.** (*c*) **4.** (*c*) **5.** (*b*) **6.** (*a*) **7.** (*c*) **8.** (*a*)

Chapter 13

PART 1

1. National Giro system	**2.** loans	**3.** first class
4. cash on delivery	**5.** account payee only	

PART 2

1. (*a*) **2.** (*b*) **3.** (*b*) **4.** (*c*) **5.** (*c*)

Chapter 14

PART 1

1. cash discount	**2.** credit worth	**3.** trade discount
4. status inquirers		

PART 2

1. (*a*)   **2.** (*c*)   **3.** (*b*)   **4.** (*a*)

Chapter 15

PART 1

1. turnover   **2.** average stock   **3.** rate of turnover, stockturn
4. gross   **5.** overheads

PART 2

1. (*a*)   **2.** (*c*)   **3.** (*c*)   **4.** (*a*)   **5.** (*a*)

Chapter 16

PART 1

1. quotation   **2.** invoice   **3.** credit note, invoice
4. advice note   **5.** debit note (supplementary invoice)

PART 2

1. (*b*)   **2.** (*c*)   **3.** (*b*)   **4.** (*a*)   **5.** (*c*)

Chapter 17

PART 1

1. assurance   **2.** mortgage protection   **3.** Corporation of Lloyd's,
4. pooling   **5.** renewal date   underwriters

PART 2

1. (*a*)   **2.** (*b*)   **3.** (*c*)   **4.** (*b*)   **5.** (*c*)

Chapter 18

PART 1

1. sidings   **2.** British Road Services   **3.** tramp, world
4. container, containers   **5.** Port

PART 2

1. (*b*)   **2.** (*b*)   **3.** (*c*)   **4.** (*a*)   **5.** (*a*)

Chapter 19

PART 1

1. middleman   **2.** distribution   **3.** Smithfield
4. store   **5.** costs, distribution

PART 2

1. (*c*)   **2.** (*a*)   **3.** (*b*)   **4.** (*b*)   **5.** (*c*)

Chapter 20

PART 1

1. unit   **2.** departmental store **3.** mail order, home
4. co-operative, dividends **5.** multiple, central

PART 2

1. (*c*)   **2.** (*a*)   **3.** (*c*)   **4.** (*c*)   **5.** (*a*)

Chapter 21

PART 1

1. supermarket   **2.** trading   **3.** Descriptions
4. wholesaling   **5.** consumer, deal

PART 2

1. (*b*)   **2.** (*a*)   **3.** (*b*)   **4.** (*c*)   **5.** (*a*)

Chapter 22

PART 1

1. branded goods   **2.** sales   **3.** increase, information
4. commercial, advertising   **5.** marks, brand

PART 2

1. (*a*)   **2.** (*a*)   **3.** (*b*)   **4.** (*c*)   **5.** (*b*)

Chapter 23

PART 1

1. credit, pay   **2.** cash   **3.** deferred
4. trading, credit   **5.** deposit

PART 2

1. (*b*)   **2.** (*a*)   **3.** (*b*)   **4.** (*c*)   **5.** (*a*)

Index